Virginia Woolf's Novels and the Literary Past

Jane de Gay

Edinburgh University Press

© Jane de Gay, 2006, 2007

Edinburgh University Press Ltd
22 George Square, Edinburgh

First published in hardback by Edinburgh University Press in 2006.

Typeset in 10.5/13 Adobe Sabon
by Servis Filmsetting Ltd, Manchester, and
printed and bound in Great Britain by
Biddles Ltd, King's Lynn

A CIP record for this book is available from the British Library

ISBN 978 0 7486 3302 9 (paperback)

Contents

Acknowledgements

Quotations from Virginia Woolf's novels by permission of The Society of Authors as the Literary Representative of the Estate of Virginia Woolf. Excerpts from *Night and Day*, copyright 1920 by George H. Doran and Company and renewed 1948 by Leonard Woolf, reprinted by permission of Harcourt, Inc. Excerpts from *To the Lighthouse* by Virginia Woolf, copyright 1927 by Harcourt, Inc. and renewed 1954 by Leonard Woolf, reprinted by permission of the publisher. Excerpts from *Orlando* copyright 1928 by Virginia Woolf and renewed 1956 by Leonard Woolf, reprinted by permission of Harcourt, Inc. Excerpts from *Between the Acts* by Virginia Woolf, copyright 1941 by Harcourt, Inc. and renewed 1969 by Leonard Woolf, reprinted by permission of Harcourt, Inc. Quotations from *The Diary of Virginia Woolf* edited by Anne Olivier Bell, *The Letters of Virginia Woolf* edited by Nigel Nicolson and Joanne Trautmann, *Moments of Being* edited by Jeanne Schulkind, *Collected Essays*, all published by Hogarth Press and reprinted by permission of The Random House Group Ltd. Every effort has been made to obtain permission for all quotations: persons entitled to fees for any matter included here are invited to apply in writing to the publishers.

This book has had a long gestation and many people have helped and encouraged me along the way. Early research trips and conference visits were funded by the Open University Arts Faculty Research Committee. Trinity and All Saints' College funded trips to the annual Virginia Woolf Conference and a short period of study leave (special thanks to Joyce Simpson and Sally Dawson for their support). I value the encouragement and feedback of Woolfians and other colleagues, including: Richard Allen, Ann Ardis, Jessica Berman, Jane Goldman, Mark Hussey, Laura Marcus, Eleanor McNees, Andrew McNeillie, Rosemary Mitchell, Vara Neverow, Stephen Regan, Bonnie Kime Scott and Pierre-Eric Villeneuve. Thanks to the staff at the Bodleian Library, Oxford and Stephen Crook of the Berg Collection, New York Public Library for assistance. Thanks to Karen V. Kukil of the Rare Books Room, Smith College for help and picture research. Many thanks to all family and friends for support.

Special thanks to Suzanne Raitt for her honest and sound advice and stimulating conversations, and to Lizbeth Goodman, for her belief in my work from the start and her continued support and encouragement. Finally, many thanks to Wayne Stote for his love and patience in living with this book for as long as I have.

This book is dedicated with love and gratitude to my parents – to my father, Edmund, and to the memory of my mother, Joan. It is also dedicated to the memory of Marjorie Reeves, who was a great inspiration and in whose household much of the text was written.

Abbreviations

Texts are by Virginia Woolf, unless stated otherwise.

3G   *Three Guineas*, intro. Hermione Lee ([1938]; London: Hogarth Press, 1986).

Anon '"Anon" and "The Reader": Virginia Woolf's Last Essays', ed. and intro. Brenda R. Silver, *Twentieth-Century Literature*, 25:3–4 (1979), 356–441.

Apology   Leslie Stephen, *An Agnostic's Apology and Other Essays* (London: Smith & Elder, 1893).

BA   *Between the Acts*, ed. and intro. Frank Kermode ([1941]; Oxford: Oxford University Press, 1992).

CE   *Collected Essays*, 4 vols (London: Hogarth Press, 1966–67).

D   *Diary*, ed. Anne Olivier Bell, asst. ed. Andrew McNeillie, 5 vols (London: Hogarth Press, 1977–84).

E   *Essays*, ed. Andrew McNeillie (London: Hogarth, 1986–).

English   Leslie Stephen, *English Literature and Society in the Eighteenth Century* (London: Duckworth, 1904).

History   Leslie Stephen, *History of English Thought in the Eighteenth Century*, 2 vols (London: Smith & Elder, 1876).

HD   *The Waves: The Two Holograph Drafts*, transcribed and ed. John W. Graham (London: Hogarth Press, 1976).

JR   *Jacob's Room*, ed. and intro. Kate Flint ([1922]; Oxford: Oxford University Press, 1992).

L   *Letters*, ed. Nigel Nicolson, asst. ed. Joanne Trautmann Banks, 6 vols (London: Hogarth Press, 1975–80).

MB   *Moments of Being: Unpublished Autobiographical Writings*, ed. and intro. Jeanne Schulkind (London: Triad/Granada, 1978).

MBk   *Sir Leslie Stephen's Mausoleum Book*, intro. Alan Bell (Oxford: Clarendon Press, 1977).

MP   Jane Austen, *Mansfield Park*, ed. Tony Tanner ([1814]; Harmondsworth: Penguin, 1966).

MD   *Mrs Dalloway*, ed. and intro. Claire Tomalin ([1925]; Oxford: Oxford University Press, 1992).

ND   *Night and Day*, ed. and intro. Suzanne Raitt ([1919]; Oxford: Oxford University Press, 1992).

O   *Orlando*, ed. and intro. Rachel Bowlby ([1928]; Oxford: Oxford University Press, 1992).

OHD   *To the Lighthouse: The Original Holograph Draft*, transcribed and ed. Susan Dick (London: Hogarth Press, 1983).

P   *Persuasion*, ed. and intro. D.W. Harding ([1818]; Harmondswoth: Penguin, 1965).

PP   Jane Austen, *Pride and Prejudice*, ed. Tony Tanner ([1813]; repr. Harmondsworth: Penguin, 1972).

QB   Quentin Bell, *Virginia Woolf: A Biography*, 2 vols (London: Hogarth Press, 1972).

Room   *A Room of One's Own* ([1929]; London: Grafton, 1977).

TL   *To the Lighthouse*, ed. and intro. Margaret Drabble ([1927]; Oxford: Oxford University Press, 1992).

VC   Anne Thackeray Ritchie, *The Village on the Cliff* (London: Smith & Elder, 1867).

VO   *The Voyage Out*, ed. and intro. Lorna Sage ([1915]; Oxford: Oxford University Press, 1992).

W   *The Waves*, ed. and intro. Gillian Beer ([1931]; Oxford: Oxford University Press, 1992).

Works   *The Collected Works of Samuel Taylor Coleridge*, 16 vols, gen. ed. Kathleen Coburn (London and Princeton, NJ: Routledge & Kegan Paul; Bollingen Series LXXV, Princeton University Press, 1969–).

Introduction

Virginia Woolf has long been celebrated as an innovative novelist and a radical thinker who broke with the aesthetics of earlier generations and challenged their values; some critics have even suggested that she anticipated ideas and approaches which emerged long after her time. However, it is less widely acknowledged that Woolf also looked backwards; that she was immersed in the literary past and her intellectual heritage as a reader and critic; and that this had an impact on her fiction. Although Beth Carole Rosenberg has drawn attention to Woolf's dialogue with other writers in her essays and fiction, and Sally Greene's edited collection, *Virginia Woolf: Reading the Renaissance*, has demonstrated that the strength of Woolf's interest in the Renaissance can be seen in both her scholarship and her fiction,[1] many scholars are none the less reluctant to see the presence of the literary past in the novels. So, for example, although Elena Gualtieri and Juliet Dusinberre have drawn attention to Woolf's intimacy with the literary past in her essays, both resist applying these insights to her novels: Gualtieri makes a distinction between the essay, which 'remained for her attached to the paternal figure and therefore became the arena where the relationship between tradition and modernity was explored', and the novel, which 'represented the possibility of experimenting with new forms and shapes'; and Dusinberre argues that Woolf 'used the past for a purpose, as an empowering model for herself as woman writer, and particularly as a writer not of fiction but of criticism and literary history'.[2]

This book will demonstrate that Woolf's preoccupation with the literary past had a profound impact on the content of her novels, on her philosophies of fiction and on certain aspects of her fictional method. It will explore how Woolf continually engaged with the literary past in her fiction: by revisiting and revising plots which had made an impression on her as a reader, by using densely packed literary allusions and even by using her fiction as a forum for exploring literary history. As a result, her drive towards innovation may be seen to be tempered by an impulse to maintain intimate connections with the literary past so that, in many cases, her route towards innovation came not through rejecting the literary past but through drawing upon it. The book will examine this process by exploring ways in which Woolf played out within her novels some of the ambivalences, tensions and resolutions in her engagement with her literary and scholarly heritage.

This book views Woolf's novels as haunted spaces in which the literary past was alive and commanded attention, spaces in which she grappled with traditional narrative structures and with questions of canonicity, as well as entering into dialogue with a host of writers who had gone before her. The idea is drawn from the conclusion to *A Room of One's Own* in which Woolf urges women scholars to 'look past Milton's bogey' to find lost women writers, for 'great poets do not die, they are continuing presences; they need only the opportunity to walk among us in the flesh' (*Room*, 108). The formulation conjures up two contradictory kinds of spectral presence: a traumatic and terrifying image which arises without being summoned, and a nostalgic picture cherished and expanded upon in the imagination. The former is an encounter with unhelpful elements of past literature, the latter a strategy for imaginatively constructing more positive and supportive views of tradition and the literary past. As we will see, Woolf's novels are marked by both processes.

In viewing Woolf's engagement with the literary past in her fiction as a dynamic process which was often undergone quite consciously, this book deliberately pushes at the boundaries of thinking about intertextuality. Burgeoning theoretical studies of intertextuality have drawn our attention to the fact that all works of literature are replete with echoes of the literary past (along with fragments of other social and cultural discourses, past and current): Julia Kristeva noted that 'any text is constructed as a mosaic of quotations; any text is the absorption and transformation of another',[3] and Roland Barthes elaborated upon this to argue that a text is a 'multi-dimensional space in which a variety of writings, none of them original, blend and clash. The text is a tissue of quotations drawn from the innumerable centres of culture.'[4] While these earlier formulations discounted the importance of the author (Kristeva stated that the 'notion of *intertextuality* replaces that of intersubjectivity' (ibid.), and Barthes famously pronounced the 'death of the author'), some recent studies have seen the author as an important channel for literary culture: as Michael Worton and Judith Still have noted, intertextuality recognises that 'the writer is a reader of texts (in the broadest sense) before s/he is a creator of texts, and therefore the work of art is inevitably shot through with references, quotations, and influences of every kind'. The writer is not merely a cipher, for the process of intertextuality is 'emotionally and politically charged'.[5] Also, as Raphaël Ingelbien has pointed out, intertextuality is more evident in some works than others, and modernist fiction is particularly rich in this respect.[6]

So, whilst the transmission and transformation of past works may be an 'inevitable' process for all writers, it is particularly marked in Woolf's work, for she read extensively and intensively, and her reading was intertwined with her writing. Woolf's diaries show that she was making an extensive study of literature for *The Common Reader* whilst writing *Mrs Dalloway*, and that she underwent a programme of reading for 'Phases of Fiction' whilst writing *Orlando*. Furthermore, reading notes are often inserted into drafts of novels, including *Night and Day, Mrs Dalloway* and *Between the Acts*, so that Woolf's engagement with other writers worked in close proximity to her own creative writing. Some of the impact of this reading on Woolf's fiction has been demonstrated and explored by Beverly Ann Schlack, Alice Fox and Gillian Beer, and various critical editions of the novels have also shown that they are peppered with allusions to the works she had read.[7] This study will expand on this research by examining how Woolf engaged with a range of different writings across her career.

In gauging Woolf's responses to the literary past, this book will consider how her social, cultural and political contexts affected her reading for, as Melba Cuddy-Keane has argued, Woolf 'historicises' the reading process as 'her own reading in her own time and as therefore differing from the various historical readings that have preceded and will follow her'.[8] Broadly, the book will view Woolf as actively engaged in reading texts from the position of an early twentieth-century woman writer whose world-view was marked in certain complex ways by her Victorian upbringing, by her acute awareness that she did not share the privileges enjoyed by the men of her generation and class, by her intimacies with other women and by the events she witnessed unfolding in European politics. It will argue that Woolf was exercised by the need to question the institutions and ramifications of patriarchy so that textual battles were often closely implicated in social and political ones.

While theories of intertextuality have alerted us to the fact that, in Graham Allen's words, 'all texts are potentially plural, reversible, open to the reader's own presuppositions, lacking in clear and defined boundaries',[9] the comparative studies in this book will attempt to posit culturally and historically-specific meanings within Woolf's source texts, and then explore how she questioned those meanings and uncovered new ones as she drew on phrases and ideas derived from others. This approach begs the question of the criteria by which particular sources have been selected for scrutiny and by which those texts are interpreted. As Cuddy-Keane has pointed out, the kinds of connection made in source criticism or influence study involve a three-dimensional process: if Woolf is placed on the vertical axis and her influences on the horizontal axis, then the position of the critic in a third dimension affects her perception of the relations between Woolf and her precursors.[10] It will therefore affect which sources are selected as significant, even which ones are spotted at all, and it will also affect how a critic views both Woolf's texts and those counted as her sources. This study aims to address these problems by using for the most part Woolf's essays, diaries, notebooks and letters as evidence of what works she read, and as an indication of how she read them. It will also seek to examine how Woolf's response to particular writers was conditioned by prevailing critical debates about their work.

This introduction first considers Woolf's essays about reading to outline the processes by which her reading was transformed into creative writing, then sets out a framework for the discussion by sketching some significant contexts which impinged on Woolf's reading experience.

I

Several of the essays demonstrate that for Woolf the act of reading was a creative process for which the reader needed to use her imagination to develop a sense of empathy with the writer and the work. As Hermione Lee has noted, 'the heart of the pleasure of reading' for Woolf was 'the delight in a free union, like a very intimate conversation or an act of love'.[11] 'Reading' (1919) is a demonstration of this empathetic, sympathetic response to books for it is both literary criticism and creative writing, presenting a first-person narrative of a reader recalling days spent in the library of a country house, in a state of heightened sensibility in which the figures of past authors and scenes from their work are as vivid as the room in which she sits and the countryside beyond:

> instead of being a book it seemed that what I read was laid upon the land-scape, not printed, bound, or sewn up, but somehow the product of trees and fields and the hot summer sky . . . even the gardener leading his pony was part of the book . . . This man took his place naturally by the side of those dead poets. (*CE*, II. 13)

The essay muses on history as evoked through reading works such as Richard Hakluyt's *Voyages* and the narrative enters into the world described in those old texts:

They talk of commodities and there you see them; more clearly and separately in bulk, colour, and variety than the goods brought by steamer and piled upon docks; they talk of fruit; the red and yellow globes hang unpicked on virgin trees; so with the lands they sight; the morning mist is only just now lifting and not a flower has been plucked. (*CE*, II. 21)

Woolf's use of free indirect discourse, shifting clause by clause between what 'they' describe and what the reader envisages, reinforces this sense of intimacy between reader and writer. The essay demonstrates that the reader's experiences outside the library also influence her reception of books: the speaker closes Hakluyt and goes moth-hunting, continuing her dream-like state, but in the morning wants a different sort of book to read, something 'hard as gem or rock with the seal of human experience in it' (*CE*, II. 26), and so turns to Sir Thomas Browne. This principle of matching reading matter to mood also underlies Woolf's later essay, 'Phases of Fiction' (1928).

In 'How Should One Read a Book?' (1926), Woolf hints at a degree of intimacy at which the distinction between reader and author is transcended, for she argues that the first stage of reading should involve total immersion in a book:

If we could banish all . . . preconceptions when we read, that would be an admirable beginning. Do not dictate to your author; try to become him. Be his fellow-worker and accomplice. If you hang back, and reserve and criticise at first, you are preventing yourself from getting the fullest possible value from what you read. (*CE*, II. 2)

The act of reading is one of constructing the book for oneself, making the creative effort of attempting to 'become' the author, or entering into partnership with him. However, she goes on to say that this empathetic reading is only the first stage – an 'admirable beginning' – which must be followed by assessment from a critical distance, for the process of reading is 'completed' when we 'pass judgement upon [our] multitudinous impressions' (*CE*, II. 8). Yet, the sort of judgement she prescribes is a subjective one, for the reader reviews her feelings about what she has read, considering her *impressions* of the book and not the book *per se*. Thus a book is not completed on turning the final page, but when the *reader* makes the book into a coherent whole: as Woolf noted in 'On Re-reading Novels', our observations about a book assemble themselves after we finish reading it (*CE*, II. 125).

Woolf's unpublished manuscript 'Byron & Mr Briggs' (1922) throws further light on her view of the reader's creative partnership with the writer. As an early exploration of the themes developed in *The Common Reader* (a collection which included 'How Should One Read a Book?'), it offers a more spontaneous view of the reading process than the polished, prescriptive account in that later essay. In 'Byron & Mr Briggs', Woolf attacks the way in which literary critics seek to act as intermediaries between text and reader, and champions the common reader, defending the validity of the ordinary reader's responses to literature by emphasising the intimacy between reader and author: 'It is I who have read the play. I hold it in my mind . . . I am . . . directly in touch with Shakespeare' (*E*, III. 478). The notion of direct contact with an author is a fantasy: indeed, Woolf's description of the reading process suggests that the reader supplements the text as she goes along. She notes that our reading is 'always urged on' by an 'instinct' to 'complete what we read': this process of completion requires us 'to supply background, ~~significant~~ relationship, motive, while we are rounding the whole with a running commentary <or ~~significance~~ of our own>' (*E*, III. 482–3). The reader's mental effort in bringing the text to life can result in her anticipating outcomes, but significantly Woolf expresses this the other way round, for she suggests that Shakespeare 'anticipates whatever we are about to say' (*E*, III. 498). The exchange between reader and writer described here becomes a kind of internal dialogue of the sort described by Patrocinio Schweickart, whereby the 'subjectivity roused to life by reading, while it may be attributed to the author, is nevertheless not a separate subjectivity but a projection of the subjectivity of the reader'.[12]

'Byron & Mr Briggs' also offers a clue as to how Woolf's lively reading flowed over into her writing practices, for it demonstrates how literary quotations can be used as a way of maintaining the intimacy between reader and writer. In a discussion of the anonymous Middle English lyric 'Western wind, when will thou blow | The small rain down can rain?', Woolf notes that critical analysis is frustrating because it puts the poem at a distance: 'I am tempted directly I begin to analyse to get far away from what I feel' (*E*, III. 486). Initially, she suggests that the only way to retain emotional contact with the poem is to repeat it over and over again, but finds that even this palls. She notes that some of these feelings return later when she recalls lines from the poem spontaneously, possibly when they seem appropriate to a situation: 'later I shall think involuntarily of "the small rain" ~~with curiosity~~, for it describes rain that I have seen but never thought of calling ~~small~~' (*E*, III. 486–7). This quotation suggests a kind of shared feeling between reader and writer as the words of a writer loom up to describe phenomena Woolf experiences.

Certain entries in Woolf's diary give evidence of how her imaginative response to other writers had an impact on her own creativity. For example, while reading *Roxana* and *Moll Flanders* in 1919, she described seeing London 'through the eyes of Defoe. . . . Yes, a great writer surely to be thus imposing himself upon me after 200 years' (*D*, I. 263). The observation suggests she was aware that her imagination was being shaped by Defoe. If this example suggests that Woolf was at ease with the sense of being influenced by an earlier author, a diary comment on reading Marcel Proust after completing *Mrs Dalloway* suggests elements of Bloomian anxiety and conflict:[13]

> I wonder if this time I have achieved something? Well, nothing anyhow compared with Proust, in whom I am embedded now. The thing about Proust is his combination of the utmost sensibility with the utmost tenacity. . . . He is as tough as catgut & as evanescent as a butterfly's bloom. And he will I suppose both influence me & make me out of temper with every sentence of my own. (*D*, III. 7)

Here, Woolf measures her own progress against the strengths of the work she is reading, admiring Proust critically, whilst being aware that he may affect her creative process adversely. However, in recognising Proust's influence, Woolf also judges him according to her own criteria: the combination of firmness with subtlety she valued in Proust was a balance she sought to achieve in her own writing, for she had envisaged the finale to *Mrs Dalloway* as 'a complicated *spirited solid* piece' (*D*, II. 312; emphasis added), and in her next novel, *To the Lighthouse*, she would describe Lily Briscoe's painting as a quest for something 'feathery and evanescent, one colour melting into another like the colours on a butterfly's wing; but beneath the fabric must be clamped together with bolts of iron' (*TL*, 231). Both are examples of the vacillation between granite and rainbow which Ann Banfield has shown to characterise Woolf's work.[14] As will be suggested throughout this study, Woolf's exchanges with her literary precursors were more complex and subtle than those accounted for by Harold Bloom's tropes whereby writers enact radical swerves away from the work of earlier authors in order to assert their originality.

Woolf's treatment of literary quotations alone suggests a gradational series of responses to the literary past, ranging from her sympathetic reading of 'O western wind' to more dynamic and transformative appropriations of other writers' words. Again in 'Byron & Mr Briggs', she notes that words can have a sensory impact which may not be directly related to meaning. She describes reading a poem by Robert Herrick 'somnambulistically', which is 'not reading, but only striking notes one after another and letting each one sound. Still since the sounds are pure, echoes come back' (*E*, III. 492). The musical metaphor suggests that the words and their meanings have been lost, but have been translated into sound. In this particular essay, Woolf develops the analogy in a manner reminiscent of Romantic theory by arguing that this transmutation of words into echoes has the effect of taking emotions and putting them in harmony with a wider whole, 'a profound and comprehensive gaze' (*E*, III. 492–3).

Woolf points to a more radical reading of literary quotations in 'On Being Ill' (1930), where she comments that when reading during illness, 'we rifle the poets of their flowers. We break off a line or two and let them open in the depths of the mind' (*CE*, IV. 199). The flower metaphor for the literary quotation is exploited in contradictory ways to suggest both desecration and creativity. The patient seizes particular lines, neglecting the meaning of the poem as a whole and thus despoiling the poem as one might damage a plant; and new meanings evolve as she meditates on isolated lines, like a severed flower taking root when placed in water. She suggests that such a reading goes beyond words and meanings to uncover something less 'meagre': 'a sound, a colour, here a stress, there a pause' (*CE*, IV. 200). The unconventional and idiosyncratic readings which can be produced under the influence of illness provide other ways in which the reader may transcend the opinions of critics and gain intimacy with the writer, for illness 'leaves nothing but Shakespeare and oneself' (*CE*, IV. 201). Yet, since this is a product of illness rather than health, there is a sense that such encounters may also be troubled and troubling: as Daniel Mark Fogel has pointed out, Woolf often used illness as a metaphor for literary influence, as in her comment that 'some writers are far more infectious than others'.[15]

This study seeks to understand Woolf's use of allusions in a dynamic way. An allusion can be seen as a point at which the words of an earlier writer are introduced into a text and so function as a link between her work and that of another. But the meaning of the fragment may differ significantly from its meaning in the source texts, for as Linda Hutcheon notes, 'no integration into a new context can avoid altering meaning'.[16] These points of difference will be read as part of a dialogue – a negotiation of meaning – between Woolf and earlier writers.

A sense of dialogue is strongly illustrated in Woolf's fiction and non-fiction at the moments where she casts the author as a character with whom the reader can engage. In her early reading notes she conjures up from William Cowper's poetry 'a slim young man, with melancholy eyes, – a gleam of humour in them – an anxious expression – beautiful hands'; she sees John Keats as 'gentle and strong. Most loveable character.'[17] When discussing Sir Thomas Browne in 'Reading', she almost goes as far as to propose that one can enter into conversation with an author. She elaborates on the fact that Browne was a doctor to imagine consulting him, speculating that 'his consolations must have been sublime', although, significantly, the sense of dialogue slips as she imagines that he would have spoken 'mostly in soliloquy' (*CE*, II. 27) – perhaps recollecting that she is, after all, discussing the written word.

A similar process is found in some of Woolf's novels, where she caricatures other authors in order to bring them alive in writing; as Bakhtin has noted, the process of 'turning persuasive discourse into speaking persons' in a novel may be a liberating experience.[18] There are three highly significant cases of extended caricatures of writers Woolf had known: her step-aunt, Anne Thackeray Ritchie, is depicted in Mrs Hilbery in *Night and Day*; her father, Sir Leslie Stephen, is represented by Mr Ramsay in *To the Lighthouse*; and her lover, Vita Sackville-West, is turned into the eponymous hero/ine in *Orlando*. Significantly, all three novels reflect the interests of the writers they depict: thus Mrs Hilbery appears in (and appears to direct) a romantic comedy of manners of the kind that Ritchie wrote; Mr Ramsay's intellectual concerns, particularly the problem of 'subject, object and the nature of reality', resemble those of Stephen and are explored within *To the Lighthouse*; and *Orlando* presents a fictionalised version of Sackville-West's own account of her family history. Although Woolf had known these writers, her attention to the preoccupations of their work suggests that she had also come to know them in a different way through their work, much as Woolf's imaginative picture of Sir Thomas Browne is formed through engagement with his writings. The process of caricaturing these writers while responding to their work can be read in terms of an imaginary dialogue with them – one in which, of course, they could not answer back.

Woolf's appropriation and re-working of plot-lines and scenarios from the works of earlier writers, like her use of literary quotations, gives evidence of a combination of sympathetic, creative and resistant readings. In this respect, Linda Hutcheon's theory of parody offers a more useful approach than the Bloomian model, for it accounts for sympathetic readings of an earlier writer's work as well as resistant ones: as Hutcheon points out, parody is not always practised at the expense of the parodied text for, while the usual etymology of parody is 'counter-song', the morpheme 'para' can also mean 'beside', thus suggesting accord or intimacy as well as contrast.[19] Hutcheon defines parody as 'extended repetition with critical difference' which may be 'overtly signalled or economically inscribed', thus encompassing a range of ways in which earlier works may be incorporated into later ones, from short, local echoes to longer rehearsals of narratives or ideas.[20] As will be demonstrated, Woolf's revisions of plots and situations may involve active criticism: changing aspects of a plot being a way of negotiating past ideas, making earlier plots relevant to present-day concerns, or exposing ways in which past plots have become outdated. In this way, Woolf's invocation of past literature (like Hutcheon's view of parody) involves a process of coming to terms with the literature, values and ideas of the past.

Whilst Woolf's essays express a strong desire to attain intimacy with the literary past, they also demonstrate a recognition that we can do so only by coming to terms with the mediating framework of literary history. In 'Reading', Woolf attempts to circumvent the historicising process by bringing the literary past to life dramatically:

> If I looked down at my book I could see Keats and Pope behind him, and then Dryden and Sir Thomas Browne – hosts of them merging in the mass of Shakespeare, behind whom, if one peered long enough, some shapes of men in pilgrims' dress emerged, Chaucer perhaps, and again – who was it? some uncouth poet scarcely able to syllable his words; and so they died away. (*CE*, II. 13)

Woolf envisages a text not simply as a palimpsest of earlier writings, but as a physical space in which past writers are present and active. Past literature is made current by placing it at a *spatial* rather than a temporal distance from the present: so, for example, Pope and Keats are seen together in the same place, even though they lived a century apart. Many writers are seen to 'merge in the mass of Shakespeare', as though he is a colossal figure whose stature obliterates our view of others. The focus extends beyond this to envisage earlier writers: Chaucer and his predecessors are set spatially behind him, and his anonymous precursor (sketched in mid-process of trying to articulate his thoughts) stands behind him. Woolf's attempt to see beyond the layers of history to reclaim lost origins anticipates her argument in her late essay 'Anon' (1940), in which she traces the origins of English literature not to famous authors, but to the forgotten balladeers of an oral tradition, the poets who were part of the common people and sang for them: 'Anon is sometimes man; sometimes woman. He is the common voice singing out of doors' (*Anon*, 382).

Like many of Woolf's accounts of literary history, this model is strategic. Her sketch of literary history as a kind of pageant attempts to evade ideas of hierarchy: unlike the popular notion of literary tradition as a hierarchical structure, with ancient writers positioned high up and passing ideas and themes *down* to later generations, Woolf places all writers on the same level, thus giving each potentially the same degree of importance. As a result, obscure past writers need not be lost but can be reclaimed if the present-day reader or writer moves into a position from which those precursors might be seen.

The dynamic, strategic approach to literary history in 'Reading' anticipates Woolf's conclusion to *A Room of One's Own*, where she urges female Cambridge students to 'rewrite history' in order to 'think back through our mothers' and uncover a lost tradition of women writers, represented in the essay by the fictional figure of Shakespeare's sister whose creativity would have been stifled by the limited opportunities available to her as a woman. The process would entail learning to 'look past Milton's bogey, for no human being should shut out the view' (*Room*, 108), implying that the woman reader needs to shift her position so that she can see past his gigantic figure.

A Room of One's Own is generally celebrated as a critique of patriarchal values and a championing of female over male writers, but the essay can be seen to employ more complex strategies, which in turn reveal how Woolf sought to place her own work within literary history. The overtly feminist argument of the essay belies an ambivalence towards female precursors. Indeed, when Woolf discusses *actual* female precursors such as Lady Winchilsea, the Duchess of Newcastle, Dorothy Osborne and Aphra Behn, she names them as though they have been forgotten. Even when she mentions later and better-known precursors such as Jane Austen and George Eliot, Woolf emphasises that they were suppressed or silenced in certain ways. She narrates the anecdote about Austen feeling compelled to keep her writing secret by hiding her manuscripts when visitors arrived and she stresses Eliot's suffering as a woman, particularly the social ostracism brought about by her relationship with a married man, George Lewes. Furthermore, as Alison Booth has pointed out, Woolf overlooks almost a century of scholarship on women writers when she identifies a need to 'rewrite history' to include women.[21] Thus, although *A Room of One's Own* is generally taken to hail an inspiring and supportive female tradition of writing in place of an inhibiting male one, a closer look reveals that Woolf was also sceptical and suspicious of the legacy of some of her female precursors.

The essay furthermore gives evidence of a stronger affinity with male precursors than is suggested by the attack on Milton, for it shows that Woolf also 'thought back' through male writers. Woolf's famous quotation about thinking back through our mothers continues: 'It is useless to go to the great men writers for help, however much one may go to them for pleasure' (*Room*, 72). The cost of such pleasure for Woolf was that it led her to value a tradition of 'great' English writers in which female writers were marginalised. As I will argue, Woolf's valuation of her female precursors was compromised by her respect for a male-dominated tradition. The ambiguities and tensions of this position are revealed in *A Room of One's Own* when she interrupts her discussion about women and writing to introduce the problematic idea of 'androgyny', defined as the presence of masculine and feminine attributes in the same mind, in order to admit male precursors into the tradition she has invented. Woolf draws the concept of androgyny from the work of Coleridge and she uses it to claim Shakespeare as one of the great androgynous writers. Elaine Showalter has argued that, in adopting androgyny, Woolf failed to engage with feminist ideas on writing and consequently should not not be considered as part of a 'women's tradition'.[22] However, Woolf's attempt to draw on both female and male precursors can be seen as an attempt to place herself within two traditions, to lend credence to her own writing by tracing her heritage back to the male authors whose greatness was already firmly accepted.

However, even when Woolf turned to male writers, she sought to read them on her own terms as a woman, as Jane Marcus, Beth C. Schwartz and Miriam Wallace have pointed out.[23] This concern comes to the fore in *Three Guineas* (1938) where, having established that women have consistently been denied the educational privileges accorded to men, and by extension may be said to have received their cultural education second-hand through their fathers and brothers, Woolf urges women to read and write for themselves (*3G*, 103). Such a move, she argues, would help preserve culture from fascism – a movement which was threatening to take over Europe and one she closely associated with the patriarchal family.

II

Although the familial metaphors Woolf uses in *A Room of One's Own* and *Three Guineas* are popularly used to express literary relationships (Bloom's theory of influence, for example, is based on the Oedipal conflict between father and son), her own practices as reader and writer were bound up with complicated responses to members of her own family. Woolf was conscious of the fact that she had been denied a formal education, and felt that her access to literature was second-hand, partly through her brother Thoby Stephen, who gave her books and discussed with her what he had learned at school and university, but chiefly through her father, who played a key role in her education.[24]

The influence of Leslie Stephen on Woolf's reading and writing was complex and multidimensional, and will form a major underlying concern of this study. On a personal level, Stephen introduced Woolf to works of literature at an early age through his practice of reading aloud novels and plays and of reciting poetry to his children from memory: in an appreciation written for Frederic Maitland's *Life and Letters of Leslie Stephen* (1906), Woolf recalled him reading *Tom Brown's Schooldays*, *Treasure*

Island, the works of Walter Scott, Jane Austen, Carlyle, Hawthorne and Shakespeare and reciting poetry by William Wordsworth, Alfred Tennyson, John Keats, Matthew Arnold, John Milton, George Meredith, Arthur Lyall, Rudyard Kipling and Henry Newbolt.[25] This practice made Stephen an important medium through which she first encountered literature: as she put it, he had not simply memorised but 'acquired' or appropriated the work of the poets and recited their words as his own. As a result, Woolf identified her father with the great writers: 'many of the great English poems now seem to me inseparable from my father'.[26] While this characteristic put Stephen in a position of power, it also took on an elegiac or memorial function, for the memoir is a list of his preferred reading, as though Woolf recalled her father through the books he loved. This adds a further layer to Woolf's use of literary quotations in her novels, not least when she recalls her father in *The Voyage Out* where Ridley Ambrose is heard to recite Milton's 'Nativity Ode', and in *To the Lighthouse* when Mr Ramsay declaims lines from Cowper and Tennyson, among others. Leslie Stephen continued to mediate the young Virginia's access to literature even when she began to read books for herself: he took over her education when her mother died and he lent her books from his library.

In the public sphere, Stephen's published criticism, literary histories and biographical work (most notably the *Dictionary of National Biography*), had contributed to the wider intellectual context into which Woolf entered. Although she was critical of Stephen's intellectual legacy, she frequently turned to his works: her reading notes for her literary essays, for example, reveal that she often began her preparation by reading the *DNB* entry on the author under review. The extent of Woolf's use of Stephen's works has yet to be fully appreciated, although Beth Carole Rosenberg's work has made an important contribution towards this. Woolf's reading of Stephen provided an important mechanism by which she reviewed her intellectual heritage, debated with it and found her own way forward.

Leslie Stephen's impact on Woolf as a reader can be seen in her essays on reading. In 'Hours in a Library' – an essay which shares its title with Stephen's three-volume collection of criticism (1874–79) – Woolf gives a description of the 'true reader' which reads as a character sketch of him. Such a reader, she says, is 'essentially young. He is a man of intense curiosity; of ideas; open-minded and communicative, to whom reading is more of the nature of brisk exercise in the open air than of sheltered study; he trudges the high road, he climbs higher and higher upon the hills until the atmosphere is almost too fine to breathe in; to him it is not a sedentary pursuit at all' (*CE*, II. 34). Woolf's equation of reading with physical exercise recalls Stephen's passions for reading, walking and

Alpinism. Stephen himself had drawn close connections between moun-
taineering and reading: for example, he noted that 'Shelley's poetry is in
the most complete harmony with the scenery of the higher Alps; and I
think it creditable to the mountains that they should agree so admirably
with the most poetical of poets'.[27] Stephen is even invoked by Woolf's
description of the true reader as youthful, for she remarked that, 'My
impression as a child always was that my father was not very much older
than we were'.[28]

Woolf's advice on reading in 'How Should One Read a Book?' echoes
ideas Stephen had expressed in an essay on Sterne: where Woolf encouraged the reader to start by trying to 'become' the author, Stephen urged
the reader to 'read a book in the true sense – to read it, that is, not as the
critic but in the spirit of enjoyment – is to lay aside for the moment one's
own personality, and to become part of the author'.[29] Thus, ironically,
Woolf's longing for intimacy with the authors she read was overdetermined by the views of the critic who had first fired her love of reading.

A recognition of Stephen's influence goes some way towards explain-
ing some of the complexities of *A Room of One's Own*. Three of the
female writers who feature prominently in *Room* had already been discussed at length by Stephen: he wrote the *Dictionary of National
Biography* entry on Jane Austen; he published a book-length study of
George Eliot (ironically, for the 'English Men of Letters' series); and
wrote lengthy essays on Eliot and Charlotte Brontë, collected in *Hours
in a Library*. Stephen's admiration of Austen for accepting the narrow
confines of a woman's life, and his qualified sympathies for Brontë in
whose work he found an air of 'indescribable pathos' which 'leaves us
with a sense of something morbid and unsatisfactory', and Eliot, 'so sensitive a woman, working so conscientiously and with so many misgiv-
ings',[30] can all be seen to have an impact on Woolf's ambivalent valuation
of her female precursors in *Room*, even as she claims them for a female
tradition.

On the other hand, later essays suggest that Woolf worked through
some of the inhibiting aspects of Stephen's influence, so that she also
came to reclaim some of his ideas as empowering. Thus, in 'The Leaning
Tower', a talk given to the Workers' Educational Association in 1940,
she quoted Stephen to encourage a working-class audience to read as
widely as they wished, to challenge élitist conceptions about literature:

> let us bear in mind a piece of advice that an eminent Victorian who was also
> an eminent pedestrian once gave to walkers: 'Whenever you see a board up
> with "Trespassers will be prosecuted", trespass at once.'
>   Let us trespass at once. Literature is no one's private ground; literature is
> common ground. (*CE*, II. 181)

Reading here becomes both personal and political: social change might come about when those who had been denied a formal eduation read more widely and learned things which traditionally had been the preserve of the more privileged classes. The process by which Woolf moved from being inhibited by Stephen to being empowered by his ideas will be an important underlying theme of this book.

Woolf's use of the literary past in her work was bound up in different ways with her problematic reactions to her fellow modernists. Whilst she read past literature avidly and extensively, Woolf was a reserved, suspicious and resistant reader of contemporary literature. For example, she claimed in a letter to Ethel Smyth that she was reading D. H. Lawrence for the first time in the year after his death: 'Now I realise with regret that a man of genius wrote in my time and I never read him' (*L*, IV. 315). The assertion is untrue, for Woolf had reviewed *The Lost Girl* in 1920, but it suggests that she could not take Lawrence's work seriously until he was dead and no longer a rival. Woolf suggested a complex reason as to why she had avoided him: 'the fact about contemporaries (I write hand to mouth) is that they're doing the same thing on another railway line: one resents their distracting one, flashing past, the wrong way – something like that: from timidity, partly, one keeps ones eyes on one's own road' (ibid.). Woolf had expressed a similar sentiment towards James Joyce in a diary entry made while she was struggling with *Jacob's Room*: 'what I'm doing is probably being better done by Mr Joyce' (*D*, II. 69).

One of Woolf's responses to the perceived threat of contemporary literature was to set the weight of the literary past against it. This can be seen in her reaction to *Ulysses* when she read it for the first time in 1918–19 whilst thinking about her own methods and formulating theories about the future of the novel for the essay 'Modern Novels'. Woolf takes *Ulysses* as an example of the kind of modern novel she aspires to write – one which can convey 'life' or 'spirit', 'truth' or 'reality' – and yet she draws back from wholehearted praise of Joyce by comparing him unfavourably with Laurence Sterne and the Victorian novelists. She argues that *Ulysses* excludes or ignores too much of life, whereas reading Sterne's *Tristram Shandy* or Thackeray's *Pendennis* leaves her 'convinced that there are other aspects of life, and larger ones into the bargain' (*E*, III. 34). The comparison suggests that Woolf sets up these canonical authors as figureheads of a tradition which she herself supports and which Joyce, by implication, has failed to uphold. Thus, she draws freely and deeply on the literary past whilst belittling the work of a contemporary.

Woolf made similarly unfavourable comparisons between T. S. Eliot and earlier writers, particularly in 'The Narrow Bridge of Art' where, although she is considering the way forward for literature, she mocks contemporary works and praises earlier ones, seeing Eliot's description of a nightingale singing 'jug jug jug to dirty ears' in *The Waste Land* as inferior to Keats' 'Ode to the Nightingale', and noting that 'There trips along by the side of our modern beauty some mocking spirit which sneers at beauty for being beautiful' (*CE*, II. 223). There are also some sly asides in her diary, such as when she notes that he 'cant read Wordsworth when Wordsworth deals with nature' (*D*, II. 68), or when she recalls telling him: 'We're not as good as Keats' (*D*, II. 103–4).

Woolf's prizing of past literature over contemporary writing is complicated by the fact that many of her contemporaries drew on the literary past themselves. Contrary to the popular but simplistic conception of modernism as a movement which sought to effect a break with the past, scholarship of the past fifteen years has revealed intricate sets of links between modernists and their precursors: Bonnie Kime Scott in particular has sketched a web of intertextual connections linking various modernist writers with one another and with earlier writers.[31] Joyce and Eliot in particular drew on the literary past for their own writings, *Ulysses* and *The Waste Land* being well-known examples, and Pound wove fragments from a vast array of other texts into his poetry, leading May Sinclair to remark that 'there never was a poet more susceptible to influence'.[32]

Kevin Dettmar has argued that, for some modernist writers, an initial radical stance was followed by a form of literary criticism which attempted to give it academic credibility by linking it to established traditions:

> Critics of the second moment in an attempt to argue for the work's greatness, ironically blur the distinctions between the new work and the tradition against which it believes itself to be rebelling. This creates the uncomfortable situation in which the maverick work of new writers is made to look as traditional as possible, in order that it might be read.[33]

Eliot's notes to *The Waste Land* may cynically be read in this way, as a means of convincing a less than enthusiastic reading public of the merits of the work, and his essay 'Tradition and the Individual Talent' (1919) as giving theoretical credibility to this stance.

Woolf's denigration of writings by her contemporaries may therefore be read as a counter-strategy for questioning their claims to a place in the tradition. Her writings on female traditions in *A Room of One's Own* can be seen as a way of constructing an alternative tradition to theirs, whilst her theory of androgyny and her use of quotations and allusions in her own work become ways of establishing her rights to a literary tradition in opposition to theirs.[34] There is no space in this book to examine these strategies in detail, but some significant examples will be indicated briefly in the chapters that follow.

This book looks at eight of Woolf's novels, in the order in which they were written, examining how she engages with the literary past in each, and exploring how her reception of that past was conditioned by personal, intellectual and political contexts. Chapter 1 examines how *The Voyage Out* developed out of Woolf's reading experiences, and particularly out of her exploration of what it meant to read as a woman; Chapter 2 demonstrates how Woolf attempted to place herself within both male and female traditions in *Night and Day*. Chapter 3 demonstrates how Woolf's revolutionary modernist texts *Jacob's Room* and *Mrs Dalloway* drew on literature as far back as the Greek classics in order to mourn both cultural and personal losses and seek forms of renewal. Family influences are shown to underlie all of these works, but Chapters 4 and 5 will focus on the ways in which Woolf responded to and came to terms with the literary legacy of her father especially in *To the Lighthouse* and *Orlando*. The final two chapters demonstrate how Woolf's concerns and preoccupations with her personal history and intellectual pasts gave way to an investigation of the possibilities of wider cultural survival in *The Waves* and, more urgently, in *Between the Acts*, written at a time when the prospect of world war threatened to obliterate literature and culture as she had known them.

Notes

1. Rosenberg, *Woolf and Samuel Johnson*; Greene (ed.), *Woolf: Reading the Renaissance*. See also *Woolf Studies Annual* 9 (2003) and 10 (2004): Special Issues on Virginia Woolf and Literary History, ed. Lilienfeld, Oxford and Low, sections II, 'Storming the Library: Taking Back the Texts'; and III, 'Emerging Narratives of Gender'.
2. Gualtieri, *Woolf's Essays*, p. 15; Dusinberre, *Woolf's Renaissance*, p. 1.
3. Kristeva, 'Word, Dialogue and Novel' (1966), in *The Kristeva Reader*, ed. Moi, p. 37.
4. Barthes, 'The Death of the Author' (1968), in *Image–Music–Text*, p. 146.
5. Worton and Still (eds), *Intertextuality: Theories and Practices*, p. 1.
6. Ingelbien, 'Intertextuality, Critical Politics and the Modernist Canon', pp. 279–80.
7. Schlack, *Continuing Presences*; Fox, *Woolf and the Literature of the English Renaissance*; Beer, *Arguing with the Past* and *Woolf: The Common Ground*. See also Lyons, 'Textual Voyages'.

8. Cuddy-Keane, 'Virginia Woolf and the Varieties of Historicist Experience', p. 74.
9. Allen, *Intertextuality*, p. 209.
10. Cuddy-Keane, 'Thinking Historically about Historical Thinking'.
11. Lee, *Virginia Woolf*, p. 410.
12. Schweickart, 'Reading Ourselves', p. 627.
13. See Bloom, *The Anxiety of Influence*.
14. Banfield, *The Phantom Table*, p. 153.
15. Fogel, *Covert Relations*, p. 70.
16. Hutcheon, *A Theory of Parody*, p. 8. Mikhail Bakhtin has similarly noted that 'the speech of another, once enclosed in a context is – no matter how accurately transmitted – always subject to certain semantic changes' (*The Dialogic Imagination*, p. 340).
17. Reading notes, January 1909–11, at the back of Chapters 11–17 of the holograph draft of *Night and Day* pp. 4, 24. Berg Collection, New York Public Library.
18. Bakhtin, *The Dialogic Imagination*, p. 348.
19. Hutcheon, *A Theory of Parody*, p. 31.
20. Ibid., pp. 7, 19.
21. Booth, 'Virginia Woolf and Collective Biographies of Women'.
22. Showalter, *A Literature of Their Own*, pp. 263–97.
23. Marcus, *Virginia Woolf and the Languages of Patriarchy*; Schwartz, 'Thinking Back Through our Mothers'; Wallace, 'Thinking Back Through our Others'.
24. For an account of Woolf's education, see Hill, 'Virginia Woolf and Leslie Stephen'.
25. Maitland, *Leslie Stephen*, p. 475.
26. Ibid., p. 476.
27. Stephen, *The Playground of Europe*, p. 63.
28. Maitland, *Leslie Stephen*, p. 474.
29. Stephen, *Hours in a Library*, III. 139.
30. Stephen, 'Charlotte Brontë', *Hours in a Library*, III. 28–9. *George Eliot*, pp. 173–4.
31. Scott, *Refiguring Modernism*. See also Schneidau, *Waking Giants*; Laity, *H.D. and the Victorian Fin de Siècle*; Pierce and de Voogd (eds), *Laurence Sterne in Modernism and Postmodernism*.
32. Sinclair, 'The Reputation of Ezra Pound', in Scott (ed.), *The Gender of Modernism*, p. 469.
33. Dettmar, *Rereading the New*, p. 7.
34. Woolf's use of literary allusion has been compared with that of Joyce and Eliot: see Ames, 'The Modernist Canon Narrative'; and Zwerdling, '*Between the Acts* and the Coming of War', p. 231.

Chapter 1

From Woman Reader to Woman Writer: *The Voyage Out*

The year after *The Voyage Out* was published, Woolf wrote in 'Hours in a Library' that 'the great season for reading is the season between the ages of eighteen and twenty-four' (*CE*, II. 34). In her own case, that six-year period led up to her beginning *Melymbrosia*, the first draft of *The Voyage Out*, in 1907, at the age of twenty-five (*L*, I. 315 n.; *QB*, I. 125). Quentin Bell suggests that *Melymbrosia* 'may have had its beginnings in Virginia's imagination' in 1904 (*QB*, I. 125) and indeed, Woolf herself suggested that she had a 'vision' of her first book whilst visiting Manorbier in March 1904, which means that the novel was conceived in the midst of this period of intensive reading. In 'Hours in a Library', Woolf notes that 'scarcely any of the contemporary writers' are among the authors she read during that time, except George Meredith, Thomas Hardy and Henry James, who (she argues) had classic status, although they were still alive (*CE*, II. 36). This insight into Woolf's reading habits suggests that she began her own writing career by immersing herself in the work of others – almost exclusively writers from past eras. The process of writing *The Voyage Out* can thus be seen as a period of transition from reading books by earlier authors to writing her own. Woolf's reading of past literature and her reflections on the nature of reading had significant effects on the novel.

There is an important biographical subtext to Woolf's transition from reader to writer: Leslie Stephen died in February 1904, a month before she first conceived *Melymbrosia* and halfway through this period of intensive reading. Her first article – on Haworth and the Brontës – was published later that year. Woolf suggested much later that her father's death had enabled her to become a writer: on the day he would have turned ninety-six she noted in her diary that she would not have become a writer had he lived (*D*, III. 208). Yet, if her writing was a sign of her independence of her father, she also saw it as a way of remaining close to him. As Juliet Dusinberre has noted, Woolf may have turned to writing in 1904 as consolation for Stephen's death: 'Work was to be in Woolf's experience inseparable from personal loss.'[1] (There were, of course, other losses: of her mother and step-sister in the 1890s and her brother Thoby in 1906.) She may also have continued her intensive reading as a form of consolation: Woolf closely associated her father with the reading experience,[2] and several of the writers and texts alluded to in *The Voyage Out* – including John Milton, Edward Gibbon, William Cowper and Jane Austen – were among his favourite writers. As we will see, Woolf's readings of these writers in *The Voyage Out* display tensions between respecting Stephen's memory and seeking independence from him.

Woolf relives some memories of Stephen in *The Voyage Out* in the figure of the scholar, Ridley Ambrose. He exhibits Leslie Stephen's habit of reciting poetry aloud and is heard to recite one of Stephen's favourite poems, Milton's ode 'On the Morning of Christ's Nativity'. As Woolf noted in her memoir of Stephen: 'Milton of old writers was the one he knew best; he specially loved the "Ode on the Nativity", which he said to us regularly on Christmas night' (ibid., p. 475). The phrase 'said to us' suggests that she saw Stephen as having special intimacy with Milton's work: it is as though he was speaking his own words rather reiterating those of Milton. Woolf's recollection of this custom exhibits a tension between criticising Stephen for appropriating Milton and a desire to remember him through Milton's words.

Woolf's description of Ambrose ensconced in his library as a keeper of books also has a basis in her recollections of Stephen. Woolf sketched a scene for Vita Sackville-West several years later, in which she pictured herself

> tapping at my father's study door, saying very loud and clear 'Can I have another volume, father? I've finished this one'. Then he would be very pleased and say 'Gracious child, how you gobble!' . . . and get up and take down, it may have been the 6th or 7th volume of Gibbons complete works, or Speddings Bacon, or Cowper's Letters. 'But my dear, if its worth reading, its worth reading twice' he would say. (*L*, IV. 27)

The incident demonstrates how Stephen mediated the young Virginia's access to literature: he is the custodian of literature; Virginia has to knock for permission to enter his study and ask for another book. Her reading earns both praise and admonishment as he advises her to read the volume twice. Woolf plays out a similar scene, more critically, in *The Voyage Out*, where Ambrose sits behind a closed door 'alone like an idol in an empty church', expecting others to keep quiet as they pass. The daughterly interruption comes when his niece Rachel enters his room, calls him twice and asks for Gibbon's *History of the Roman Empire* (which has been recommended to her by a man, St John Hirst, in the first place). Ambrose does not oblige for he does not have a copy, and anyway disapproves of the choice – 'Gibbon! What on earth d'you want him for?' – and instead makes a series of recommendations of his own (*VO*, 192). The scene draws attention to the paternal custodianship of literature and the unequal position of the young woman reader.

Gibbon's work becomes a form of currency in the cultural economy of Rachel's circle, and references to him continue to raise anxieties about female exclusion from the reading experience. Gibbon is first mentioned when St John Hirst urges Rachel to read him, a recommendation which shows his ignorance of and patronising attitude towards women:

> 'About Gibbon,' he continued. 'D'you think you'll be able to appreciate him? He's the test, of course. It's awfully difficult to tell about women,' he continued, 'how much, I mean, is due to lack of training, and how much is native incapacity.' (*VO*, 172)

St John assigns women a negative value in the patriarchal system, as 'lacking' education and being intrinsically incapable. Rachel is understandably offended by this, but Gibbon becomes a means of dividing male and female experience, and asserting male dominance. Woolf describes how female characters try to deny Gibbon's cultural value. Mrs Thornbury remembers eschewing Gibbon's work in order to resist fatherly influence: 'My dear father was always quoting it at us, with the result that we resolved never to read a line' (*VO*, 224). Rachel reads Gibbon in a resistant, disinterested way. She opens a page and finds the words 'vivid and so beautiful'. Savouring sounds like 'Arabia Felix' and 'Aethiopia', she sets off on a flight of imagination along 'roads back to the very beginning of the world, on either side of which the populations of all times and countries stood in avenues, and by passing down them all knowledge would be hers'. Her excitement takes her away from the book, for 'she ceased to read' (*VO*, 196). Rachel's imaginative, expansive approach to reading does not help her to resist patriarchal valuations but merely marks her as an outsider to the cultural economy, for when she tells Hirst that she does not like Gibbon, she feels as though 'her value as a human being was lessened because she did not happen to admire the style of Gibbon' (*VO*, 226). The problem of how to valorise a female approach to reading underlies much of the novel.

Woolf further exposes the perils of imaginative, resistant reading in a passage where she describes Rachel reading Cowper:

> Next, she had picked up *Cowper's Letters*, the classic prescribed by her father which had bored her, so that one sentence chancing to say something about the smell of broom in his garden, she had thereupon seen the little hall at

Richmond laden with flowers on the day of her mother's funeral, smelling so
strong that now any flower-scent brought back the sickly horrible sensation
(*VO*, 33)

We need to distinguish between between Rachel's and Woolf's experiences of Cowper, for Woolf chose to re-read Cowper in 1908–9, suggesting that she did not share Rachel's view of him as dull. The passage does
suggest, however, that Woolf identified separate male and female strategies of reading. The idea of a 'prescribed' text in this passage indicates
that Willoughby Vinrace seems to think that the book will somehow do
Rachel good, whether she likes it or not. 'Pre-scribing' suggests writing
the plot in advance; the plot here is that of a male author of the eighteenth century whose experience is very different from that of a young
woman of the early twentieth. Rachel attempts to resist her father's prescription by reading the text imaginatively, but she retreats into funereal
thoughts, which, centring on her dead mother, emphasise female mortality and suggest that Cowper's male narrative could offer no useful course
for a female reader to follow.

An exploration of the part played by reading in Rachel's growth into
womanhood is central to the novel's *Bildungsroman* of her progress from
an 'unlicked girl' (*VO*, 19) to a young woman about to be married and
the curtailment of that process in her death (from a tropical disease)
shortly after her engagement. Early in the novel, we find Rachel sitting
in a room of her own reading Ibsen's *A Doll's House*. She is totally
engrossed in the play and continues to feel part of it, even after lifting her
eyes from the page. She stops reading to ask aloud, 'What's the truth of
it all?', a question asked 'partly as herself, and partly as the heroine of
the play she had just read' (*VO*, 136). As her absorption in the book
fades, Rachel goes on to formulate her own ideas about its themes, for
'she went on thinking of things that the book suggested to her, of women
and life' (*VO*, 137). The process of alternation between being carried
with the flow of a book and standing back to think for herself contributes to Rachel's development as a person:

She came to conclusions which had to be remodelled according to the adventures of the day, and were indeed recast as liberally as anyone could desire,
leaving always a small grain of belief behind them. (*VO*, 138)

As Kate Flint notes, this passage combines an acknowledgement of the
degree to which a reader can become absorbed in a book with 'a recognition (which the reader is expected to share) that such habits of identification, slipping into the skin and mind of a fictional character, can go
hand in hand with a self-awareness of the process which is taking place'.[3]

It also reflects Woolf's view of reading as expressed in 'How Should One Read a Book?', of allowing oneself to be caught up by the book first before passing judgement on one's impressions (*CE*, II. 8). The fact that Rachel is reading drama emphasises the degree to which she 'acts out' the text she reads. As Brownstein comments, Rachel learns about life 'by doing mysterious solitary researches into her own importance by becoming, as she reads fiction, a heroine'.[4] Rachel's attempt to read beyond the text of *A Doll's House* is significant, for that play presents Nora's decision to leave her husband as stepping outside received, especially written, wisdom: 'I've had enough of what most people say, what they write in books. It's not enough. I must think things out for myself, I must decide.'[5] The play cannot give Rachel guidance on what to do, for although Rachel, like Nora, steps outside the institution of marriage, it is by dying and not by leaving to start a new life.

Woolf's invocation of past plots in *The Voyage Out* may likewise be seen partly to demonstrate a concern to develop and authenticate female-centred responses to books she has read. A major factor in this process is the absence of women, or a silence about the realities of their lives, in earlier writings. *A Doll's House* is a case in point, for Ibsen's play does not depict Nora building a new life. A further instance is Woolf's rewriting of the outward voyage and inward journey of Joseph Conrad's *Heart of Darkness* to include a female protagonist in place of the male-centred narrative of Marlow and Kurtz which, as Nina Pelikan Strauss has pointed out, gives the novel an 'extremely masculine historical referentiality', an 'insistence on a male circle of readers'.[6] Woolf may be said to be providing a revision of *Heart of Darkness* which seeks to include female readers within its circle and tries to give substance to the figure of an engaged woman by seeing her as more than someone else's 'intended'. However, in her focus on a young woman's journey towards engagement, Woolf grapples in a more troubled and complex way with a problematic narrative form in which women *were* included: the long tradition of the courtship narrative.

I

The Voyage Out is a courtship novel at odds with the genre. Jane E. Miller has noted that the traditional courtship narrative was one in which the heroine develops psychologically, reaching a state of maturity symbolised by her marriage.[7] Rachel's development takes place in private, through reading and playing music, rather than in society, and her engagement is almost an accident, for Rachel and Terence's companions eagerly brand them as an engaged couple before they have fully taken this on board themselves. The betrothal is not a sign of Rachel's emotional and social maturity but, in effect, curtails her growth, and the novel ends not in marriage but in her death. The engagement takes place part-way through the novel, and the narrative might be expected to follow what Miller has described as a 'wedlock plot' in which married couples are shown in the process of learning to live with one another.[8] However, Rachel and Terence find it impossible to get to know one another, and indeed they wonder whether it is possible for men and women to understand one another at all.

Although Woolf was not unique among early twentieth-century novelists in seeking to adapt and critique courtship and marriage narratives and in questioning the validity of marriage as an institution, her critique was more oblique than that found in some novels of the recent past. *The Voyage Out* does not follow the trend of the 'New Woman' novels of the 1890s, which had foregrounded issues such as women's economic inequality, their rights over their children and their right to work, and often featured independent women who (like Nora in *A Doll's House*) left their husbands or led unconventional lives.[9] It also eschews the Edwardian pattern of the 'marriage problem novel', which depicted the frustrations of married people, although rarely depicting divorce and holding back from a full-scale attack on marriage as an institution:[10] indeed, we know from 'Modern Fiction' that Woolf particularly disliked the Edwardians Arnold Bennett and John Galsworthy, both of whom wrote social realist 'marriage problem' novels. Although *The Voyage Out* might be located within a trend, identified by Miller, of novels in which marriage was seen as 'a locus of frustration, confusion, unhappiness and violence . . . an unsettling rather than a stabilizing force',[11] it lacks the frankness of D. H. Lawrence's treatment of marriage in *The Rainbow* (or later, *Women in Love*) or the cynicism of E. M. Forster in *The Longest Journey*. Indeed, with its curtailed courtship plot, *The Voyage Out* is significantly silent on what might happen after marriage: rather than depicting Rachel seeking fulfilment elsewhere or rejecting marriage directly, Woolf simply lets her die.

If criticism or rejection of marriage was essentially a social issue for Woolf's immediate predecessors and her contemporaries, Woolf treated it also as a textual problem, for the literary past, in the shape of Jane Austen (a prominent figure in the history of the courtship narrative), becomes a key point of reference for the critique of marriage in *The Voyage Out*. Austen is recommended to Rachel by Richard and Clarissa Dalloway, who, in different ways, try to initiate Rachel into society and the marriage market: Clarissa reads *Persuasion* to her and later gives her a copy (*VO*, 64, 83).

Although Rachel's antipathy towards Austen may be read as a function of her rejection of society's expectations, these allusions may also be read in terms of Woolf's own negotiations with the legacy of a female literary tradition. The first reference to Austen raises concerns about the patriarchal custodianship of literature, and it is significant that Woolf associated Austen (like Gibbon and Cowper) with Leslie Stephen.[12] The chauvinistic Richard Dalloway persuades Rachel to read Austen, whom he describes as 'incomparably the greatest female writer we possess', because 'she does not attempt to write like a man. Every other woman does; on that account, I don't read 'em.' Dalloway pushes Austen outside masculine configurations into the marginalised category of 'woman writer'. As Dalloway's wife Clarissa points out, he does not read Austen himself: 'it's no good *your* pretending to know Jane by heart, considering that she always sends you to sleep!' (*VO*, 64). Thus Dalloway advises Rachel to read Austen, whom he dismisses as a woman writer (or a 'woman's writer'), thereby marginalising women's writing and their reading experience.

Dalloway's view of Jane Austen as a woman writer reflects an idea about writing and the separate spheres which had been widespread since the nineteenth century. For example, George Lewes criticised those women writers who wrote 'from the man's point of view, instead of from the woman's . . . women have too often thought but of rivalling men. It is their boast to be mistaken for men, – instead of speaking sincerely and energetically as women.'[13] Thus it can be seen that the 'female' perspective was itself defined by patriarchy and that Austen's popularity stems from the fact that, by keeping to that perspective, she was thought not to rival men in literary territories they claimed as their own: Lewes advocated Austen's seeming passivity as an antidote to 'angry' women writers, and he famously prescribed for Charlotte Brontë 'a course of reading in Jane Austen' in order to teach her to counterbalance her powerful feelings with observation of human nature.[14] Leslie Stephen viewed Austen as superior to Charlotte Brontë, and held her up as an example for women writers to follow:[15] these views are echoed by Clarissa Dalloway, who rates Austen more highly than the Brontës (*VO*, 59).

Patriarchal approval marginalised Austen as much as it valued her. Stephen (like George Lewes and Woolf's Richard Dalloway) praised her awareness of 'the precise limits of her own powers', limits which confined her to the home, and produced the 'unconscious charm of the domestic atmosphere of the stories'.[16] Stephen did not value the domestic sphere highly: 'allowing all possible praise to Miss Austen within her own sphere, I should dispute the conclusion that she was therefore entitled to be ranked with the great authors who have sounded the depths of human passion, or found symbols for the finest speculations of the human intellect, instead of amusing themselves with the humours of a country tea-table.'[17] Critical opinions such as these sought to define Austen restrictively as a 'woman writer', suitable reading material for 'women readers' and a suitable model for female writers to follow. As Bonnie Costello notes: 'Male praise [often] undermined women writers by isolating them in conventional gender categories that diminished their power', for example, by associating them with confined spaces and domesticity.[18]

Woolf's satire of Dalloway, then, critiques a patriarchal critical tradition which mediated her own reception of Jane Austen, but that legacy was too pervasive and wide-ranging to be dismissed so easily. The Jane Austen praised by the Dalloways was in many ways an invention of the Victorian culture into which Woolf was born. As B. C. Southam points out, Austen was reinvented and her popularity soared with the publication in 1870 of the first extended biographical account, a memoir by her nephew, J. E. Austen-Leigh. Anne Thackeray Ritchie famously reviewed the memoir in the *Cornhill* magazine and became influential in the popularisation of Austen. Leslie Stephen also played a part in establishing her as a prescribed author by writing the entry on her in the *Dictionary of National Biography*. Southam notes that, after 1870, Jane Austen was 'prescribed in . . . salutary terms'. Her novels were hailed as approved reading for the family circle because they conformed to John Ruskin's ideas of 'good books': they were seen to lack sensation and to endorse a domestic role for women.[19]

The key reason why Austen's major novels had such strong approval from Victorian society is the centrality of the courtship narrative within them: they were seen to endorse the values of marriage and domesticity. As Rachel Blau Du Plessis argues: 'Narrative outcome is one plane where . . . the word "convention" is found resonating between its literary and social meanings.'[20] She argues from Althusser that narrative is prescriptive, for it 'may function on a small scale the way that ideology functions on a large scale – as a "system of representation by which we imagine the world as it is"'.[21] The prescription of Austen by Victorian society can thus be seen as an attempt to 'pre-scribe' the lives of its young women.

Although Woolf satirised Richard Dalloway's view of Austen, her essays suggest that she had internalised male critical views. She echoes Lewes in *A Room of One's Own* when she praises Austen and Emily Brontë because they 'wrote as women write, not as men write', preferring them to Charlotte Brontë whose books are 'deformed and twisted' because she is 'at war with her lot' (*Room*, 71, 67). Woolf shared Stephen's approval of Austen's acceptance of her limitations and her use of a narrow environment to its fullest potential: she later wrote that from infancy, Austen 'knew not only what the world looked like, but had already chosen her kingdom. She had agreed that if she might rule over that territory, she would covet no other' (*CE*, I. 146). Woolf took these principles to heart in *The Voyage Out*, for she sets the novel in limited, enclosed environments – a ship, an isolated villa, a hotel and a river-boat – and develops her narrative through a series of exchanges at dances, expeditions, dinners and social gatherings. Like Austen, Woolf mentions world events tangentially rather than focusing on them.

Elements of Woolf's style in *The Voyage Out* suggest that she may have looked to Austen as a role-model for making veiled social criticism whilst apparently keeping within the culturally accepted limits for women writers. Indeed, Woolf has frequently been compared with Austen, starting from a review of *The Voyage Out* in 1915, which noted that 'One of [Woolf's] greatest gifts is satirical, and this side of her work makes it hard to refrain from a comparison with Jane Austen'.[22] Although Daniel Fogel has argued that the satire in *The Voyage Out* owes more to Henry James's comedies of manners than to those of Austen,[23] the complexities of Austen's position as a female role-model should not be ignored because they make her a powerful point of reference. Woolf recognised that Austen's greatest strength was her ability to satirise: 'when she is pointing out where [things and people] are bad, weak, faulty, exquisitely absurd she is winged and inapproachable' (*E*, II. 13), and a number of comments in *The Voyage Out* suggest that Woolf had studied Austen's method and put some of her techniques into practice. Like Austen, Woolf belittles characters by using reported speech to imply that what they actually said is not worth repeating. Austen, for example, dismisses the bookish Mary Bennet in *Pride and Prejudice*:

> [Elizabeth and Jane] found Mary, as usual, deep in the study of thorough bass and human nature; and had some new extracts to admire, and some new observations of thread-bare morality to listen to. (*PP*, 105)

Woolf gives similar short shrift to the pedantic Mr Pepper who gives a talk, which interests no one, on the submarine world, going on 'with considerable detail and with such show of knowledge, that Ridley was disgusted, and begged him to stop' (*VO*, 19). In both quotations, the satire is intensified by the ironic combination of praising and diminishing phrases. Although we are told that Mary's collection of quotations is to be admired, the implication is that she asks for, rather than deserves, admiration; similarly, Pepper does not impress people with his knowledge, but self-indulgently shows it off.

Austen also combines a demonstration of folly with a direct comment on it, extending the comic effect but also giving a false sense of authorial naïveté by directly acknowledging something which the reader will have noticed much earlier on. Austen spends two chapters in *Pride and Prejudice* presenting the pompous and sycophantic Mr Collins in a thoroughly ridiculous light, but rounds it off with the direct authorial comment that 'Mr Collins was not a sensible man, and the deficiency of nature had been but little assisted by education or society' (*PP*, 114). Woolf treats Evelyn Murgatroyd in *The Voyage Out* in a similar way: she begins by depicting Evelyn's excessive keenness to become friendly with every man she meets, but then goes on to gloss this account with an ironic authorial statement:

> The full and romantic career of Evelyn Murgatroyd is best hit off by her own words, 'Call me Evelyn and I'll call you St John.' She said that on very slight provocation – her surname was enough – but although a great many young men had answered her already with considerable spirit she went on saying it and making choice of none. (*VO*, 143)

Woolf's satire here not only takes on Austen's tone, but carries a conservative message, implicitly criticising Evelyn for flouting accepted standards of female behaviour. Rather than arguing for sexual freedom, as many of her contemporaries were doing, Woolf treats Evelyn with the suspicion that Austen directs towards man-hunters such as Lydia Bennet in *Pride and Prejudice* or Mary Crawford in *Mansfield Park*.

However, Woolf's use of Austenian satire and irony is uneven, for *The Voyage Out* resists the didactic structure found in Austen's novels (a constraint hinted at in Rachel's description of Austen as 'so like a tight plait' (*VO*, 59)), where Austen makes clear distinctions between characters who have her approval and those who do not. Woolf's disruption of the courtship narrative may be read in part as a reaction against Austen's didactic structure. Specifically, certain elements of the plot-line in *The Voyage Out* may be read as disruptions of the narrative pattern of *Pride and Prejudice*. In that novel, Austen brings about four marriages: Elizabeth Bennet and Fitzwilliam Darcy; Jane Bennet and Charles Bingley; Lydia Bennet and George Wickham; and Charlotte Lucas and William Collins. The serious side of the novel explores and justifies Elizabeth and Jane's motivations for choosing their husbands. The more satirical side criticises Lydia and Charlotte: the former brings scandal on her family by eloping; the latter makes the 'disgracing' decision to marry a man she does not like for the sake of material comfort (*PP*, 166). Austen also makes it clear that marriage is an economic imperative in her society: Elizabeth, Jane and Lydia cannot expect to inherit from their father because his estate is entailed on their cousin, William Collins. In the case of Elizabeth and Jane, Austen shows how it might be possible for women to maintain self-respect and build positive relationships as well as gaining economic security. She draws a careful contrast between these characters and Charlotte Lucas, who cynically sees marriage as an economic necessity only one step removed from prostitution: 'the only honourable provision for well-educated young women of small fortune' (*PP*, 163). Austen brings the moral and economic dimensions of marriage together when she hands out a system of 'rewards' to her four couples: Elizabeth wins the richest man in the book, with the highest social standing. Jane, the secondary heroine, marries Bingley, the 'single man in possession of a good fortune' described in the famous opening sentence. Charlotte marries Collins, a clergyman of only moderate social standing and income; and Lydia marries Wickham, a servant's son who is deeply in debt.

In *The Voyage Out*, Woolf begins to parallel this structure, for the novel also features a quartet of couples: Susan Warrington and Arthur Venning; Evelyn Murgatroyd and Mr Perrott; Helen Ambrose and St John Hirst; and Rachel and Terence. However, whereas marriage was a given in Austen's society, and so her critical comparison is directed at the spirit in which characters enter into it, Woolf uses her four couples to question the validity of marriage as an institution. The first couple, Susan and Arthur, become engaged and will presumably be married, but Woolf's satirical treatment of their engagement suggests her discomfort in seeing marriage as a positive outcome. Woolf's picture of Susan and Arthur veers from sympathy to ridicule. Her description begins sympathetically: in the scene when we first meet Susan we are made privy to her thoughts and she cuts a sad figure as a thirty-year-old spinster who would very much like to be married but has to endure the hardship of looking after her selfish invalid aunt. It is made clear that she is genuinely very fond of Arthur and, in the scenes that follow, we see his kindnesses towards her and his attempts to draw her out of her servitude. Not only are we shown that their relationship is founded on genuine affection, but Woolf implies that Susan stands to gain, rather than lose, freedom, by getting married. Their engagement scene begins sympathetically by presenting Susan's feelings as genuine and intense, an awareness of 'the excitement of intimacy' and a feeling that 'no human being had ever come so close to her before' (*VO*, 154). It then lapses into ridicule. Susan asks Arthur what first attracted him to her; Elizabeth Bennet poses a similar question when she asks Darcy what made him fall in love with her (*PP*, 388). Whereas Darcy replies that it was a gradual process, Arthur states that he was attracted by a buckle Susan had worn and by the fact that she did not take peas with her meal. The Austenian satire continues: 'From this they went on to compare their more serious tastes, or rather Susan ascertained what Arthur cared about, and professed herself very fond of the same thing' (*VO*, 155). The phrase 'professed herself', which is often used by Austen to expose hypocrisy, implies that Susan is trying hard to impress Arthur in order to secure him as a husband, so that she can 'escape the long solitude of an old maid's life' (*VO*, 155). This is an odd interpretation of Susan's behaviour – for she has just secured an offer of marriage – and it conflicts with the tone Woolf had taken towards the couple before their engagement.

Woolf tears apart the neat pattern of *Pride and Prejudice* with the other couples in the novel, for the prospect of marriage is forestalled in all three cases. The second relationship, between Evelyn Murgatroyd and Mr Perrott, ends in a proposal, but no engagement. Evelyn spends the whole of the novel trying to win a husband, but when Perrott proposes in the closing pages, her romantic notions wither away: 'Now that he was actually asking her, in his elderly gentle words, to marry him, she felt less for him than she had ever felt before' (*VO*, 426). The reason she gives for her refusal is a questioning of monogamy: 'I sometimes think I haven't got it in me to care very much for one person only' (*VO*, 427). The third couple, Helen Ambrose and St John Hirst, represent a radical opposition to marriage in themselves, for Helen is already married. Their relationship is never developed beyond flirtation and a feeling of mutual understanding, but they are frequently seen together and, like Jane and Bingley in *Pride and Prejudice*, they make a central quartet with the two main protagonists. In these two relationships, Woolf may be seen to share the concerns of Woolf's contemporaries: for example, Forster's criticism of monogamy in *The Longest Journey* and Lawrence's endorsement of adultery in *Sons and Lovers*. Yet, Woolf treats these issues ambivalently: Evelyn is not a sympathetic character and her rejection of Perrott is seen as capricious rather than principled; Helen and St John's relationship is not discussed, and Helen is never led to question openly her loyalty to her husband. The fourth couple are Terence and Rachel, who get engaged, but then face the greatest emotional problems rather than being given the greatest rewards.

Woolf's adoption of a courtship narrative and an Austenian style in *The Voyage Out* suggests that she had partly internalised prevailing ideas about the role of the 'woman writer'. Her disruption of the narrative, and her uneven use of Austenian satire, suggest that she was also uneasy about accepting the limitations inherent in that role, and ambivalent about winning patriarchal approbation by following the paradigm male critics such as Ruskin, Lewes and Stephen had identified in the works of Jane Austen. As Du Plessis has argued, there is an 'aggressive' element in

Woolf's rupturing of the marriage narrative with Rachel's death; it reacts against narrative convention – 'the plot "tyranny", that avalanche of events moving to "satisfactory solutions"'.[24] Ironically, then, Woolf's invocation and rejection of Austen's narrative technique suggests a violent assault on the legacy of her female precursor: a dismissal of Austen along with a rebuttal of the male critics.

However, Woolf's curtailment of Rachel and Terence's engagement in her untimely death is not such a radical rejection of Austen as it may appear. By not depicting their marriage, Woolf does not provide 'the drama of their problems, their developments, their mutual interaction' after marriage, which E. M. Forster saw as essential to a modern novel;[25] she even evades such descriptions of marital unhappiness as may be found in predecessors like George Eliot, Thomas Hardy and Henry James. By ending Rachel and Terence's relationship in the limbo of betrothal, Woolf was actually replicating the ending of Austen's novels, for, to all intents and purposes, Austenian heroines only ever get *engaged*. In all six novels, a brief account of the marriage takes place in the final chapter; *Emma* ends simply with the wedding. Marital happiness can be assumed, but often there are grounds to suspect otherwise. For example, in *Pride and Prejudice*, Darcy and Elizabeth are apart for much of the novel: the major shifts in Elizabeth's attitude towards him happen in his absence, and there are hints that it is easier for them to relate to one another when they are apart: for example, Elizabeth's feelings towards Darcy intensify whilst looking at his portrait – 'as she stood before the canvas, on which he was represented, and fixed his eyes upon herself, she thought of his regard with a deeper sentiment of gratitude than it had ever raised before' (*PP*, 272) – but when she meets him face-to-face moments later, she is embarrassed and unable to communicate. Woolf takes up these questions in *The Voyage Out*: by placing Terence and Rachel's engagement part-way through the novel, she attempts to probe what happens when a couple sets out towards marriage, and much of the central part of the book is concerned with their conversations together and their faltering attempts to get to know one another better.

Rather than rejecting Austen's narratives outright, then, Woolf affirms what Austen hints at: that marital happiness is easier to assert in a conclusion than to demonstrate in a developed narrative. Ironically, happiness is found in a concluding moment in *The Voyage Out*, for after Rachel's death, Terence briefly experiences 'happiness . . . perfect happiness. They had now what they had always wanted to have, the union which had been impossible while they lived' (*VO*, 412). Nick Smart has pointed out that this description echoes the closing words of Austen's

Emma, where we are told that the wishes and hopes of the friends who watched the wedding ceremony 'were fully answered in the perfect happiness of the union'.[26] The phrase 'perfect happiness' is used in *Northanger Abbey* as a synonym for marriage: 'To begin perfect happiness at the respective ages of twenty-six and eighteen is to do pretty well.'[27] In each of these novels, the heroine's achievement of 'perfect happiness' marks her disappearance from the narrative; just as Rachel disappears into death. Rachel's death can thus be read as a replication of, and a critical commentary on, the courtship narrative: in Linda Hutcheon's terms, it is a parody or 'extended repetition with critical difference'.[28]

Woolf's exploration of Terence and Rachel's efforts to get to know one another constitutes an effort to explore a subversive, a feminine aesthetic. In their exchanges, Terence and Rachel try to communicate through ideas which reach beyond language: he tells her of his plans to write a novel 'about Silence . . . the things people don't say' (*VO*, 249), and she talks about finding expression in music, for 'music goes straight for things. It says all there is to say at once' (*VO*, 239). These constitute hints at a semiotic order beyond the symbolic order. Shortly after finishing *The Voyage Out*, Woolf suggested that she associated Jane Austen with this kind of exploration:

> Only those who have realised for themselves the ridiculous inadequacy of a straight stick dipped in ink when brought in contact with the rich and tumultuous glow of life can appreciate to the full the wonder of her achievement, the imagination, the penetration, the insight, the courage, the sincerity which are required to bring before us one of those perfectly normal and simple incidents of average human life. (*E*, II. 14)

Here, Woolf reclaims Austen as a positive role-model, a female novelist who is able to wield the phallic 'straight stick' in order to capture the semiotic 'rich and tumultuous glow of life'. Woolf seeks to identify herself with Austen as a fellow novelist: the qualities she picks out for comment – imagination, penetration, insight, courage and sincerity – are not technical but personal, and so she seeks to restore the woman behind the writer. As Judith Lee argues, Woolf claims privileged knowledge of Austen and tries to '"express" a character through whom we can understand experience instead of describing a figure we merely observe'.[29] Yet Woolf's essays on Austen also suggest that she found her impossible to know: she describes her as 'inscrutable', yielding only 'blankness' despite Woolf's wish 'to know everything that it is possible to know about her' (*CE*, II. 275; *E*, II. 10). In effect, Austen comes to represent what Woolf seeks for herself: her analysis of Austen's writing prefigures her own ideas about using fiction to explore the 'luminous halo' of life in 'Modern Fiction' (*CE*, II. 106); in Schweickart's theory of reading, the 'subjectivity roused to life by reading', although it is attributed to Austen, is 'not a separate subjectivity but a projection of the subjectivity of the reader'.[30] Woolf's identification, then, becomes an imaginative attempt to develop an alternative Austen; this re-reading is made possible precisely because Austen had become an unknown quantity as her legacy was marginalised and circumscribed by patriarchal culture.

II

The Voyage Out can be seen as Woolf's novel about silence: a novel about the silencing of female experience, particularly the silence surrounding female sexuality. Such a silence is part and parcel of the courtship narrative, for it traditionally ends as the heroine enters marriage and faces the prospect of losing her virginity. An awakening of sexual consciousness is part of Rachel's personal development. This is first seen on board ship when Richard Dalloway seizes her and kisses her passionately, so that 'she felt the hardness of his body and the roughness of his cheek printed on hers' (*VO*, 80). Both parties are initially shocked by the encounter, but when Rachel goes outside, she is elated and amazed at the possibilities life holds for her. However, that night she is haunted by nightmares in which she finds herself wandering down 'a long tunnel' with 'damp bricks on either side', and finds herself with 'a little deformed man who squatted on the floor gibbering, with long nails', and then fears that the ship is being attacked by 'long barbarian men' (*VO*, 81–2).

In her account of this experience, Woolf uses literary allusions from male writers in innovative ways in order to figure the female sexual experience they often occlude. The figure in Rachel's nightmare is comparable to Milton's Comus, a hairy creature who threatens a lady's virtue; the figure of Comus was, in turn, based on Caliban from Shakespeare's *The Tempest*, who attempted to rape Miranda. Both these texts, read from the point of view of the female protagonist, set out an impossible choice between two evils: suffering a sexual assault or being rescued by men who have their own agendas (Miranda's father Prospero saves her from Caliban, only to steer her into a marriage which is dynastically favourable to himself; the Lady's brothers implicitly have similar economic interests in preserving their sister's virginity). Rachel's nightmare, which returns when she lies dying of a fever, can be seen as an expression of this dilemma in adverse reactions to her awakening sexuality: the first a response to Dalloway's kiss, the second a retreat from her forthcoming marriage.

The Voyage Out critiques the way in which patriarchy has rendered women strangers to their sexual selves. Although Schlack has read Rachel's death as an escape from marriage, a resisting of romance which, in Nancy K. Miller's words, enacts a *'bypassing* of the dialectics of desire' to produce 'a peculiarly feminine "act of victory"',[31] Rachel is also terrified of female sexuality, the spectre of the sexualised woman she has become. Louise De Salvo has noted that Woolf exhibits a concern with male views of sexuality and sexual relations from early in the composition process. She notes that the earliest known draft includes references to the heroine reading Sir Thomas Browne and becoming depressed by his cynicism about love and the possibility of men and women having meaningful relationships. Woolf read Browne in a similar way: as she wrote in 'The Elizabethan Lumber Room', Browne could force the mind to explore its darker side (*CE*, I. 51–2). As De Salvo notes, part of the heroine's process of self-discovery involves grappling with the ways in which men see her: she argues that the heroine here becomes 'not Everyman, but Every*woman* – or, to be more precise, Everyman's view of Everywoman which Everywoman rages against and accepts, in part as being a true assessment of her nature'.[32] In the draft of 1909–10, Woolf placed these anxieties in a modern setting, where Rachel rages against her father for keeping her confined to the house because there were prostitutes in London. The fear of prostitutes (a visible symbol of female sexuality) communicates itself to Rachel: in the final version of the novel, she names the 'women one sees in the streets' among the fears a young woman has to face (*VO*, 247). The fear and loathing generated by male control of female sexuality is thus shown to underlie apparently anodyne prescriptions of domesticity and decorum enshrined in courtship narratives.

If Woolf uses literary allusions as part of her critique of the problem of male control of female sexuality, she also uses them to help address that problem. The most liberating of these are drawn from the work of Walt Whitman. The drafts of the novel indicate that Woolf deliberately sought to include references to his work in this novel: she worked a series of references to his 'Passage to India' into the drafts and quotes from 'Calamus' in the final version. Whitman may have appealed to Woolf because he held democratic principles and because, as an American, he offered a perspective from outside her own culture. Chiefly, however, his poems may have appealed to Woolf for their homosexual content: although his celebration of the 'beautiful and sane affection of man for man' in his introduction to *Leaves of Grass* may seem androcentric, he wrote about experiences which went beyond heterosexual and patriarchal configurations. This consideration helps to explain a brief moment of happiness which Rachel experiences in her relationship with Terence, when she has a sense of 'peace between them. It might be love, but it was not the love of man for woman' (*VO*, 367). The references to Whitman, therefore, offer ways of speaking about love and sexuality which evade society's prescriptions.

Although 'Calamus' is quoted just once in the final version of *The Voyage Out*, certain congruences between themes in the poem and Woolf's portrayal of Terence and Rachel's relationship suggest that she had continued to think about the poem when writing this part of the novel. Terence reads it to Rachel on the river voyage when they first declare their love:

> Whoever you are holding me now in your hand,
> Without one thing all will be useless! (*VO*, 312)

Terence is interrupted by 'malicious' animal sounds before the 'one thing' is explained, but in turning to the next lines from 'Calamus' we can see that the missing element is knowledge of the other person:

> I give you fair warning before you attempt me further
> I am not what you supposed but far different.[33]

The missing lines explain why Terence should feel uneasy, mocked and threatened, and he proceeds to try to tell Rachel about 'the worst' about himself (*VO*, 347). Rachel, too, is unknowable, for she escapes from Terence during a mock fight in which her dress is torn: '"I'm a mermaid! I can swim!", she cried, "so the game's up!"' (*VO*, 347). The sequence, with its sexual overtones, prefigures Woolf's account of Rachel's death. This echoes a theme of elusiveness in 'Calamus':

> Even while you should think you had unquestionably caught me, behold!
> Already you see I have escaped from you.[34]

The theme of unknowability may function as a way of resisting paradigms in this relationship. Like the lovers in 'Calamus', Terence and Rachel recognise a tension between the way they construe their relationship and the way society sees it.

Although the allusions to Whitman offer some hope for resisting patriarchal heterosexual understandings, the last chapters are dominated by Woolf's critique of male control of female sexuality in an extended series of references to Milton's 'Comus' which permeate the account of Rachel's illness, as Beverly Ann Schlack and Louise De Salvo have shown.[35] Woolf enacts a radical rewriting of the poem, for 'Comus' ostensibly celebrates the ideal of female chastity: it tells the story of a virgin Lady who is threatened by the lustful spirit Comus but is rescued by Sabrina, a chaste river-nymph, before she can be deflowered. Schlack suggests that the theme of chastity threatened but saved is relevant to Rachel's dilemma as an inexperienced young woman terrified at the prospect of marriage, and reads Rachel's death as a means of both escaping marriage and preserving her chastity. However, Woolf's reading of 'Comus' is not this straightforward, for whereas in Milton's poem the Lady's life and chastity are saved, Rachel dies and is lost to Terence and St John, whose position parallels that of the two brothers. The re-reading explores at length the young woman's impossible choice between becoming sexually active (and thus 'fallen' in patriarchal terms) and remaining chaste and therefore still enclosed.

Schlack and De Salvo do not appear to notice that, in general, the allusions to 'Comus' appear in the reverse order from Milton's poem, so that Milton's tale of an encounter with danger and a rescue is rewritten as a delivery into danger and death. The first reference to 'Comus', which occurs as Rachel falls ill while Terence recites the poem to her, comes from the conclusion of the poem, when the Lady is about to be saved:

> There is a gentle nymph not far from hence,
> he read,
>   That with moist curb sways the smooth Severn stream.
>   Sabrina is her name, a virgin pure;
>   Whilom she was the daughter of Locrine,
>   That had the sceptre from his father Brute. (VO, 380; 'Comus', l. 823)

Terence continues his recitation with the song in which the Lady's Attendant Spirit calls for Sabrina to come from under the 'glassy, cool, translucent wave', and 'listen and save' the Lady (VO, 381; 'Comus', ll. 858–65). Rachel finds that the words 'sounded strange', and instead of experiencing the reassurance of this moment of rescue, she sets off 'upon curious trains of thought suggested by words such as "curb" and "Locrine" and "Brute", which brought unpleasant sights before her eyes, independent of their meaning' (VO, 380–1). Significantly, two of the words Rachel lights upon in her misreading of the poem conjure up images of restraint by force: the saviour Sabrina is represented as a conspirator in the patriarchal control of women. While listening to the poem, Rachel begins to suffer from the headache which proves to be the first symptom of her illness: the disjuncture between the happy conclusion to Milton's poem and Rachel's illness is emphasised by juxtaposing the last line of the quotation, 'Listen and save', with Rachel's response, 'But her head ached' (VO, 381).

After this initial quotation, Milton's poem is thoroughly disrupted, as fragments are woven into Woolf's text: in Schlack's words, the quotations are 'no longer set off with quotation marks as . . . "foreign"' but are 'thoroughly integrated into Woolf's own narrative'; and as they are repeated, they are subjected to 'further development and expansion'.[36] Yet, rather than preserving Milton's original meaning, as Schlack suggests, Woolf continues to twist Milton's ideas, wrenching them out of their original context. Milton's depiction of Sabrina is consistently subverted: in 'Comus', the Lady trusts in 'the sun-clad power of chastity' (l. 781) to protect her, but Rachel cannot bear sunlight or whiteness, and finds her bedroom wall 'painfully white' (*VO*, 382), as her illness takes hold; Milton's Lady is released from Comus's spell by Sabrina's 'chaste palms moist and cold' ('Comus', l. 917), but Rachel shrinks from the touch of the nurse's cold hands (*VO*, 385). Sabrina is associated with positive, underwater images (she lives under a 'glossy, cool, translucent wave' (l. 860), and she once jumped into the Severn to escape from the wrath of her stepmother). Rachel, on the other hand, imagines her nurse living 'under a river' in slimy tunnels, and later has feverish dreams with ugly images of an underwater tunnel with 'little deformed women sitting in archways' and walls that 'oozed with damp'. Her fever becomes 'a deep pool of sticky water, which eventually closed over her head', although this does free her from the faces of her 'tormentors' (*VO*, 386, 397).

Woolf's negative readings of 'Comus' extend from Rachel's delirium into Terence's thoughts: here, they become even more troubled and also take on elegiac qualities of loss and sorrow. When Rachel says that she has a headache, Terence hears 'the shiver of broken glass which, as it fell to earth, left him sitting in the open air' (*VO*, 381). This echoes an earlier scene from 'Comus' when the Lady's brothers try to rescue her, but though they shatter Comus's glass of potion and cause him to flee, they cannot release her from his paralysing spell. Schlack argues that this action could be read as Rachel's refusal to give Terence sexual pleasure (for Comus's potion has aphrodisiac properties), but Woolf's narration emphasises Terence's distress rather than Rachel's potential freedom. The shattering of the glass in 'Comus' is the first stage in the Lady's rescue, but in *The Voyage Out* it sounds an ominous note at the onset of Rachel's illness.

The next allusion to Milton after the glass-breaking scene comes as Rachel wakes with a fever, a few hours later. Reversing the sequence of 'Comus', this scene alludes to Milton's episode in which the Lady is tempted by Comus. That encounter is suggested both by Rachel's feeling that there is an animal in the room (Comus is here elided with the effect of his potion, which turns people into animals) and by the visit from Dr Rodriguez, the untrustworthy doctor, who is described as hairy and like

Comus is a purveyor of potions. Rachel is not tempted by the Comus figure, but shrinks from the doctor (the sexualised racial other), who has the power to make her well but in doing so would deliver her into marriage.

The focus shifts to Terence in the next cluster of allusions. He confronts Dr Rodriguez about his treatment of Rachel, and his loss of trust in the doctor is confirmed as he too becomes aware of his bestial appearance. Shortly afterwards, Terence also loses trust in Nurse McInnes, who 'seemed to shrivel beneath one's eyes and become worthless, malicious, and untrustworthy' (*VO*, 401). The process of unmasking alludes to a scene earlier in Milton's masque, when the Attendant Spirit tells the brothers that he has seen the Lady with Comus, and 'knew the foul enchanter though disguised' as a shepherd ('Comus', l. 644).

The allusions culminate in a scene where Terence and St John fear for Rachel's life, which parallels a sequence towards the beginning of the masque where the Lady's brothers fear for their missing sister. Like the brothers, who are not significantly distinguished from one another (they are nameless and only ever seen as a pair), Terence and St John are mistaken for one another as Dr Lesage addresses them 'equally, as if he did not remember which of them was engaged to the young lady' (*VO*, 406). By distorting the sequence of 'Comus' in her allusions, Woolf takes the Lady's story back to the brothers' wanderings in search of their sister. Going back further might present Rachel, like the Lady, wandering freely; but instead Rachel effectively disappears from the narrative. By showing both Rachel and Terence re-reading 'Comus' – one in a state of delirium, the other in a troubled emotional state where 'pain lies, quiescent, but ready to devour' (*VO*, 402) – and by gradually shifting the focus away from Rachel towards Terence, the novel emphasises loss and desolation, rather than escape.

The focus on Terence introduces an elegiac quality to the novel which dilutes its critical edge. This becomes even more pronounced as Woolf goes on to describe Rachel's death and its aftermath from Terence's point of view, using a series of allusions to Milton's 'Ode on the Morning of Christ's Nativity'. As with 'Comus', the meaning of this poem is distorted, for the allusions to the 'Ode' in the context of Rachel's death subvert Milton's theme of Christian consolation. Like 'Comus', the Ode is introduced by a character in the novel: Terence and St John overhear Ridley Ambrose reciting it as Rachel's illness nears its crisis. Their reaction imposes negative meanings on a hopeful poem: the 'Nativity Ode' celebrates the birth of Christ, but Terence and St John find its words 'strangely discomforting' (*VO*, 409). The poem reappears in buried allusions during Woolf's description of Rachel's death:

It was nothing: it was to cease to breathe. It was happiness, it was perfect happiness. They had now what they had always wanted to have, the union which had been impossible while they lived. . . . It seemed to him that their complete union and happiness filled the room with rings eddying more and more widely. (*VO*, 412)

Here, Milton's words are interspersed with Jane Austen's phrase 'perfect happiness', for the swirling 'rings' echo Milton's song of celestial jubilation at the Nativity, 'Ring out, ye crystal spheres' ('Nativity Ode', l. 125). The moment of happiness and union with Rachel which Terence experiences at her death ironically echoes Milton's description of Christ's birth:

Nature that heard such sound
Beneath the hollow round
  Of Cynthia's seat, the airy region thrilling,
Now was almost won
To think her part was done,
  And that her reign had here its last fulfilling;
She knew such harmony alone
  Could hold all heaven and earth in happier union. ('Nativity Ode', l. 101)

Cynthia, the moon goddess, is invoked in the moonshine which lights the scene in Woolf's novel (Cynthia was also Woolf's original choice of name for the heroine of *Melymbrosia*). The description of Rachel's death matches the Ode rhetorically: each presents a brief moment of stasis and peace which gives way to pain: Milton cuts across the jubilation with the reminder that it is Christ's death, not his birth, which will save mankind, for the smiling infant 'on the bitter cross | Must redeem our loss' ('Nativity Ode', l. 152). Milton also writes of the sorrow of the pagan gods forced to relinquish their posts. In *The Voyage Out*, Terence's moment of happiness is shattered when he is dragged by anonymous hands from Rachel's side and realises with horror that 'here was a world in which he would never see Rachel again' (*VO*, 413). Terence's grief echoes the sorrow of the pagan gods in Milton's poem, for as he is jostled from the room, he 'shrieks' Rachel's name, echoing the departure of the pagan gods: 'Apollo from his shrine | Can no more divine | With hollow shriek the steep of Delphos leaving' (l. 176). The ending of *The Voyage Out* is one of loss without consolation: it emphasises desolation and makes no mention of the poem's affirmation of Christian hope. Rachel's absolute disappearance from the narrative and the lack of consolation for her death make it difficult to claim the ending of her story in Nancy Miller's terms as a 'feminine "act of victory"'.[37] Even the dream-world of the delirium in which Rachel re-reads Milton is not sustained, for the novel ends anticlimatically with an account of the ordinary lives of the minor characters at the hotel.

Woolf's extended reading of Milton 'against the grain' in her account of her heroine's death seems to amount to the same as Rachel's reading of Cowper, which strayed from the text to thoughts of her dead mother. However, something more dynamic has happened in this series of allusions. In her adaptation and internalisation of Milton's words, Woolf does not refer *out* to another text, but brings elements of that text *in* to her own novel. This radically alters the nature of authority implicit in the act of reference. Annette Wheeler Cafarelli, in a discussion of Ann Radcliffe, suggests that Miltonic allusions serve the dual purpose of promoting 'an intellectual lineage for the novel' at a time when it was becoming increasingly associated with women writers and women readers; and of staking 'territory for women in the mainstream of male literature'.[38] She concludes that women novelists such as Radcliffe did not reject male texts but appropriated them in order to claim access to the mainstream of literature. Woolf uses Miltonic allusions in *The Voyage Out* in a diametrically opposite way: she appropriates Milton's words for a kind of writing which is constructed as an alternative to 'mainstream' literature.

Milton's words become vulnerable in the process of being incorporated into *The Voyage Out*. This vulnerability is seen when the 'Nativity Ode' is introduced as Terence and St John overhear Ridley Ambrose reciting it while Rachel lies dying:

> Ridley paced up and down the terrace repeating stanzas of a long poem, in a subdued but suddenly sonorous voice. Fragments of the poem were wafted in at the open window as he passed and repassed. (*VO*, 409)

In this sequence, the 'Ode' (which is not named) is broken down from a 'long poem' into 'stanzas', and it is interrupted and broken up as Ridley's voice fades in and out. Woolf's use of Milton's 'Ode' to talk of pain and illness challenges Leslie Stephen's view of literature as healthy, in that the 'true power' of great writers 'rests upon their utterance of the ennobling and health-giving emotions'.[39]

However, this is not a full-scale challenge to the patriarchal power of Milton or Stephen, for the sequence has an elegiac dimension which goes beyond the context of Rachel's death. Describing Stephen's love of the 'Nativity Ode' in her memoir for Maitland, Woolf added that it was 'the last poem he tried to say on the Christmas night before he died; he remembered the words, but was then too weak to speak them.'[40] Ridley's broken recitation in *The Voyage Out* can be read as a fictional replaying of this incident. Patriarchal authority, then, may be rendered vulnerable and even shattered, but the note of sorrow and mourning on which Rachel's story ends suggests that Woolf's loss of her father (figured in

Rachel's death and Terence's mourning) also left a void which could not be filled.

III

The Voyage Out is a novel about absence, loss and silence. It was planned during a time when Woolf experienced two close bereavements, and its plot ends in death and loss. Woolf's engagement with the literary past in the novel is similarly concerned with absence and silence: the novel engages problematically with a female literary tradition which had been marginalised by critics, and seeks to address areas such as female sexuality on which much past literature was silent. Whereas Woolf probes silences within a female tradition, represented by Jane Austen, she creates gaps in a male one, breaking the works of Cowper, Gibbon and Milton into fragments to re-work them imaginatively, but often in ways which tend towards images of death or negation.

The specific juxtaposition of Austen and Milton in *The Voyage Out* is not coincidental, for Woolf continued to play them off against one another. She used them to represent male and female traditions, respectively, in *A Room of One's Own*, when she urged women readers and writers to look back through Austen as a literary mother, and to 'look past Milton's bogey' (*Room*, 72–3, 108). Although Woolf appears here to polarise their influence into female/supportive versus male/threatening, another allusion in the essay suggests a more fluid connection.[41] Woolf characterised the lost female tradition in the figure of 'some mute and inglorious Jane Austen' (*Room*, 48): as Alice Fox has pointed out, this complex allusion parodies a line in Thomas Gray's 'Elegy Written in a Country Church Yard' which speculates that 'Some mute and inglorious Milton here may rest'.[42] In Woolf's phrase, Austen takes the place of a silenced Milton, only to be silenced herself. The tradition Woolf envisages thus depends upon both precursors being silenced and re-made in her imagination.

If silence is a precondition for creation, it is also a problem to be solved: Woolf is frustrated by Austen's 'inscrutable' nature, and she invests her allusions to Milton, Cowper and Gibbon with an elegiac strain. Literary creation becomes a way of making up for loss: a compensation for personal loss, as Dusinberre has suggested, but also for a lost literary past. *The Voyage Out* thus sets a pattern which will be seen to mark much of Woolf's later engagement with the literary past: a tension between a desire to break and reform and a temptation to restore and reclaim.

Notes

1. Dusinberre, *Woolf's Renaissance*, pp. 16–17.
2. See Maitland, *Leslie Stephen*, pp. 474–6.
3. Flint, *The Woman Reader*, pp. 272–3.
4. Brownstein, *Becoming a Heroine*, pp. 8–9.
5. Ibsen, *A Doll's House*, III. 574.
6. Strauss, 'The Exclusion of the Intended', p. 173.
7. Miller, *Rebel Women*, p. 45.
8. Ibid., p. 45.
9. Pykett, *Engendering Fictions*, pp. 57–8. See also Ardis, *New Women, New Novels*.
10. Miller, *Rebel Women*, p. 40.
11. Ibid., p. 83.
12. Maitland, *Leslie Stephen*, p. 475.
13. Allott (ed.), *Brontës: Critical Heritage*, p. 162.
14. Ibid., p. 24.
15. See, for example, his criticism of Anne Thackeray Ritchie: 'Had she . . . any share of Miss Austen's gift for clearness, proportion, and neatness, her books would have been much better' (*MBk*, 14).
16. Stephen, 'Jane Austen', *Dictionary of National Biography*, I. 732.
17. Stephen, 'Humour', pp. 324–5.
18. Costello, 'Response to [Gilbert and Gubar's] "Tradition and the Female Talent"', p. 28.
19. Southam (ed.), *Jane Austen: Critical Heritage*, II. 8–9.
20. Du Plessis, *Writing Beyond the Ending*, p. 3.
21. Ibid., p. 3.
22. Majumdar and McLaurin (eds), *Woolf: The Critical Heritage*, p. 63. Many reviewers saw *Night and Day* as a pale reflection of Austen, as will be discussed in Chapter 2. See also Blain, 'Narrative Voice and the Female Perspective in Virginia Woolf's Early Novels'; Todd, 'Who's Afraid of Jane Austen?'; and Lee '"Without Hate, Without Bitterness . . ."'.
23. Fogel, *Covert Relations*, p. 124.
24. Du Plessis, *Writing Beyond the Ending*, p. 50.
25. Miller, *Rebel Women*, p. 39.
26. Austen, *Emma*, p. 465; Smart, '"Never See Rachel Again": Virginia Woolf and Domestic Fiction'.
27. Austen, *Northanger Abbey*, p. 243.
28. Hutcheon, *A Theory of Parody*, p. 7.
29. Lee, '"Without Hate, Without Bitterness . . .", pp. 111, 112.
30. Schweickart, 'Reading Ourselves', p. 627.
31. Miller, *Subject to Change*, pp. 31–2.
32. De Salvo, *Woolf's First Voyage*, p. 21.
33. Whitman, *Leaves of Grass*, p. 97.
34. Ibid., p. 97.
35. Schlack, *Continuing Presences*, pp. 20–7; and De Salvo, *Woolf's First Voyage*, pp. 137–46, 149–52.
36. Schlack, *Continuing Presences*, p. 24.
37. Miller, *Subject to Change*, p. 32.

38. Cafarelli, 'How Theories of Romanticism Exclude Women', p. 87.

39. Stephen, *Men, Books and Mountains*, p. 227.

40. Maitland, *Leslie Stephen*, p. 475. Earlier versions make it clear that Woolf wanted to use a quotation she associated with her father at this point in the narrative. De Salvo points out that a margin note in the holograph reads: 'Keats The Ode to a Nightingale or the poems of Milton' (*Virginia Woolf's First Voyage*, p. 141): Woolf named Keats as one of Stephen's favourite poets in her memoir for Maitland. In the typescript, Ridley Ambrose quotes a line from Henry Newbolt's 'Drake's Drum', another favourite poem of Stephen's which he often read aloud (ibid., pp. 147–8; *L*, I. 47 and n).

41. Low similarly questions Woolf's view of Milton as a 'bogey' and suggests that Woolf echoes 'feminist' dimensions in his work in her fiction, in 'Two Figures Standing in Dense Violet Light', pp. 144–5.

42. Fox, 'Literary Allusion as Feminist Criticism in *A Room of One's Own*', p. 150.

Chapter 2

Tradition and Exploration in *Night and Day*

It is doubtful whether in the course of the centuries, though we have learnt much about making machines, we have learned anything about making literature. We do not come to write better; all that we can be said to do is to keep moving, now a little in this direction, now in that, but with a circular tendency should the whole course of the track be viewed from a sufficiently lofty pinnacle.

Woolf, 'Modern Novels' (*Times Literary Supplement*, 10 April 1919)

Katherine Mansfield criticised *Night and Day* for being old-fashioned on its first publication in 1919, describing it as 'a novel in the tradition of the English novel. In the midst of our admiration it makes us feel old and chill: we had never thought to look upon its like again!'[1] As a courtship drama, which reaches a comic conclusion in the engagement of two couples, the novel can be read as conservative not only for following an age-old narrative pattern but also for appearing to endorse the conservative social imperative of marriage. It thus seems to undo the progress made by Woolf's contemporaries and immediate precursors, from the so-called 'New Woman' novels to the radical sexual agenda of D. H. Lawrence.[2] With its structured plot, conventional ending, rounded characters and setting in pre-war London, *Night and Day* sits oddly with modernist writings of the time (such as Mansfield's own work). It also reads as an aberration in Woolf's development as a novelist: it takes fewer risks with plot and characterisation than her first novel *The Voyage Out*; and is an unlikely predecessor to *Jacob's Room*, in which character and plot are fragmented and decentred. For these reasons, *Night and Day* has often been dismissed for its apparent reversion to tradition in subject-matter and narrative form, or at best seen as an unsatisfactory experiment which convinced Woolf of the need for reform and innovation in narrative fiction.

Night and Day also appears to conflict with ideas about the novel as a genre which Woolf was developing at the same time, particularly in

'Modern Novels', published shortly before the novel (and later collected as 'Modern Fiction'). In the essay, Woolf speculates about the kind of novel which might be written 'if one were free and could set down what one chose', and suggests that (unlike *Night and Day*) such a novel would have 'no plot, little probability, and a vague general confusion in which the clear-cut features of the tragic, the comic, the passionate, and the lyrical were dissolved beyond the possibility of separate recognition' (*E*, III. 33). 'Modern Novels' has been taken as Woolf's rejection of *Night and Day*,[3] and her criticism of novels in which 'we go on perseveringly, conscientiously, constructing our thirty-two chapters after a design which more and more ceases to resemble the vision in our minds' (*E*, III. 33) could be read as a hint at her frustration in writing the thirty-four chapters of *Night and Day*.

Woolf's choice of an old-fashioned style goes hand-in-hand with her depiction of a social world which no longer existed. As Suzanne Raitt notes in her introduction to *Night and Day*, 'Virginia was simply too fragile mentally to allow herself to document the destruction of the pre-War world towards which she had such intense and complex feelings' (*ND*, xv). Although Woolf wrote the novel during the closing stages of the First World War, many details (such as the mention of the Welsh Harp Reservoir, which closed its gates in 1910 (*ND*, 546)), as well as the absence of any reference to the war, set the action in a pre-war world. In turning back time to overlook the destruction caused by the war, Woolf also evokes the gender relations of an earlier era: in particular, looking back to an era before the vote was won. Thus, Woolf's use of the outmoded literary style of the courtship narrative (which in itself placed central importance on marriage, domesticity and the reproduction of the patriarchal family) can be seen as a way of immersing herself in, and examining in writing, the social order into which she had been born.

However, as this chapter will argue, *Night and Day* is not a complete capitulation to convention, for it attempts a negotiated return to the literary past: in other words, it can be read as parody. In *Night and Day*, Woolf attempted to reform the traditional novel from within, particularly by consciously invoking the plots of her female precursors in order to make their legacy easier to deal with. In Linda Hutcheon's terms, *Night and Day* offers an 'extended repetition' of the form with 'critical difference' by which its norms are questioned. The process was not without its problems, for there is a danger of endorsing older values by repeating traditional patterns. A narrative ending in marriage, like the marriage ceremony itself, can be seen in terms of what Judith Butler has described as 'ritualized production', an act which brings individuals into conformity with society's norms unless the norms or rituals are cited ironically.[4] I will argue that although *Night and Day* critiques the narrative patterns it parodies, it does not manage fully to ironise or subvert these patterns and their underlying values. On the other hand, we will see that there are further allusive layers in the novel – references to Shakespearean comedy and an invocation of Romantic ideas about the workings of the mind in particular – which serve to unsettle the parameters of the traditional novel and point towards future reforms.

I

The necessity of dealing with literary, personal and familial pasts is established as a theme in the opening chapters of the novel in the figure of Mrs Hilbery, the daughter of a famous Victorian poet, Richard Alardyce. Woolf uses Mrs Hilbery to explore the difficulty of living under the weight of the literary past, particularly the problems arising from having a well-known writer as a father. A room in the Hilbery home is set aside as a shrine containing a collection of Alardyce's manuscripts and possessions, and Mrs Hilbery, assisted by her daughter Katharine, spends her life trying to write his biography. Woolf shows that the weight of the past can be oppressive and the writing of the biography stifling and frustrating. Katharine sees herself as a Bloomian latecomer, 'one forced to make her experiment in living when the great age was dead' (*ND*, 35), but also takes pleasure in her distinguished family, for she enjoys dreaming of her ancestors, seeing herself as 'the companion of those giant men, of their own lineage' (*ND*, 10).

Woolf's account of Mrs Hilbery's attempts to write, in particular, shows how illustrious forebears can inhibit the writing of those who come afterwards, particularly women. Mrs Hilbery's biography seems destined never to progress beyond disjointed fragments, with its variety of alternative opening paragraphs and long digressions (*ND*, 38). These problems are akin to the predicament of the Victorian woman writer which Sandra Gilbert and Susan Gubar have called the 'anxiety of authorship': the fear that 'the act of writing will isolate or destroy her'.[5]

The character of Mrs Hilbery is based on Woolf's step-aunt, the Victorian novelist Anne Thackeray Ritchie (*D*, I. 247 n2). The portrait of Mrs Hilbery as a failing writer was something of a travesty, because Ritchie herself was prolific and successful: she completed eight novels, including *The Story of Elizabeth*, *The Village on the Cliff* and *Old Kensington*; a biography of Mme de Sévigné; and many essays and memoirs. However, Mrs Hilbery's struggles with the biography are true of Ritchie: she wrote episodically about her father, William Makepeace

Thackeray, in *Chapters from Some Memoirs*, in deference to his wish not to be the subject of a biography; and, like Mrs Hilbery, she was anxious about offending her father's memory either by making private issues public or by the failure of her own ventures.[6]

Ritchie played an important part in Woolf's attempt to recall and deal with a pre-war world which resonated for her personally and as a writer. She was the sister of Leslie Stephen's first wife, Minny; she shared their home at Hyde Park Gate and stayed on for two years after Minny's death, until her marriage to Richmond Ritchie in 1877. Although Ritchie was alive when Woolf began to write *Night and Day*, her death in February 1919 prompted Woolf to reflect that she had lost a link with her personal past: 'Father cared for her; she goes down the last, almost, of that old 19th Century Hyde Park Gate world' (*D*, I. 247). This comment suggests that Woolf's feelings for Ritchie were strongly overdetermined by her relationships with other people. Woolf found Ritchie as a person 'a little distant, & more than a little melancholy' and felt that she 'showed very little anxiety to see one' (*D*, I. 247), but she valued her because Leslie Stephen liked her, and because she represented the family pre-history of Stephen's life before his marriage to Julia Duckworth and the births of Virginia and her full-blood siblings.

Woolf recognised that Ritchie provided links with, and indeed embodied, a literary past which included both female and male precursors. Besides being Thackeray's daughter, she was a friend of Henry James, Alfred Tennyson, Thomas and Jane Carlyle, and Robert Browning and Elizabeth Barrett Browning.[7] In an obituary for the *Times Literary Supplement*, Woolf suggested that Ritchie would become 'the transparent medium through which we behold the dead. . . . Above all and for ever she will be the companion and interpreter of her father, whose spirit she has made to walk among us not only because she wrote of him, but because even more wonderfully she lived in him. It would have pleased her well to claim no separate lot for herself, but to be merged in the greater light of his memory' (*E*, III. 18). Where Woolf's personal memories of her aunt were intimately connected with her feelings for Leslie Stephen, she saw Ritchie as integrally linked with *her* father, William Thackeray.

The account of Mrs Hilbery's struggle with the past can also be seen to reflect Woolf's attitude towards famous members of her own family. The Hilbery family, with its colonial administrators, judges, philanthropists and writers, closely resembles Woolf's own family. The description of Mrs Hilbery and her struggles with her family history may thus be seen to identify, and perhaps make light of, the weight of patriarchy. Mrs Hilbery's problems may even reflect Woolf's own difficulties in writing about Leslie Stephen, for shortly after his death she commented that 'all this stupid writing and reading about father seems to put him further away' (*L*, I. 131). She told Violet Dickinson that she found it difficult to write her memoir for Maitland's *Life*: 'I really did get depressed about that thing, as I especially wanted it to be good' (*L*, I. 176).

Ritchie had helped to create a female literary tradition, for she had played an influential role in defining the legacy of the earlier generation of women writers by helping further Jane Austen's reputation among the Victorians in a landmark essay of 1870.[8] Although the essay panders to Victorian tastes in its readings of Austen, it also displays an early attempt to sketch out a female literary tradition, not by tracing lines of inheritance but by testifying to the intimacies which develop between writer and reader, and between writers. This is exemplified by Ritchie's digression on her own fondness for, and identification with, characters such as Anne Elliot in *Persuasion*:

> Looking at oneself – not as oneself, but as an abstract human being – one is lost in wonder at the vast complexities which have been brought to bear upon it; lost in wonder, and in disappointment perhaps, at the discordant result of so great a harmony. Only we know that the whole diapason is beyond our grasp . . . [W]e seize a note or two of the great symphony, and try to sing; and because these notes happen to jar, we think all is discordant hopelessness. Then come pressing onward in the crowd of life, voices with some of the notes that are wanting to our own part – voices tuned to the same key as our own, or to an accordant one; making harmony for us as they pass us by.[9]

Here, the collective body of writers is described in terms of a vast choir; sympathy with another writer in terms of singing in harmony. Ritchie's work can thus be seen as a prototype for Woolf's more historically grounded account of the female tradition in *A Room of One's Own*.

As we will see, Ritchie's own fiction, which was influenced by Austen in certain ways, forms an important intertext in Woolf's response to the legacy of her female precursors. Woolf's attempt to grapple with her heritage from earlier women writers is worked out through a series of specific allusions to the work of Jane Austen, George Eliot and Anne Thackeray Ritchie herself.

II

If Woolf wrote *The Voyage Out* under the weight of a male Victorian critical tradition which hailed Jane Austen as a paradigm, she wrote *Night and Day* under the additional pressure that her first novel had been compared with Austen.[10] *Night and Day* was also compared with both

Austen and Eliot on its first publication. Katherine Mansfield noted that 'it is impossible to refrain from comparing *Night and Day* with the novels of Miss Austen', and Clive Bell remarked that the novel deals with 'a subject for Jane Austen, into which she could have fitted all her curious knowledge of the upper-middle-class heart. But Mrs Woolf is not a born story-teller'. Ford Madox Hueffer heard within it 'the voice of George Eliot'.[11] All three reviewers judged Woolf to be inferior to her precursors. In returning to forms used by earlier women writers, then, Woolf responds not only to her precursors' fame but to critics of her own generation.

Gilbert and Gubar have described the characters in *Night and Day* as performing 'an Austenian courtship dance throughout the work',[12] finding the 'right' partner through the instructive experience of making choices which transpire to be unwise: Katharine ends her unsatisfactory relationship with William Rodney to become engaged to Ralph Denham, in much the same way as Elizabeth Bennet is disabused of her attraction to George Wickham in *Pride and Prejudice*; Anne Elliot rejects advice to marry Mr Elliot in *Persuasion*; and Fanny Price resists pressure to accept Henry Crawford in *Mansfield Park*. As in Austen, too, we have the juxtaposition of a couple who are taken seriously (Katharine and Ralph) against a couple who are treated satirically (William and his eventual fiancée, Cassandra).[13]

The parodic value of Woolf's work emerges on closer inspection, for she subverts the Austenian pattern by making her heroine lose rather than gain financial status through marriage and giving her the chance to escape the limiting conventions of her upbringing by marrying outside her social class. Where William Rodney is 'strictly conventional where women were concerned' (*ND*, 256), Katharine's relationship with Ralph promises to be unconventional – Ralph even claims not to believe in marriage – offering her the means of escape from her family home and the ghostly domination of her grandfather.

A further level of critical difference can be seen in the character of Ralph. *Night and Day* can be read as a cross-cast version of *Mansfield Park*, for Ralph Denham takes the role of Fanny Price, the girl from a poor family who marries a wealthy man. Fanny is taken away from her impoverished parents and eight siblings to be brought up by her rich uncle, Sir Thomas Bertram; Ralph Denham, from a middle-class family of 'six or seven brothers and sisters' (*ND*, 20) who have fallen on hard times becomes involved with the privileged literary set at the Hilbery home. Both Fanny and Ralph are outsiders in their new environment: Fanny refuses to take part in the Bertrams' theatricals; Ralph is excluded as the 'dumb note in a sonorous scale' at the Hilbery home (*ND*, 8). Both

Fanny and Ralph are attracted to the most important member of the younger generation: Fanny likes Edmund, Sir Thomas's son, and Ralph is attracted to Katharine, the great poet's only granddaughter. Both watch helplessly as the person they love becomes involved with a rival: Ralph watching Katharine with William Rodney, and Fanny seeing Edmund become captivated by Mary Crawford. Both face expulsion from their new circle when their intentions become known: Sir Thomas sends Fanny home in an attempt to force her to accept an alternative offer of marriage, and Mr Hilbery threatens to banish Ralph from his house (ND, 500). Both characters end up being reinstated in the family circle and engaged to the partner of their choice. By assigning this particular role to a male character, Woolf transposes the motif of the economically disadvantaged outsider and thus evades the issue prevalent in many courtship dramas – Mansfield Park included – where a woman needs to marry for economic security.

Woolf enacts a further and altogether more problematic revision of the Austenian paradigm in the figure of Mary Datchet, who declines a half-hearted proposal from Ralph and remains single. There are verbal echoes of Austen in this part of the novel, for the Datchet family is described with a satirical detachment characteristic of Austen's writings. Mary's sister Elizabeth resembles Elizabeth Elliot in Persuasion (who also has a sister called Mary), for they both live with a widowed father whom they take after: Elizabeth Datchet 'already much resembled [her father] in dry sincerity and methodical habit of mind' (ND, 185), while Elizabeth Elliot gets on well with her father, because she is 'very like himself' (P, 37). Each has an inheritance from her mother: Austen writes that 'Elizabeth had succeeded, at sixteen, to all that was possible, of her mother's rights and consequence' (P, 37). Woolf parodies this to make her Elizabeth inherit only domestic responsibility: the 'late Mrs Datchet had left an excellent cupboard of linen, to which Elizabeth had succeeded at the age of nine-teen, when her mother died, and the charge of the family rested upon the shoulders of the eldest daughter' (ND, 185). Thus the patriarchal system which gives Lady Elliot 'rights and consequence' is replaced with a more onerous matrilineal system of household management.

Woolf draws on Austen's approach to her characters' interiority to accord Mary some volition in absenting herself from the courtship pattern of the novel. Mary, like Fanny Price (and also Anne Elliot), has a deliberative rather than an active role. Throughout the novel, her thoughts are concerned with her relationship with Ralph: initially she hopes that their friendship might develop into something deeper; then she realises that Ralph cares more for Katharine than he does for her; and, finally, she attempts to adjust her feelings towards him and to channel her energies in new directions. Jane Austen frequently describes such reflective moments in her heroines as attempts to 'compose' themselves. Although the term describes the heroines' efforts to control emotion (as Mary does), it also suggests their attempt to take control over their future, to write their own narratives. Major changes of plot are conceived by Austen's heroines long before the events take place. For example, villains are often suspected by the heroine before they are exposed publicly, as when Fanny Price suspects that Henry Crawford is unreliable and predicts that he will seduce Maria Bertram. Mary Datchet occupies a similar position: she suspects that something is wrong between Katharine and William and when she sits down to consider the situation, she realises Ralph's affinity with Katharine (*ND*, 182). This understanding gives Mary a degree of control over her own future, for it gives her the wisdom to reject Ralph's offer of marriage.

By describing Mary and her family in an Austenian manner, Woolf seeks Austen's authority for a plot-line ending in confirmed spinsterhood rather than marriage. Although this might seem to reverse the view Austen presented in her novels, Mary enacts a potential ending of *Mansfield Park* which Austen did not pursue. Fanny's engagement to Edmund takes place very suddenly – within a single sentence – a few pages from the end of *Mansfield Park*. We are told that Edmund 'scarcely had . . . done regretting Mary Crawford' when he begins to wonder

> whether Fanny herself were not growing as dear, as important to him in all her smiles, and all her ways, as Mary Crawford had ever been; and whether it might not be a possible, an hopeful undertaking to persuade her that her warm and sisterly regard for him would be foundation enough for wedded love. (*MP*, 454)

The ending of *Mansfield Park* is ambiguous as to whether it ultimately validates sibling love (Fanny's 'warm and sisterly regard' for Edmund) or marriage. Although the equation of romantic love with sibling affection may reinforce the status quo by suggesting that the ideal marriage is one which replicates the birth family, the ending also has empowering potential. As Rachel Brownstein notes, Fanny has 'a brother who adores her, and a lover who feels toward her as a brother'; and Austen uses this to revise romance, by invoking 'men's brotherhood with women to claim that the sexes are equal, which is to say well matched'.[14] The relationship between Katharine and Ralph may be thought of as sibling love, for, as we have seen, Mary perceives a similarity between them. Mary Datchet, too, enjoys sibling love (*ND*, 197–8), and her story could also be read as enacting the unrealised potential ending to *Mansfield Park* of Fanny finding a valid alternative to marriage. Mary's story could then be read as a critique on the contrived nature of the actual ending of *Mansfield Park*, and as a reading of a potential ending which Austen gestured towards but did not carry through.

Woolf also draws on George Eliot in her attempt to present alternatives to marriage: in this case, by alluding to a moment in *Middlemarch* when the concluding marriage between Dorothea and Will Ladislaw was not yet inevitable. The allusion occurs during a reverie in which Mary renounces personal happiness and the prospect of marrying Ralph. Walking among the crowds Mary shifts from 'an acute consciousness of herself as an individual . . . to a conception of the scheme of things in which, as a human being, she must have her share' (*ND*, 271). This echoes the passage in *Middlemarch* in which the widowed Dorothea Brooke learns to ignore her own problems and concern herself with the sufferings of humankind: the dawning of a consciousness of 'the largeness of the world and the manifold wakings of men to labour and endurance' and the realisation that she was 'part of that involuntary, palpitating life, and could neither look out on it from her luxurious shelter as a mere spectator, nor hide her eyes in selfish complaining'.[15] In both passages, the protagonist is offered a chance to escape from a previously confined existence by taking a role in society. However, where Dorothea's involvement in the community in *Middlemarch* results in her meeting Ladislaw, Mary's decision leads her to reject marriage entirely. This is confirmed in a later reverie when she realises that she no longer loves Ralph and that she has gained 'independence of the tyranny of love' (*ND*, 472–3). Mary absents herself from the courtship plot to discover that 'there are different ways of loving', replacing romance with a more altruistic way of caring, as 'another love burned in place of the old one' (*ND*, 471) and she throws herself into the campaign for female suffrage.

However, the conventional narrative pattern ultimately is too strong for these alternatives to be presented in a truly positive light. Woolf does not treat Mary's commitment to political causes as positively as might be expected: as Anna Snaith has noted, Woolf expresses ambivalence towards the suffrage campaign in *Night and Day*;[16] indeed the campaign is shown to be in a state of disarray, even though women over thirty-five were granted the vote while Woolf was writing the novel. In our last glimpse of Mary, she is enclosed in her room, 'working out her plans far into the night – her plans for the good of a world that none of them were ever to know' (*ND*, 533), a comment which implies that her work will not bear fruit in her lifetime. Where Katharine's marriage can be viewed as a 'reward', offering her an escape from conventionality and from the confines of her family, Mary's choice of altruism over romance seems to rob her of personality and lead her to back to confinement, with little prospect of success in her ventures. The happy couples gain from marriage; the spinster is left out of the celebrations.

Makiko Minow-Pinkney has suggested that Woolf's modernist experiments with form and her critique of social conventions were parallel feminist challenges to patriarchy: her fiction is 'a feminist subversion of the deepest formal principles – of the very definitions of narrative, writing, the subject – of a patriarchal social order'.[17] Such subversion is not fully realised in *Night and Day*: Woolf's difficulty in presenting Mary's fate as a positive one suggests that even the deliberate negotiation of past narratives she conducted in *Night and Day* could not fully subvert the limited definitions of women's role which were inherent in the courtship narrative. Woolf's frustration with these conventions contributed to her realisation while writing *Night and Day* that 'as the current answers don't do, one has to grope for a new one' (*D*, I. 259), and fuelled the reforming ideas she articulated in 'Modern Novels'.

Woolf's ambivalence towards a female novelistic tradition is also evident in her treatment of Anne Thackeray Ritchie and her works. In this case, her ambivalence extends to earlier attempts to reform the courtship plot, for Ritchie had anticipated Woolf re-workings of Austen: specifically, *The Village on the Cliff* may be seen to prefigure Woolf's re-reading of *Mansfield Park*. *The Village on the Cliff*, like *Night and Day*, is a courtship drama focusing on how the protagonists sort themselves into couples. The plot of Ritchie's novel parallels that of *Mansfield Park*, for its main protagonist, a governess, 'poor little Catherine George', is an impoverished outsider in a wealthy home. Like Fanny Price, Catherine is attracted to the most powerful member of the younger generation of the family, falling in love with Richard Butler, her employer's nephew and heir to the family estate. Where Fanny absents herself from the Bertrams' theatricals on moral grounds and wins Edmund's approval for doing so, Ritchie depicts Catherine George's exclusion from family musical soirées: she describes Catherine watching flirtations taking place under the cover of the entertainment and notes that Richard is drawn to her when he senses her exclusion and disapproval: 'You don't think it quite right, do you, Miss George?' (*VC*, 70). Like Fanny, Catherine is deterred from marrying the man she loves: she watches helplessly as Richard falls in love with Reine Chrétien and she is later sent to another post to keep her away from Richard and cajoled into marrying an elderly widower, M. Fontaine.

Ritchie, however, is more successful than Woolf in her attempt to present the single life as a positive outcome. At the end of *The Village on the Cliff*, Fontaine dies and it looks likely that Catherine will marry Richard, who has begun to lose hope of marrying Reine. As in *Mansfield*

Park, there is a last-minute twist to the tale, but rather than granting marriage to the heroine, Ritchie allows Richard to marry Reine after all, and grants Catherine a happy ending with the security of her late husband's money and the love of her young sisters.[18] Thus Ritchie opens up the subversive potential of Austen's ending by conferring marriage on Reine, her secondary heroine, but giving her main protagonist the reward of familial love from doting and trusting children. Reine and Catherine enact respectively the potential and the actual endings of Fanny's story: the outcome which looks likely until the closing pages, in which she would give up hope of marrying Edmund and continue to live as her aunt's helper and companion; and the actual ending where she marries Edmund after all.

There are echoes of *The Village on the Cliff* in *Night and Day*: for example, Woolf's description of Ralph as a 'dumb note in a sonorous scale' (*ND*, 8) resembles Ritchie's image of Catherine as a 'dumb note in the music' (*VC*, 70). Yet, if Woolf used Ritchie's work as a model for reworking an Austenian narrative, she disguised this by representing Ritchie in Mrs Hilbery as a failing author and as sentimental and conventional woman who believes in marriage, thus obscuring the subversive potential of Ritchie's work and undermining her achievement. In using the figure of Mrs Hilbery to mock Ritchie, Woolf makes her the target for satire and irony which she could not direct towards better-known female writers.

Woolf uses her humorous sketch of Mrs Hilbery in an attempt to undermine the institution and binding power of marriage by rendering the courtship process as a theatrical performance. The Hilbery home is described as a theatre: one wall of their drawing-room is draped with a large curtain from which characters – particularly Mrs Hilbery – make surprise appearances. Katharine, who often feels isolated from her family, looks in on them as though they were actors in a play:

> The dream nature of our life had never been more apparent to her, never had life been more certainly an affair of four walls, whose objects existed only within the range of lights and fires, beyond which lay nothing, or nothing more than darkness. (*ND*, 371)

Here, the social world is described as a theatre: a confined, lighted space, and as a consequence, its imperatives are dismissed as fictions.

Within this setting, the courtship process becomes a drawing-room drama directed by Mrs Hilbery. This may be seen very early in the novel when she sends Katharine and Ralph off together and then watches them secretly 'with a smile of expectancy on her face, as if a scene from the drama of the younger generation were being played for her benefit' (*ND*,

15). As Joanne Zuckerman points out, Mrs Hilbery is 'virtually permitted to take over and write the end of the plot',[19] for she plays a significant role in uniting the two couples. She rescues Ralph from his banishment and brings him to Katharine, and she encourages William and Cassandra to become engaged. Thus the courtships and their outcomes are presented as scenes in a play directed by Mrs Hilbery rather than as realistic social possibilities endorsed by Woolf herself. Mrs Hilbery's involvement in the conclusion of *Night and Day* suggests that the ending may be read as a parody of Ritchie's work. By representing Ritchie in the figure of Mrs Hilbery, and by making her a focal point in the courtship plot, Woolf uses her as a target for her ambivalence towards her inheritance from her female precursors and the limited contexts in which they worked.

The ending of the novel is ironic, for although a traditional closure is offered, much remains unresolved, not least the fact that Ralph and Katharine have always had difficulties in knowing one another, and there is little to suggest that this situation will change. Against this, the trappings of the wedding service seem superficial, as Mrs Hilbery eagerly anticipates how 'the noble cadences, the stately periods, the ancient eloquence of the marriage service would resound over the heads of a distinguished congregation gathered together near the very spot where her father lay quiescent with the other poets of England' (*ND*, 515). (The reference to Poets' Corner here reminds us that the institution of marriage is endorsed by literary tradition as well as cultural and religious practices.) The absurdity of convention is further highlighted by a chaotic scene in which Katharine tries to hand back her engagement ring for William to give to Cassandra, but someone drops it and farce ensues as the couples hunt for it. However, the novel also hints ominously that something will change, that convention will creep in, for we are told that part of Ralph's motivation for marrying Katharine is 'to dominate her, to possess her' (*ND*, 515). Here Woolf shows an awareness of the process later theorised by Judith Butler whereby performances and rituals can and do have a regulatory impact on the individuals who take part in them.

Although theatrical metaphors enable Woolf to critique the imperatives of courtship narrative, even these may be seen to engage with terms from *Mansfield Park*, which is also preoccupied with drama. Early in the novel, the Bertram family and their guests take part in a drawing-room performance of Elizabeth Inchbald's *Lovers' Vows*. The conduct of the play becomes the means by which relationships between the characters are revealed: it gives Mary Crawford the chance to approach Edmund, for she plays a character who tries to seduce his; Henry Crawford plays the scoundrel he is later revealed to be; and Maria and Julia Bertram vie over the part of leading lady, as they will later compete for Henry's attentions.

Drama in *Mansfield Park* serves a didactic purpose which it does not fulfil in *Night and Day*. If the characters in *Night and Day* remain steeped in theatricality, the more enlightened characters in *Mansfield Park* disdain it. Thus, Edmund initially argues against the plan to stage a play, although he later reluctantly agrees to take part, and Fanny resolutely stays out of the production. They agree that the theatre is disreputable and are drawn together by that shared opinion. Fanny is saved from being lured into Henry Crawford's trap by her ability to distinguish between performance and reality: she is briefly entranced by his reading of a scene from *Henry VIII*, but only until he looks up, when 'the book was closed, and the charm was broken' (*MP*, 335). Edmund's illusions are not dispelled until the end of the novel when Mary Crawford's attentions to him prove to be as contrived as her performance in *Lovers' Vows*.

Joseph Litvak has provided a reading of theatricality in *Mansfield Park* which renders its project closer to Woolf's in *Night and Day*. He argues that, although the plans to stage *Lovers' Vows* are scuppered by the return of Sir Thomas Bertram, the site of theatricality merely shifts from the makeshift set to Mansfield Park itself.[20] Although Sir Thomas deplores the project of putting on a play, his attempt to stage-manage Fanny's marriage to Henry Crawford makes him complicit in theatricality. Even though Fanny marries Edmund rather than Henry, the ending is none the less in Sir Thomas's interests: theatricality-as-subversion has thus been replaced by theatricality-as-conventionality.[21] *Night and Day* similarly rejects the prospect of Katharine marrying William as a piece of farcical theatre, but it endorses her marriage to Ralph, which is presented as subversive but is potentially conventional, for as we have seen Woolf hints that their relationship will replicate the power imbalances of the conventional marriage they appear to have rejected.

The theme of the complex and ambivalent relationship between theatre and society, illusion and reality ultimately has its roots in the Shakespearean adage that 'all the world's a stage' (*As You Like It*, II. vii. 138). This connection was made more explicitly by Anne Thackeray Ritchie when she used Shakespearean allusions to expose the absurdities of real life in *The Village on the Cliff*. Catherine George's isolated existence is made bearable by her lively imagination, to the extent that her dreams seem more real than the everyday lives of those around her, and Ritchie describes Catherine's wish to be part of the Butler family as a desire 'to be acting a part ever so small in this midsummer night's dream'

(*VC*, 70). Ritchie alludes to *A Midsummer Night's Dream* later when Catherine senses that she has fallen out of favour with her employers, and asks: 'Had some malicious Puck squeezed some of the juice of Oberon's purple flower . . . to set them all wandering at cross purposes all through this midsummer's day?' (*VC*, 96). Here, the dream-world functions doubly as an escape from patriarchal society and as a critique of that society by rendering it as an absurd delirium from which the heroine eventually escapes to attain economic security outside of marriage.

Woolf, too, picks up on this theme in *Night and Day* when she articulates an ironic antithesis between the 'night' world of imagination which is more real than ordinary life; and the 'day' world of ordinary relationships which often appears illusory. This is seen when Katharine becomes aware of the 'dream nature of our life' (*ND*, 371), which is a faint echo of Demetrius's comment on waking from his midsummer night's dream: 'Are you sure | That we are awake? It seems to me | That yet we sleep, we dream' (IV. i. 192). Like Demetrius, Katharine and Ralph, in part, remain in the dream-world even at the end of the novel: they distrust one another's feelings because those feelings are based on dreams rather than experience, but Mrs Hilbery advises them to learn to believe in romance; to exchange dreams rather than try to get to know one another better. The emphasis on dream here, as in Ritchie's novels, works to undermine the binding power of marriage.[22]

Shakespeare becomes a touchstone for resisting patriarchal constructions for both Anne Thackeray Ritchie and Woolf. In *Night and Day*, Woolf links Shakespeare with Ritchie specifically (and, by extension, with women writers in general) when she makes Mrs Hilbery the nexus for many of the Shakespearean references in *Night and Day*: Mrs Hilbery encourages people to read Shakespeare, plans to stage his plays and visits Stratford-upon-Avon. She even appears to enact scenes from his plays, particularly in her return from Stratford covered in foliage from Shakespeare's grave, parodying the army which descends on Macbeth, bearing branches like a moving forest.[23]

Mrs Hilbery also claims Shakespeare for a 'female' literary tradition, in her 'theory that Anne Hathaway had a way, among other things, of writing Shakespeare's sonnets'; she then had 'come half to believe in her joke, which was, she said, at least as good as other people's facts' (*ND*, 320). This refers to an anecdote about Ritchie making a similar comment to Samuel Butler, as a riposte to Butler's suggestion that the *Odyssey* was written by a woman.[24] The joke unsettles the authority of 'fact', and imaginatively points to the possibility of female authorship for Shakespeare's texts and so threatens to displace Shakespeare as a male literary icon and claim him as a role-model for women writers.

Shakespeare has often been assumed to fulfil a paternal role for Woolf,[25] but her attempts to forge connections between Shakespeare and Anne Thackeray Ritchie through Mrs Hilbery suggest that she wanted to claim him for a female literary tradition. As Beth Schwartz points out, Woolf 'reimagines Shakespeare as the cornerstone of the incipient tradition of women writers'. Although Schwartz argues that Shakespeare's 'mothering influence' is most evident in *A Room of One's Own* and *Orlando*, the origins of this process may be seen as early as *Night and Day*.[26]

III

Woolf's references to Shakespeare's plays, especially his comedies, in *Night and Day* help problematise the courtship narrative. The institution of marriage is critiqued in a cluster of references to *Measure for Measure*, a play greatly concerned with changing codes of sexual morality. In Shakespeare's play, Claudio is faced with the death penalty for making his lover pregnant. His defence is that they consider themselves married, without having undergone a ceremony:

> [U]pon a true contract
> I got possession of Julietta's bed.
> . . . she is fast my wife
> Save that we do the denunciation lack
> Of outward order. (I. ii. 134–8)

The injustice of Claudio's situation becomes a harsh critique of Puritan values. In *Night and Day*, Katharine's aunt, the ridiculous Mrs Cosham, asks Ralph to explain a passage from *Measure for Measure*, during a visit when she is enlisting support for her campaign to force her nephew Cyril to marry the woman who lives with him and has borne his children. Here, the severe rule of the Puritans is re-written comically as the gossiping of a fussy old woman. However, Woolf provides an innovative reading of the passage Ralph has been asked to construe, for as Mrs Cosham reads the speech, Ralph gleans from the ongoing conversation that Katharine is officially engaged to William Rodney:

> *To be imprison'd in the viewless winds,*
> *And blown with restless violence round about*
> *The pendant world* (ND, 158; *Measure*, III. i. 123–5)

This speech is made by Claudio as he awaits execution and envisages the horrors he will encounter after death. Ralph associates these words with his own mood, for he imagines himself, with vagrants on the street, being wafted about by the lightest breath of wind. For the substantial world, with its prospect of avenues leading on and on to the invisible distance, had slipped from him, since Katharine was engaged. . . . All things turned to ghosts; the whole mass of the world was insubstantial vapour. (*ND*, 161, 162)

This passage echoes Claudio's images of being blown about the world in a deathly state. Ralph sees the loss of the chance of a relationship with Katharine as a death sentence, so that pre-war society's injunctions against unconventional relationships are compared directly with the harsh attitudes of Jacobean Puritans.

Woolf also alludes to *As You Like It* to undermine the imperatives of gender, courtship and marriage. Katharine, who is twice described as masculine (*ND*, 139, 298), is the cross-dressed comic heroine; her intimacy with Mary Datchet (seen particularly when Mary fingers the hem of Katharine's dress (*ND*, 287)) hints at a same-sex attraction reminiscent of the sexual confusions which arise from cross-dressing in Shakespeare's comedies. Katharine is twice compared with Rosalind from *As You Like It* in ways which point to her ambiguous status as the heroine of a courtship drama.[27] Katharine is identified with Rosalind for the first time when William mocks her for pretending not to take an interest in art and literature: 'it's one of Katharine's poses . . . She pretends that she's never read Shakespeare. And why should she read Shakespeare, since she is Shakespeare – Rosalind, you know' (*ND*, 180). Rosalind poses, first in dressing as a boy in order to flee to the Forest of Arden to escape her uncle's wrath, and then in pretending to play herself, in order to mock and test Orlando. The irony of William's comment is that he does not know that Katharine's appearance as his fiancée is also just a pose. Mary Datchet has guessed as much. She notices how Katharine takes charge of pouring tea and wonders whether there is 'something maternal in this assumption of control', but then realises that Katharine's actions are a façade: 'it struck Mary that Katharine . . . in the obscurity of her character, was, perhaps, smiling to herself, not altogether in the maternal spirit' (*ND*, 179). Like Rosalind, who could mock and test Orlando in her disguise as Ganymede by pretending to be herself, Katharine silently mocks William under the cover of their engagement and keeps her self in reserve from him.

Katharine escapes from Rodney by parodying her role as his fiancée: she continues the engagement in order for him to remain within the family circle to court Cassandra. The Shakespearean implications of this position are unwittingly signalled by Mrs Hilbery who muses about putting on a play and casting Katharine as 'Rosalind – but you've a dash of the old nurse in you' (*ND*, 321). The comparison draws attention to Katharine's matchmaking, for the Nurse is the go-between for Romeo and Juliet and Rosalind is a match-maker in *As You Like It*, not only in preparing Orlando to marry her, but in reconciling the shepherding couple, Silvius and Phebe. Phebe had refused to take Silvius because she was in love with Rosalind's disguise as Ganymede. Rosalind reunites Phebe and Silvius by stepping out of her disguise; Katharine frees William to marry Cassandra and frees herself to develop her relationship with Ralph by dismissing her engagement to William as a charade.

Shakespeare is invoked ironically in the scene where the new couples are constituted, for Mrs Hilbery cuts short any actual pronouncements of the new relationships by changing the subject and asking when *Hamlet* was first performed. When the focus cuts back to the newly formed couples, we are told that the resolution has been 'sanctioned by the authority of no less a person than Shakespeare himself' (*ND*, 525). This statement is ironic, because rather than invoking Shakespeare's endorsement of the happy ending, the allusion is merely a sleight of hand to divert our attention from what is happening.

The ending of the novel invokes the conventions of festive comedy – traditionally defined as a play whose major plot involves courtship and ends with the prospect of marriage for a heroine.[28] Mrs Hilbery's role in uniting the two couples both parodies Anne Thackeray Ritchie as a purveyor of 'happy endings' and echoes Hymen who presides over the nuptials at the end of *As You Like It*. As Penny Gay points out, festive comedy is traditionally thought to be profoundly conservative, allowing 'the topsy-turveydom of carnival', before the idea of community is asserted at the end, symbolised by a marriage and the expulsion of disruptive elements.[29] At the dinner-party which follows the announcement of the engagements, Woolf notes that 'civilization had triumphed', and that Mr Hilbery 'presided over a feast' which celebrates this restoration of the status quo (*ND*, 528). Mary Datchet is excluded from this celebration (Margaret Comstock compares her with Jacques who is left out of the happy ending to *As You Like It*).[30] This furthers the view that her chosen lifestyle is not a happy one, but she also threatens to unsettle the happy resolution, for we are told that Katharine feels that her newly found sense of unity would be destroyed if she saw Mary (*ND*, 530).

Shakespeare's comedies rarely end with a complete return to normality. Although Rosalind changes out of her male costume for the dénouement of *As You Like It*, the epilogue continues the sexual ambiguity, for it is spoken by the actor playing Rosalind who partly remains in character, describing *her*self as 'the lady' and partly identifies *him*self as the boy actor ('if I were a woman' (V. iv. 198, 214)).[31] Viola in *Twelfth Night*, more radically, remains in male costume at the end of the play. Sexual ambiguity lingers at the end of *Night and Day*, for we are told that

Katharine listens to Ralph 'like a woman', as though there may be some doubt over her sex.

The ending of *Night and Day* has congruencies with that of *A Midsummer Night's Dream*. Katharine and Ralph go out into a moonlit night in June (*ND*, 528, 535), making a dream-like journey around London. Like the couples watching the mechanicals' play in *A Midsummer Night's Dream*, they are described as 'spectators of a pageant enacted for them, masters of life' (*ND*, 529), a description carrying shades of the class differences articulated in Shakespeare's play-within-a-play. They accept theatricality rather than abandoning it, as they recall the people who have played a part in their story, and visualise them as 'little figures' who 'came by in procession' (*ND*, 533), as in the finale to a play. They also affirm their dreams rather than returning to reality, as they go together into the 'the enchanted region' where (like the Athenians under the influence of the love potion in the wood) they do not know one another: 'What woman did he see? And where was she walking, and who was her companion?' (*ND*, 534). Thus, Katharine and Ralph are not fully integrated into society at the end: they continue to play roles and, like Demetrius in *A Midsummer Night's Dream* who is never released from the spell which makes him love Helena, they live in illusion even when they are engaged.

If *Night and Day* fails ultimately to provide satisfactory alternatives to marriage, the Shakespearean allusions help to unsettle the premises of the courtship narrative. Ralph and Katharine's dreamy ending attempts to evade rather than fully to undermine the social values underlying both festive comedy and the courtship narrative. As Katherine Mansfield's response shows, *Night and Day* followed novelistic conventions too closely to propose any real alternative; those conventions would need to be dismantled before they could be revisited ironically. However, *Night and Day* need not be dismissed as an aberration in Woolf's career, for it demonstrates in embryonic form ideas which would be developed further in *A Room of One's Own*. In her allusions to Jane Austen, George Eliot and Anne Thackeray Ritchie in *Night and Day* Woolf may be seen to think back through the legacies of women writers and to critique the tradition she had inherited; by layering her parody of them with references to Shakespearean comedy, she anticipated her later attempts to claim him – by means of the concept of androgyny – for a subversive feminist agenda.

IV

Woolf's mature aesthetic is also foreshadowed in the third allusive layer of *Night and Day*: her use of Romantic metaphors to explore the workings of the mind and the imagination. The most prominent of these are fire and light, particularly lamp-light which, as M. H. Abrams has demonstrated, is a Romantic analogue for the workings of the mind.[32] Like the Shakespearean references, this exploration of the life of the mind works to undermine narrative imperatives by emphasising the workings of the imagination.

Woolf uses Romantic ideas about the imagination to support Mary Datchet's rejection of romance in her reveries. These moments are examples of the process described by Nancy Miller in which feminist writers use a dream-world as a space in which to rewrite narratives and (in contrast to the scenes with Katharine and Ralph) to reject romance.[33] In her first reverie, on Charing Cross Road, Mary seeks to escape the limitations of her daily life and personality, and to 'climb the crest of existence and see it all laid out once and for ever . . . her suffering as an individual was left behind her' (*ND*, 271). She looks for a solution in the realm of the imagination, as she seeks 'this essential thing' which she lacks and other people seem to have, taking the form of 'a flame; as if a spark in the brain ignited spontaneously at contact with the things they met and drove them on' (*ND*, 270). Mary temporarily forgets her unrequited love for Ralph, but Woolf's attempt to transcend the love plot is not sustained, for the meditation ends with an awkward break as Mary goes back to considering her relationship with Ralph: 'Where was he to be placed in the new scale of life?' This question takes her away from her unified vision in which she can empathise with others, even Ralph – 'she was identified with him and rethought his thoughts with complete self-surrender' – to one in which she opposes others, as, 'with a sudden cleavage of spirit, she turned upon him and denounced him for his cruelty' (*ND*, 272). The juxtaposition suggests that although Romantic moments of self-forgetfulness may offer an escape from the conventions of patriarchal society, they can be achieved only at the expense of self-interest, which in turn risks capitulation to patriarchy in itself.

Woolf attempts to balance these issues in Mary's later reverie, which pays attention to the activities of the mind, while pursuing the narrative by revealing that Mary no longer loves Ralph:

> She looked back dazed into the room, and her eyes rested upon the table with its lamp-lit papers. The steady radiance seemed for a second to have its counterpart within her; she shut her eyes; she opened them and looked at the

lamp again; another love burnt in the place of the old one, or so, in a momentary glance of amazement, she guessed before the revelation was over and the old surroundings asserted themselves. (*ND*, 471)

The careful construction of the relationship between subject and object made here – 'the lamplight seemed for a second to have its counterpart within her' – is attuned to Romantic debates about poetic creativity. As Wordsworth puts it in *The Prelude*: 'An auxiliar light I Came from my mind, which on the setting sun I Bestow'd new splendour' (II. 368). In this meditation, Mary's mind does not simply create the scene she views, but distorts it to reflect its own state: the lamp becomes a symbol of her new love which 'burnt in the place of the old one'. In this reverie, Woolf's exploration of the workings of the mind creates a break in the narrative, by which the inexorable progress of events may be subverted and Mary's marriage plot abandoned.

These reveries are important for Woolf's development of her feminist and modernist project: they inform her argument in 'Modern Novels', for verbal echoes between the essay and Mary's reveries suggest that the two works were part of the same project. Mary's desire to be free of personality and her predicament with Ralph prefigures Woolf's argument for reaching beyond plot, personality and emotion which she attacked in 'Modern Novels' and which were shown to be confining in *Night and Day*. In Mary's reverie, as in 'Modern Novels', Woolf finds an escape from the imperatives of narrative in paying close attention to the workings of the 'mind, exposed to the ordinary course of life', and tracing the 'pattern, however disconnected and incoherent in appearance, which each sight or incident scores upon the consciousness' (*E*, III. 33–4). Mary's search for 'this essential thing' (*ND*, 270) prefigures Woolf's argument in 'Modern Novels' that literature should convey 'this, the essential thing' (*E*, III. 32); in both pieces, she uses the symbol of the flame to suggest the activity of the mind and something intangible or spiritual. Thus, the ideas Woolf presented in 'Modern Novels' did not emerge simply as an expression of Woolf's frustration with *Night and Day*, but they were actually rehearsed in the novel in Woolf's description of the workings of the mind.

Furthermore, although Woolf refers to James Joyce in the essay as an example of a modern novelist – she praises him for being 'spiritual; concerned at all costs to reveal the flickerings of that innermost flame which flashes its myriad messages through the brain' (*E*, III. 34) – the language used in the essay seeks to appropriate the critical ideas of the Romantic poets for her literary project.

Anne Thackeray Ritchie may again have provided Woolf with a model for using Romantic motifs to undermine the imperatives of plot. As

Joanne Zuckerman has suggested, Woolf found in Ritchie 'an important predecessor, confronting the same problem of reconciling the recording of experience, as it actually passes through the mind, with the demands of the conventionally structured novel'.[34] In the preface to *The Village on the Cliff*, Ritchie disclaims responsibility for the story by claiming that it is based on one she heard in the village of Petitport in Normandy. She writes that she is interested in resurrecting her memories of Petitport, in an exploration of 'sights, sounds and peculiarities which we thought we had scarcely noticed, which remain in the mind like magic lantern slides, and come suddenly out of the darkness, starting into life when the lamp is lighted by some chance association' (*VC*, 1). Woolf's adoption of Romantic theory for the feminist project of challenging narrative may have a direct link with Ritchie's techniques – techniques which were more subversive than Woolf formally acknowledged them to be.

Of course, Woolf engaged directly with Romantic writers, rather than experiencing them second-hand: indeed, her notebooks show that she made a systematic study of the critical writings of Wordsworth, Coleridge, Keats and Shelley while writing *Night and Day*.[35] However, a comment Woolf made to Lytton Strachey in 1922 (after he had reviewed *Jacob's Room*) suggests that her attempt to develop a feminist Romantic aesthetic may have been influenced by Ritchie:

> Of course you put your infallible finger upon the spot – romanticism. How do I catch it? Not from my father. I think it must have been my Great Aunts. But some of it, I think, comes from the effort of breaking with complete representation. (*L*, II. 568–9)

Although light-hearted, this comment suggests that Woolf recognised the romantic dimension of her modernist project and acknowledged its female provenance. Woolf's great-aunts on her mother's side included Julia Margaret Cameron, the photographer who used romantic subjects for her portraits, but from the foregoing analysis, it would not be unreasonable to imagine that the term great-aunt was used loosely, and that Woolf was alluding to (and at the same time obscuring) her step-aunt Anny Ritchie.

Night and Day demonstrates that Woolf's route towards innovation involved exploring her literary past, testing its forms and methods; the novel can be seen as a stage in her process of revolutionising the novel by drawing on the literature of the past. Certain aspects of *Night and Day* anticipate ideas which became central to Woolf's later aesthetic. In particular, Woolf's exploration of the life of the mind in *Night and Day* (which, as we have seen, draws on Shakespearean and Romantic ideas), echoes statements in 'Modern Fiction' and anticipates a key element of what Woolf came to describe as her 'method'. This would emerge in more radical ways in the dispersal of personality in *Jacob's Room*, the process of 'tunnelling' into Clarissa's memories in *Mrs Dalloway*, and Mrs Ramsay's 'wedge-shaped core of darkness' in *To the Lighthouse*.

Notes

1. Majumdar and McLaurin (eds), *Woolf: Critical Heritage*, p. 82.
2. See Chapter 1 above.
3. For example, Hafley argues that '"Modern Fiction" denies the value of *Night and Day* as a work of art, but justifies it as an exercise in classicism'; it is a 'negative demonstration' of the need to reshape the novel as a genre, 'just as her achieved works of art are positive demonstrations' (*Glass Roof*, p. 38).
4. Butler, *Bodies that Matter*.
5. Gilbert and Gubar, *The Madwoman in the Attic*, p. 49.
6. Gérin, *Anne Thackeray Ritchie*, pp. 227–8.
7. Ibid., p. v.
8. Her review of J. E. Austen-Leigh's memoir of Jane Austen was 'by far the most influential of all the popularising accounts' of her in the nineteenth century (Southam (ed.), *Jane Austen: Critical Heritage*, p. 164).
9. Ritchie, *A Book of Sibyls*, pp. 212–13.
10. See p. 27 above.
11. Majumdar and McLaurin (eds), *Woolf: Critical Heritage*, pp. 80, 141, 75.
12. Gilbert and Gubar, *No Man's Land*, III. 19.
13. Also, many of the characters have classic Austenian names – William, Henry, Mary, Katharine and Elizabeth. Cassandra has the same name as Jane Austen's sister.
14. Brownstein, *Becoming a Heroine*, pp. 110, 111.
15. Eliot, *Middlemarch*, p. 846.
16. Snaith, *Woolf: Public and Private Negotiations*, p. 31.
17. Minow-Pinkney, *Woolf and the Problem of the Subject*, p. x. Pykett similarly suggests that Woolf criticised a 'masculine tradition', and that her work in remaking or renovating language and fiction was a feminist project, for the 'life' she sought in 'Modern Fiction' was 'feminine' (*Engendering Fictions*, p. 92).
18. Intriguingly, *The Village on the Cliff* (1867) anticipates *Middlemarch* (1871–72), for Fontaine's will dictates that Catherine should lose her inheritance if she marries again. Unlike Dorothea, who sacrifices financial security by submitting to a 'hopeless love' and marrying Ladislaw, Catherine keeps her money and her freedom by not remarrying.
19. Zuckerman, 'Anne Thackeray Ritchie as the Model for Mrs Hilbery', p. 37.
20. Litvak, *Caught in the Act*, p. 3.
21. Ibid., pp. 22–4.
22. Mrs Hilbery's intervention fulfils the sort of function MacKay identifies in Ritchie's novels, in which the 'whimsical mode of her domestic fairytales

dispels the hateful but familiar conventions perpetuated by literary expectations and unconsciously adopted by society' ('Hate and Humor as
Empathetic Whimsy in Anne Thackeray Ritchie', p. 118).

23. Comstock, '"The Current Answers Don't Do"', p. 157.
24. Zuckerman, 'Anne Thackeray Ritchie as the Model', p. 34.
25. For example, J. J. Wilson suggests that Woolf sees Shakespeare as the 'one
    true father' in 'Why is *Orlando* Difficult?', p. 178.
26. Schwartz, 'Thinking Back Through our Mothers', p. 722. Froula suggests
    that Woolf's attempt to claim Shakespeare for women writers began with *To
    the Lighthouse*, in 'Virginia Woolf as Shakespeare's Sister'.
27. Comstock, '"The Current Answers Don't Do"', pp. 160–2.
28. Critics have identified patterns of festive comedy in other novels by Woolf:
    see Little, 'Festive Comedy in Woolf's *Between the Acts*', and Cuddy-Keane,
    'The Politics of Comic Modes in Virginia Woolf's *Between the Acts*'.
29. Gay, *As She Likes It*, p. 2.
30. Comstock: '"The Current Answers Don't Do"', p. 467.
31. As Rackin points out, the play's epilogue includes ambiguities which
    'involve not only gender but sex itself, and not only the character Rosalind
    but also the boy actor who played her part . . . that ambivalent figure refuses
    to choose between actor and character or between male and female but
    instead insists on the ambiguities' ('Androgyny, Mimesis, and the Marriage
    of the Boy Heroine on the English Renaissance Stage', p. 36).
32. Abrams, *The Mirror and the Lamp*, pp. 57–69.
33. Miller, *Subject to Change*, pp. 31–2.
34. Zuckerman, 'Anne Thackeray Ritchie as the Model', p. 38.
35. Woolf made notes on Wordsworth's 'Preface' to *Lyrical Ballads*, Coleridge's
    Biographia Literaria, and Shelley's 'Preface' to *Alastor*: see *Reading
    Notebooks*, Notebook XXX. She reviewed a new edition of Coleridge's
    Table Talk in the *Times Literary Supplement* (*E*, II. 221–5) and probably
    read Keats's *Letters* (*D*, I. 113).

Chapter 3

Literature and Survival: *Jacob's Room* and *Mrs Dalloway*

It is widely accepted that *Jacob's Room* (1922) and *Mrs Dalloway* (1925) are Woolf's first experimental novels, building on radical short stories such as 'Kew Gardens' and 'The Mark on the Wall' and on the theories of fiction developed in 'Modern Novels'. Woolf abandons the rigid chapter structure she criticised in 'Modern Novels', adopting in both a more flexible form built on sketches or 'moments' of varying length. She eschews a documentary approach to character in *Jacob's Room* by making the eponymous character an enigma, and in *Mrs Dalloway* by concentrating on the mental experience of her protagonists, the latter being especially radical for embracing the psychotic consciousness of Septimus Warren Smith. Woolf also wrote both novels with an awareness of the work of her contemporaries, particularly T. S. Eliot, whom she had met in 1919, and James Joyce, whose *Ulysses* she had read in draft form in 1918 and grudgingly admired.

However, as this chapter will demonstrate, alongside her innovations Woolf maintained a respect for the literary past and remained concerned about tradition and canonicity. The tension is evident within 'Modern Novels' itself, for Woolf notes that her 'quarrel . . . is not with the classics' (*E*, III. 31), levelling her criticism against the popular writers of the time: the previous half-generation of novelists represented by H. G. Wells, Arnold Bennett and John Galsworthy; and although she hails Joyce as the leading figure in a new trend, she none the less compares him unfavourably with Thomas Hardy, Joseph Conrad, Laurence Sterne and William Thackeray (*E*, III. 33–4). Furthermore, Woolf values tradition as a link with those past writings she finds sympathetic and congenial. This is partly informed by a sense of Englishness, for although Woolf expresses admiration for Russian fiction in 'Modern Novels' and offers it as an example of the kind of writing she advocates, she none the less retreats into a vision of an English tradition: she notes that Russian literature awakens in her 'a voice of protest' which is 'the voice of another and an ancient civilisation which seems to have bred in us the instinct to enjoy and fight rather than to suffer and understand. English fiction from Sterne to Meredith bears witness to our natural delight in humour and comedy, in the beauty of earth, in the activities of the intellect, and in the splendour of the body' (*E*, III. 36). The reference to an 'ancient civilisation' offers a conception of native culture which goes beyond the narrow definitions of nationhood of recent history; this aspect is highlighted in the song of the street singer in *Mrs Dalloway*, which sounds as the 'voice of an ancient spring spouting from the earth' (*MD*, 105).

While writing *Jacob's Room* and *Mrs Dalloway*, Woolf began to reflect on the continuing presence of another 'ancient civilisation' – the literature and culture of classical Greece – and its significance to the English tradition, for, as Rowena Fowler has noted, Woolf's encounter with classical Greek played a defining role in her sense of Englishness.[1] Although Woolf presented her thinking formally in 'On Not Knowing Greek', an essay she began whilst finishing *Mrs Dalloway*, we shall see that she rehearsed ideas for the essay in both novels. 'On Not Knowing Greek' takes its ostensible premise from Woolf's sense of the 'foreignness' of classical Greece, but she is at pains throughout to overcome the sense of alienation by seeking traces of the classical past in her native land. So, in reading Sophocles, she calls up 'some village, in a remote part of the country, near the sea. Even nowadays such villages are to be found in the wilder parts of England' (*CE*, I. 1). Greek literature represents an edenic state of which English literature is a pale reflection:

> Here we listen to the nightingale whose song echoes through English literature singing in her own Greek tongue. For the first time Orpheus with his lute makes men and beasts follow him. Their voices ring out clear and sharp; we see the hairy, tawny bodies at play in the sunlight among the olive trees, not posed gracefully on granite plinths in the pale corridors of the British Museum. (*CE*, I. 5)

Here, Woolf acknowledges that classical literature remains alive and relevant, and reverberates throughout English literature. She contrasts the vibrancy of Greek literature, full of words which 'must eternally endure', with the ossified remains of classical culture found in a museum. This contrast becomes a significant motif in both novels.

In 'On Not Knowing Greek', Woolf makes Shakespeare a specific point of contact between the literatures of classical Greece and modern England. Although a literary historian would locate the connection in Shakespeare's re-working of classical motifs, Woolf sees the link more in terms of affinity: she argues that the multivalency of Greek poetry can also be found in Shakespeare: 'It is necessary to take that dangerous leap through the air without the support of words which Shakespeare also asks of us' (*CE*, I. 7); she compares his later plays to Greek drama, saying that both contain 'more of poetry than of action' and 'are better read than seen' (*CE*, I. 5); and she praises the Greeks, as she would later praise Shakespeare, for being 'impersonal' (*CE*, I. 5; *Room*, 63). For Woolf, Shakespeare is the closest English approximation to Greek literature, which alone is original and perfect.

This chapter will examine Woolf's engagement with ancient Greek literature and Shakespeare as interrelated strands of her literary past in the two novels. As we shall see, Woolf seeks in both novels to engage with the vibrancy of the past works, but in both she is also critical of those who would seek to adopt the classics and Shakespeare to support narrow patriotic and patriarchal ideologies. Since the novels deal, respectively, with the causes and consequences of the First World War, Woolf also shows how such attitudes have sought to use literature to support patriotism and warmongering.

I

In *Jacob's Room*, Woolf examines and criticises the ways in which patriarchal society sought to construct culture and the literary tradition and to control who has access to it, by pointing to the educational inequalities between young men and women. Following Jacob Flanders at a distance through public school at Rugby and university at Cambridge, Woolf shows young men attaining 'culture' almost as a birthright. Jacob and his contemporaries are privileged with special access to literature, for they 'have at hand as sovereign specifics for all disorders of the soul Adonais and the plays of Shakespeare' (*JR*, 105); Fanny Elmer, by contrast, wistfully longs for an education and feels excluded from the experience of reading: 'there is something, Fanny thought, about books which if I had been educated I could have liked' (*JR*, 168).

Woolf shows that Jacob and his friends believe that their educational privilege, particularly their classical education, has put them in a position of power and instilled in them an imperialist urge to subdue and appropriate the culture of other nations. As Jacob discusses ancient Greece with his friend Timmy Durrant, the narrator comments that, 'Civilizations stood round them like flowers ready for picking. Ages lapped at their feet like waves fit for sailing' (*JR*, 101). Yet Woolf also undermines the validity of Jacob's apparent privilege by describing his reading interests ironically to show that he does not really engage with the literature on offer to him. We are told that, although Jacob and

Timmy walk down the street quoting from the classics, 'Durrant never listened to Socrates, nor Jacob to Aeschylus' (*JR*, 101). Similarly, Jacob admires Shakespeare for jingoistic reasons – 'Shakespeare had more guts than all these damned frogs put together' (*JR*, 172) – but betrays a lack of true interest when he takes an edition of Shakespeare on holiday, but fails to read a single play through and knocks the book overboard (*JR*, 60, 62).

Furthermore, Woolf suggests that Jacob's education may have instilled in him and his generation a fatalism which prepared them to become cannon fodder. As Emily Delgarno notes, 'The war in which Jacob dies is an event prepared by an education which teaches young men a destructive myth about their relationship to ancient Greece, that is compounded by their relative ignorance of Greek texts.'[2] The connection between education and death in war is underlined in Woolf's description of King's College Chapel, Cambridge, an all-male bastion where academics' wives are barely tolerated. Woolf's description aligns academia and religion with militarism:

> Look, as they pass into service, how airily the gowns blow out, as though nothing dense and corporeal were within. What sculptured faces, what certainty, authority controlled by piety, although great boots march under the gowns. (*JR*, 38)

Woolf's pun on service conflates enlistment with religious observance and suggests that established religion and education are forms of conscription, in which young men are marshalled both physically and mentally. This idea is reinforced by the image of 'great boots' marching into chapel. There is an inevitability about the procession, for the boots seem to march independently of the volition of the men who wear them. These young men are insubstantial; their gowns appear empty, reinforcing the anonymity and insignificance of the thousands who died in battle. Their 'sculptured faces' make them seem already like pieces of antiquity.

Woolf suggests that Cambridge students are trained to think in a linear way which leads them inexorably towards war and death. She describes the erudition of the don Huxtable as militaristic and deathly: his thoughts are 'orderly, quick-stepping, and reinforced, as the march goes on, by fresh runnels' (*JR*, 50). Continuing the military metaphor, Woolf adds that 'Such a muster takes place in no other brain' (*JR*, 50). Seeing Huxtable asleep, the narrator imagines that 'you might fancy that on a pillow of stone he lay triumphant' (*JR*, 51), implying that, like a dead warrior, the reward for his labours will be commemoration in (and reduction to) a stone monument.

Jacob's development to maturity is described as a process of ossification. Jacob's friend Bonamy sees him staring 'straight ahead of him, fixed, monolithic – oh, very beautiful! – like a British Admiral' (*JR*, 230), associating him with the armed forces and forecasting his death in battle. This is explicitly linked with the classics when Jacob's lover, Florinda, describes him as being 'like one of those statues . . . I think there are lovely things in the British Museum' (*JR*, 108). This reference to the statues of antiquity kept at the Museum suggests that the classical element of Jacob's education may have brought about a spiritual death, even before he dies in body. This suggestion is reinforced later in Fanny Elmer's image of Jacob which was

> more statuesque, noble, and eyeless than ever. To reinforce her vision she had taken to visiting the British Museum, where, keeping her eyes downcast until she was alongside of the battered Ulysses, she opened them and got a fresh shock of Jacob's presence. (*JR*, 238)

Coming pages before we hear of his death, Jacob is not only seen as a lifeless monument but also compared with the 'battered' hero of Homer's *Odyssey*.

Woolf suggests that Jacob's reading of English philhellenes may also have prepared him for death in war. Jacob reads a *History of the Byzantium Empire from 716–1077* (*JR*, 87) by George Finlay, an historian who supported Greek independence and died in Athens in 1875. More powerfully, Jacob has an affinity with Byron, who died of fever at Missolonghi where he had gone to support the cause of Greek independence. As a child, Jacob chooses the works of Byron as a keepsake from Mr Floyd, the local vicar (*JR*, 24): it is an influential gift, for 'the moors and Byron' become part of the reality of Jacob's life (*JR*, 44). Woolf links Byron with Jacob's death by referring to the incident in our final sighting of Jacob, where Mr Floyd passes him in the street and remembers giving him the book. (*JR*, 243). The episode immediately following this presages Jacob's death, as Woolf gives a chilling description of gunshots over Piraeus and darkness falling 'like a knife' over Greece (*JR*, 245). Although we have been told that the gunshots are a nightly ritual, this description is overladen with the shadows of war. Taken together, these allusions suggest that Jacob's admiration of Byron may have led him to his death in battle. It is significant, too, that Jacob was given Byron's works by a clergyman, thus reinforcing the links between war and established religion set up in the description of King's College Chapel.

In *Mrs Dalloway*, Woolf criticises the ways in which Shakespeare has been used ignorantly to support war and nationalism. The militaristic Lady Bruton, the epitome of the English ruling classes, 'never spoke of

England, but this isle of men, this dear, dear land, was in her blood (without reading Shakespeare), and if ever a woman could have worn the helmet and shot the arrow, could have led troops to attack, ruled with indomitable justice barbarian hordes and lain under a shield noseless in a church . . . that woman was Millicent Bruton' (*MD*, 236). Although Lady Bruton alludes to Shakespeare, she is not a reader and her nationalistic sentiment is expressed in a misquotation from John of Gaunt's eulogy to England in *Richard II*: 'this sceptred isle . . . This happy breed of men . . . this dear dear land' (II. i. 40, 45, 57).[3] The speech is well known and is often quoted for nationalistic purposes, but the irony against Bruton and her kind is that John of Gaunt was not advocating war, but defending England against its own ruler.

The end of the passage alludes to Rupert Brooke's 'Forever England', a more recent work also frequently cited for patriotic reasons: 'one could not figure her even in death parted from the earth or roaming territories over which, in some spiritual shape, the Union Jack had ceased to fly' (*MD*, 237). The classical theme from *Jacob's Room* subtly reverberates here, for Brooke was buried at Skyros, thus claiming a patch of Greek soil as 'forever England'. Lady Bruton's ambition to lie 'noseless in a church' continues the motif of statuary: the irony that victory means simply to be commemorated in a lifeless, mutilated stone effigy. Although a woman, Bruton stands for the political establishment which, like the university system satirised in *Jacob's Room*, has appropriated literature for deathly ideological purposes.

Woolf is more explicit about the ways in which the education system has appropriated literature to legitimise war and nationalism in the case of Septimus Warren Smith who, although from a very different social class from Jacob, is led into battle by his education. Septimus studies Shakespeare at an adult education college and falls in love with the lecturer Isabel Pole. Septimus volunteered to fight to 'save an England which consisted almost entirely of Shakespeare's plays and Miss Isabel Pole in a green dress walking in a square' (*MD*, 112). Woolf here shows Shakespeare being co-opted to support nationalism and the heterosexual economy which exhorted women to encourage their husbands to volunteer and challenged men to prove themselves by joining up.[4] Female complicity in warmongering is underlined by the detail that Miss Pole had 'reflected how she might give him a taste of *Antony and Cleopatra* and the rest' (*MD*, 110–11). The plot of that play bears a sinister similarity to what will happen to Septimus: Cleopatra entices Antony to wage a battle he lacks the resources to win; he is defeated, abandoned and disgraced, and commits suicide to restore his honour.

Woolf's examination of the ways in which the patriarchal constructions of a canon have been implicated in militarism reflects a social and cultural phenomenon of the time. As Paul Fussell has argued, the Great War took place against the background of two 'liberal' cultural forces: 'the belief in the educative powers of classical and English literature' and 'the appeal of popular education and "self-improvement"'.[5] If *Jacob's Room* describes the first cultural force, Septimus in *Mrs Dalloway* represents the second. Fussell also indicates the importance of the literary canon at this time, by pointing out that Sir Arthur Quiller-Couch's edition of the *Oxford Book of English Verse* was particularly popular among soldiers, arguing that it 'presides over the Great War in a way that has never been sufficiently appreciated' (p. 159). Although this book was taken to the Front because it was easy to carry, its format represents the prescription and canonisation of approved texts. Quiller-Couch notes in his preface that he had aimed to select pieces which have attracted universal approval: 'The best is the best, though a hundred judges have declared it so.'[6] The anthology is significantly lacking in women writers, suggesting a masculine bias in the definition of what qualifies as 'the best' writing. For soldiers who had received a formal education at public school and university, the texts selected by Quiller-Couch would be ones they had already been taught to know and value; for those like Septimus, such a selection might channel their education in certain ideological directions.

Fussell suggests that literature was a comfort; that writers such as Wilfred Owen and Herbert Reed used literary allusion to express experiences which were 'unspeakable'. However, when he suggests that the feeling of national sentiment generated by English literature was 'one of the reasons why there was no serious mutiny in the British army, even under the most appalling conditions', he hints at but does not critique the power of the cultural encoding of literature (found in the very process of canonisation) to regiment and oppress individuals.[7] Woolf's descriptions of Jacob's Cambridge and Septimus's extra-mural education can be read as critiques of these conditions. Woolf's political satire in *Jacob's Room* and *Mrs Dalloway* foreshadows her argument in *Three Guineas* that the educational system which had always discriminated against women had failed to protect 'culture and intellectual liberty', and that such a failure might be an indirect cause of war (*3G*, 98–100).

Lady Bruton's allusions to Shakespeare in *Mrs Dalloway* can be related to more specific contemporary ideological battles over literature for, as Jonathan Bate has argued, the First World War had awakened critical debates over Shakespeare's status as the 'national poet'.[8] For example, J. W. Mackail, in the British Academy Annual Shakespeare Lecture for 1916, argued that although Shakespeare was 'no teacher of patriotism', certain scenes from his plays illustrate that 'patriotism is not only differ-ent from, but also better than, want of patriotism'.[9] He used Shakespeare to voice his support for Britain's recent decision to become involved in trench warfare to defend France against the Germans: he quoted Posthumus's speech from *Cymbeline* that British soldiers 'will make known I To their approvers they are people such I That mend upon the world' (II. iv. 24). A more extreme example of the appropriation of Shakespeare in support of the establishment is Sir Walter Raleigh's lecture 'Shakespeare and England', delivered in the same series in 1918. Much of the lecture is taken up with sketching national stereotypes and denounc-ing what Raleigh sees as German characteristics. He hails Shakespeare as 'our national poet', who 'embodies and exemplifies all the virtues, and most of the faults of England. Any one who reads and understands him understands England'. He praises 'the splendid outbursts of patriotism' in *King John, Henry V,* and *Richard II,* selecting for special praise the speech by John of Gaunt which Lady Bruton misquotes in *Mrs Dalloway.*[10] While there are no explicit references to these particular lec-tures in Woolf's letters, essays or diaries, she knew of both speakers and we know from her later writings that she held Raleigh in low esteem.[11] Her satire of Lady Bruton therefore can be seen as an early instance of Woolf's antipathy towards the world-view of Raleigh and his ilk.

However, as we will see, Woolf uses strategies to counter the patriar-chal appropriation of literature in both *Jacob's Room* and *Mrs Dalloway,* for both novels seek to defend feminine ways of reading, fre-quently by offering female characters who are able to engage with liter-ature in lively and challenging ways, enabling them to use literature in the causes of peace and rebuilding.

II

Woolf's quest to develop female reading strategies against patriarchal appropriations of literature was partly driven by a more personal drama in *Jacob's Room*: sibling rivalry over literature with her brother Thoby, the model for Jacob (*QB*, I. 112), who died of typhoid fever shortly after a visit to Greece in 1906. Woolf's envy of Thoby's apparently privileged knowledge of Shakespeare is reflected in a late memoir:

> He had consumed Shakespeare, somehow or other, by himself. He had pos-sessed himself of it, in his large clumsy way, and our first arguments – about books, that is – were heated; because out he would come with his sweeping assertion that everything was in Shakespeare: somehow I felt he had it all in his grasp; at which I revolted. (*MB*, 138–9)

The language used here – 'consumed', 'possessed', 'all in his grasp' – implies that Woolf saw her brother greedily absorbing an experience which had been denied her, and jealously guarding it against her attempts to obtain it. The passage suggests that Woolf saw Thoby as inheriting the male custodianship of literature: her description of him having 'possessed himself' of Shakespeare is reminiscent of her account of Leslie Stephen having 'acquired' the great English poems.[12] Thoby's view of Shakespeare may reflect the ideologies of his education: his assertion that 'everything was in Shakespeare' betrays the same kind of overstatement that Sir Walter Raleigh made when he claimed that 'anyone who reads and understands [Shakespeare] understands England'.[13] Woolf's response is defensive, for she argues and 'revolts' against her brother.

Woolf's strategies for claiming literature for herself are revealed in a letter to Thoby in 1901, while he was a student at Cambridge. Woolf wrote to tell him of what was perhaps her first serious encounter with Marlowe and Shakespeare, or at least her first attempt to appraise their claims to greatness:

> Speaking of a certain great English writer – the greatest: I have been reading Marlow[e], and I was so much more impressed by him than I thought I should be, that I read Cymbeline just to see if there mightnt be more in the great William than I supposed. And I was quite upset! Really and truly I am now let in to [the] company of worshippers – though I still feel a little oppressed by his – greatness I suppose. I shall want a lecture when I see you; to clear up some points about the Plays. I mean about the characters. Why aren't they more human? Imogen and Posthumous [*sic*] and Cymbeline – I find them beyond me – Is this my feminine weakness in the upper region? (*L*, I. 45)

Woolf approaches these writers with a scepticism towards the traditional conception of greatness, but none the less admits to being overawed by Shakespeare. She turns to Thoby as a mediator, asking him to 'lecture' her – to pass on to her some of the knowledge he is acquiring at Cambridge – while she excuses herself by putting her critical comments down to 'feminine weakness'. However, Woolf's deference to Thoby and her confession to intellectual 'weakness' are partly façades, for she goes on to make her own critique of *Cymbeline*. She argues that the characters lack humanity and that Shakespeare's greatest strength lies in writing good lines: she picks out 'the best lines in the play – almost in any play I should think –' and quotes them: 'Think that you are upon a rock and now throw me again! . . . Hang there like fruit my soul, till the tree die' (*L*, I. 45–6; *Cymbeline*, V. v. 262). Having reduced Shakespeare to isolated lines she can admire him, for she adds, 'Now if that doesn't send a shiver down your spine . . . you are no true Shakespearian!' (*L*, I. 46).

Where Woolf saw Thoby as having literature 'all in his grasp', her approach is the more tentative one of extracting lines from Shakespeare's plays. The quoted lines are also a way of taming and controlling Shakespeare's 'greatness': Woolf does not accept him as a great author because of his canonical position, but because she has a strong sympathetic reaction to his words. Having appropriated Shakespeare in this way, she can use his greatness to challenge Thoby's educational privilege, for she dares him to match her sensitive critical appreciation. Woolf's sense of the superiority of her own approach to literature is confirmed in the memoir where she writes that Thoby 'was not, as I was, a breaker off of single words or sentences . . . he was much more casual and rough and ready and comprehensive' (*MB*, 139). This appraisal suggests that although Thoby's command of Shakespeare seems more complete, his approach was more coarse than her own careful attention to the details of language.

Woolf also associated Thoby with classical Greek literature, for he was the person who introduced this literature to her (*MB*, 126). The occasion was Thoby's first return home from boarding school, and the conversation about Greek literature helped them renew their friendship after their separation:

> The day after he came back from Evelyns the first time he was very shy; unfamiliar; yet affectionate, glad, in his queer speechless way, to be home; and we went walking up and down stairs together, and he told me the story of the Greeks: about Hector and Troy. I felt he was shy of telling it; and so must keep walking up and down; and we kept on going upstairs and then downstairs, and he told me about the Greeks, fitfully, excitedly. (*MB*, 126)

Sibling rivalry is less immediately apparent here: Thoby seems more open about sharing his knowledge of the classics, and talking about the Greeks brings brother and sister together rather than dividing them. Although Rowena Fowler once cited this passage as an instance of a process whereby the acquisition of classical languages 'marked a transition from childhood to manhood and was associated, like other puberty rites, with sexual aggression and male bonding',[14] she has since rightly rejected Ong's position,[15] for the passage does not mark Thoby's initiation into a male world, but his reintegration into the home. Thoby shares what he has learned at school with his sister, so that the occasion blurs the boundaries between public and private, privilege and exclusion. None the less, it is marked by a sense of distance found in most of Woolf's writings on Thoby: he breaks his silence, but talk of the classics is a substitute for sharing anything more personal.

Thoby appears to have inspired and encouraged the teenaged Virginia's classical studies. She wrote to tell him about her Greek classes with Janet Case, which began in 1897, appearing deferential to his knowledge at first, enlisting his help and asking him to recommend further reading (*L*, I. 10, 42). Her remarks to Thoby about the Greeks are shorter and less critical than her accounts of Shakespeare: 'I find to my immense pride that I really *enjoy* not only admire Sophocles. So after all there is hope for Shakespeare' (*L*, I. 42). When Thoby sent her a copy of J. W. Mackail's *Select Epigrams from the Greek Anthology* for her twentieth birthday in 1902, she wrote that 'these little Epigrams I think I appreciate most of all Greek – as the feminine mind would, according to my theory' (*L*, I. 46–7). Here she continues to develop the sketch of the 'feminine' approach to literature she had begun in her critique of *Cymbeline*: the importance of the short quotation is seen again, for these short, pithy epigrams appeal to her most.

Woolf's sense of rivalry and the superiority of her own approach emerge in her 'Dialogue upon Mount Pentelicus', inspired by the siblings' visit to Greece in 1906.[16] Here, she subtly undermines the value of a university education by satirising the presumption of two Cambridge men (based on her brothers), in claiming ancient Greek culture as their own: 'you would have supposed that each speaker had some personal conquest to celebrate.' The narrator is disparaging about their failed attempts to communicate with the locals by speaking Greek 'as Plato would have spoken it had Plato learned Greek at Harrow'. It becomes clear that the men have an ossified view of Greece: 'if there is one thing that we know about the Greeks it is that they were a still people . . . when they sat by the stream beneath the plane tree they disposed themselves as the vase painter would have chosen to depict them.' By contrast, the narrator offers a lively and vibrant vision of classical culture, with the arrival of a monk resembling Pan who brings an 'atmosphere' which did not 'begin and end with that day and that horizon, but it stretched like a lucid green river on all sides immeasurably and the world swam in its girdle of eternity'. This brings the ancient Greeks into the present, for 'Plato and Socrates and the rest, were close to them'. Alluding to Plato's image of a flame burning in a cave, the narrator sees a 'flame' in the monk's eyes, which 'had been lit at the original hearth'. The narrator therefore claims a living experience of ancient Greece, where the men had seen only relics.

By the time Woolf used Thoby as a model for the protagonist in *Jacob's Room*, her attitude towards him was tempered by loss. As Quentin Bell suggests, Woolf's longing for Thoby after his death was complicated by a sense that he had been a mystery to her when he was alive: she sought to know more about him, partly as consolation for his death and 'partly for a more complex reason – an amused yet resentful curiosity about the privileged masculine society of Cambridge' (I. 112). Sara Ruddick has suggested that Woolf's pursuit of her elusive subject in *Jacob's Room* is a function of her quest not only for the lost 'private' brother who had shared her home, but for the 'public' aspects of his life from which she was excluded.[17]

Woolf therefore partly sought to use Shakespeare and the classics in an elegiac way to compensate for what she could not know about him. Her attempt to use literature as a substitute for knowledge of Thoby is revealed in 'Old Bloomsbury', a memoir written at the same time as *Jacob's Room* (*MB*, 181; *QB*, I. 124–5n.). There, she describes how Thoby would regale her with stories of his friends at Cambridge: 'I thought about Pilkington or Sidney Irwin or the Woolly Bear whom I never saw in the flesh as if they were characters in Shakespeare' (*MB*, 190). Here, Woolf uses Shakespearean characters as a substitute for people she has not met, and thus makes him a cipher for the aspects of her brother's life which she finds mysterious and inaccessible.

Woolf's use of quotation in *Jacob's Room* is marked by a complicated interplay of three impulses: to wrest literature from the control of educated men; to embrace it for herself; and to use it for elegiac purposes. Woolf subtly uses literary quotations to attach male privilege in her description of the Cambridge don Sopwith talking to undergraduates. As Sopwith talks, 'the soul itself slipped through the lips in thin silver disks which dissolve in young men's minds like silver' (*JR*, 51). The image depicts education as a direct financial endowment, but it also picks up on a metaphor from Plato's *Republic*: 'god differentiated those qualified to rule by mixing in gold at their birth. Hence they are most to be honoured. The auxiliaries he compounded with silver, and the craftsmen and farmers with iron and brass. So endowed, each will usually beget of his own kind.'[18] Sopwith is therefore a 'silver' man, an assistant to the ruling elite. Richard Sterling and William Scott have pointed out that Plato has often been accused of élitism on the basis of this 'myth of the metals',[19] and this is clearly an issue in Woolf's description of Sopwith. However, Woolf also undermines the value of what Sopwith gives his students by extending the metaphor, for she imagines a time when they will look back and find that 'the silver disks would tinkle hollow, and the inscription read a little too simple, and the old stamp look too pure, and the impress always the same – a Greek boy's head' (*JR*, 52). Sopwith's teaching may lose its currency for it is part of a process of producing generations of graduates lacking individuality and self-motivation. The narrator notes that the students would respect Sopwith even then, but she adds significantly that a woman, 'divining the priest, would, involuntarily, despise' (*JR*, 52). Here is a hint that a woman may be able see through the tutors, thus subtly linking women with the female visionaries of Greek mythology: the oracles. The mention of priests also critiques the establishment, for it alludes to the convention that Cambridge dons were ordained Church of England clergymen.

Woolf's description of the British Museum in *Jacob's Room* is a central stage in the processes of using allusion in a new, more positive, way and undermining the claims of Jacob and the young men of his class to appropriate Shakespeare and the classics. The Museum is a symbol of British nationalism and the appropriation of culture, for prominent amidst its collection are the Elgin Marbles, taken from the Parthenon in Greece. Woolf suggests that the fruits of human knowledge and literature are not so easily appropriated:

> There is in the British Museum an enormous mind. Consider that Plato is there cheek by jowl with Aristotle; and Shakespeare with Marlowe. This great mind is hoarded beyond the power of any single mind to possess it. (*JR*, 147–8)

The great works of philosophy and literature are the products of human endeavour: there are more great works than any one person can read in a lifetime, and more great works than any one writer or thinker can produce. The passage sutures Shakespeare and Greek classical writers, for it links the words 'Plato' and 'Aristotle' with the phrase 'cheek by jowl' from Shakespeare's *Midsummer Night's Dream* (III. ii. 338), which is, appropriately, set in Athens and takes some of its characters from Greek mythology. The phrase subtly resists conventional concepts of canonisation, for it emphasises equality (in the original quotation, Demetrius says that he will not follow Lysander but go with him side by side). By setting Shakespeare and Marlowe alongside each other, Woolf refuses (as in her 1901 letter to Thoby) to accept that Shakespeare is greater than Marlowe, thus resisting received ideas of greatness. The juxtaposition of Plato and Aristotle, Shakespeare and Marlowe also denies a correlation between chronology and progress and resists both the element of ranking, which is central to the construction of the canon, and the linear chronology, which often underlies the construction of a tradition. The conjunction between the Greeks and Shakespeare is underlined over the next few pages, where the phrase 'Plato and Shakespeare' is repeated several times, and forms an important part of Woolf's own conception (spelled out more fully in 'On Not Knowing Greek') that Shakespeare continued the spirit of ancient Greece.

Woolf's strategy is to suggest that literature has a vibrancy which the canonical approach often fails to recognise. Woolf voices her ambivalence towards the traditional canon by setting up implicit contrasts between the continued vitality of great works of literature and the inanimity of stone memorials: although Woolf notes that all the names carved around the dome of the British Library are men's, she is not entirely in sympathy with the feminist Julia Hedge's comment, '"Oh damn . . . why didn't they leave room for an Eliot or a Brontë?"' (*JR*, 145). Woolf's description of Hedge as bitter and unfortunate, with 'Death and gall and bitter dust . . . on her pen-tip', seems an inappropriate response to what might be read as a valid feminist point, but taken in the context of Woolf's attack on the monolithic and the statuesque as the province of the patriarchal system, Hedge's desire to see the great women writers commemorated in stone becomes synonymous with a wish to ossify their work. Here, Woolf adopts a position which she would develop more explicitly in *Three Guineas*: the view that women should remain 'outsiders' to patriarchal institutions.

In this sequence, Woolf also suggests that the enduring works of literature provide elegiac consolation for they testify to a cultural survival which is greater than the individual. Woolf contrasts the enduring power of the ideas of Plato and Shakespeare with the mortality of the individual:

> Stone lies solid over the British Museum, as bone lies cool over the visions and heat of the brain. Only here the brain is Plato's brain and Shakespeare's; the brain has made pots and statues, great bulls and little jewels, and crossed the river of death this way and that incessantly, seeking some landing; now wrapping the body well for its long sleep . . . Meanwhile, Plato continues his dialogue . . . And Hamlet utters his soliloquy. (*JR*, 149)

Individual mortality, represented by the wrapped bodies of the mummies at the British Museum, is contrasted with the continually renewed effort of the human race in making artefacts which survive; and of great writers whose works continue to be read, and thus continue to live, so that, as in Woolf's 'Dialogue', long-dead writers are seen to have a life in the present. By contrast, the objects listed are all funerary artefacts, traditionally ceremonially dispatched across sacred rivers, suggesting individual mortality. The phrase 'river of death' also alludes to the river of Ocean in Greek mythology, over which the heroes were allowed to pass to the Islands of the Blessed or Elysium. By asserting the immortality of heroes, or great authors like Shakespeare and Plato against the mortality of individuals, Woolf suggests that individuals like Jacob and his contemporaries (or even Thoby) cannot possess the great civilisations, as their education might have led them to believe. Yet she seeks elegiac consolation in the idea that culture continues to thrive and survive: we may read this assertion as Woolf's consolation that she still has Shakespeare and the classics, whom she had discussed with Thoby, as ways of remembering him.

The passage subsumes and re-contextualises two works which discuss individual immortality. Plato's dialogue is identified in the next paragraph as *Phaedrus*, in which Socrates argues that 'All soul is deathless'.[20] Woolf does not specify a soliloquy from *Hamlet*, but 'To be or not to be . . .' (III. i. 56–88) fits the context for it also debates the question of immortality, and Woolf's description of death as a 'long sleep' echoes Hamlet's speculation that the hereafter is a ' sleep of death' (III. i. 66–8).

Woolf's treatment of *Phaedrus* is complex. The dialogue is not presented in a wholly positive light in the British Museum sequence, where Woolf describes Jacob reading in the martial way characteristic of his training:

> When at length one reads, straight ahead, falling into step, marching on, becoming (so it seems) momentarily part of this rolling, impeturbable energy, which has driven darkness before it since Plato walked the Acropolis, it is impossible to see the fire. (*JR*, 150)

The passage implies that Jacob is falling into an illusion as he reads Plato. The suggestion is reinforced by allusions to Plato's parable of the cave from Book VII of the *Republic*, where he likens the uneducated to a group of prisoners shackled within a cave, unable to see daylight, watching shadows on a wall projected from a fire behind them; true education comes when the prisoner is freed to leave the cave and sees sunlight.[21] Here, Jacob pursues Plato's offer of enlightenment, but he is still trapped in the ideologies of his upbringing, and does not notice the (metaphorical) fire which has been the source of his illusions. As Delgarno notes, the scene shows how his education has shielded him from issues of class, nation and gender.[22] The argument of *Phaedrus* also conflicts with Jacob's earlier insistence that body and intellect are inseparable: 'The problem is insoluble. The body is harnessed to a brain' (*JR*, 110). As Sue Roe notes, this position is comparable to that of the Roman philosopher Lucretius: 'The Intellect cannot spring up | Alone outside of the body, or live far from blood and sinews.'[23] Roman philosophy, unlike the Greek, did not admit of a soul or an afterlife. If Jacob favoured Lucretius, then he could not embrace Plato without contradiction.

However, allusions to *Phaedrus* are carried over into the wider context of the book in a way that fulfils the elegiac function of suggesting that something of Jacob survives in others. Woolf draws on ideas from *Phaedrus* to address the problems of death and absence: as Delgarno notes, Woolf learned from the Greeks that 'the visible is one segment of the larger invisible world that is seen by the gods and intermittently by the mad . . . In this scheme death is the event that precipitates the fundamental question: how does language name the figure who is no longer visible?'[24] In *Phaedrus*, Socrates likens the soul to a charioteer driving two horses: one virtuous the other wanton. The charioteer has to control and subdue the unruly horse – in other words, to subdue the temptations of lust – in order to live a virtuous life which will lead to happiness in an afterlife.[25] Shortly before this passage, Jacob had been seen riding a horse which becomes part of him: 'as if your own body ran into the horse's body and it was your own forelegs grown with his that sprang' (*JR*, 136). The conjunction between man and horse foreshadows the reference to *Phaedrus*; Jacob wrestles with the temptations of the flesh in his relationships with women, particularly a prostitute, Florinda, and a married woman, Sandra Wentworth Williams. The image from *Phaedrus* is recalled more strongly when Jacob visits Greece:

> Blame it or praise it, there is no denying the wild horse in us. To gallop intemperately; fall on the sand tired out; to feel the earth spin; to have – positively – a rush of friendship for stones and grasses, as if humanity were over . . . there is no getting over the fact that this desire seizes us pretty often.' (*JR*, 194–5)

The horse therefore figures as Jacob's elusive being – his life-force. These references provide a link between Plato's position and Lucretius's, for Jacob is driven by bodily urges which, in Plato's view, harm the soul.

The horse motif reappears as a symbol of Jacob at the end of the novel, when Clara Durrant stands by the statue to Achilles (another Greek hero) in Hyde Park, which commemorates the Duke of Wellington (an image which again illustrates how the patriarchal establishment has ossified classical culture and made it serve militarism). Clara is then distracted by a riderless horse running past which, according to the *Phaedrus*, implies uncontrolled desire and spiritual chaos – an image encapsulating the onset of war and presaging Jacob's death. The live horse also implies a release from ossification, and the scene quickly turns to farce as Julia Eliot sees a 'little man . . . pounding behind with his breeches dusty' trying to catch the runaway horse (*JR*, 234). The horses provide a glimpse of Jacob, even as the seeds of his death are being sown; tragedy, a genre closely associated with classical culture and the aggrandisement of the male protagonist, briefly gives way to comedy.

Jacob's mother, Betty Flanders, has similar skills of animation. While Jacob is touring modern Italy and feeling alienated by its 'fierceness, bareness, exposure' (*JR*, 186), Betty visits a Roman camp in Scarborough and imagines herself walking with the Romans:

> Did the bones stir, or the rusty swords? . . . and if all the ghosts flocked thick and rubbed shoulders with Mrs Flanders in the circle, would she not have seemed perfectly in her place, a live English matron, growing stout? (*JR*, 182)

She can also animate the more recent dead, as she reads the inscriptions on the tombstones in her local church and imagines 'brief voices saying, "I am Bertha Ruck," "I am Tom Gage"' (*JR*, 183). This is not the style of inscriptions on British tombstones, where the dead are spoken for and do not speak; it is, however, very much the style of the ancient Greek inscriptions collected in the *Greek Anthology* which Woolf had enjoyed as a young woman. Many Greek epitaphs were written as though the deceased were addressing the reader: 'I am an Athenian woman; for that was my city'; others were written as though the stone itself were speaking: 'I am the tomb of one shipwrecked.'[26] The dead are given a kind of immortality in that they speak directly to the reader, and Betty Flanders is aware of this: 'Tom Gage cries aloud so long as his tombstone endures' (*JR*, 184). From this, we can deduce that it was the animated nature of the epigrams, as well as their brevity, which caused Woolf to think that they appealed especially to 'the feminine mind' (*L*, I. 46).

Through Betty Flanders, Woolf develops a view of how a woman's reading might enable cultural regeneration by endorsing a fluid and suggestive relationship with literature. This relationship, which embodies Woolf's engagement with individual lines from Shakespeare, is suggested in Betty's thoughts of her dead husband:

> Seabrook lay six foot beneath, dead these many years; enclosed in three shells; the crevices sealed with lead, so that, had earth and wood been glass, doubtless his very face lay visible beneath, the face of a young man whiskered, shapely (*JR*, 15)

Although Seabrook is buried in a churchyard, his maritime name, his burial in shells (inner coffins) and Betty's fantasy about seeing his face through glass all evoke a submarine world. These images hint at the presence behind Woolf's text of Ariel's song from *The Tempest*:

> Full fadom five thy father lies;
>   Of his bones are coral made;
> Those are pearls that were his eyes:
>   Nothing of him that doth fade,
> But doth suffer a sea-change
>   Into something rich and strange.
> Sea-nymphs hourly ring his knell . . .
> Hark! now I hear them, – Ding-dong, bell. (I. ii. 399)

As in the song, Betty imagines that her husband has not decayed but has somehow been preserved underground. The echo from *The Tempest* continues as she hears a church bell and thinks of it as 'Seabrook's voice – the voice of the dead'. She hears her son, Archer, calling, and 'Sounding at the same moment as the bell, her son's voice mixed life and death inextricably, exhilaratingly' (*JR*, 16). The echoes of Shakespeare give Ariel's song new vitality by working it into a new context, and the song itself speaks of regeneration, for the character elegised in *The Tempest* – Ferdinand's father, Alonso – is not dead but has been rescued by Prospero. The synchronicity of the voices of the living and the dead described here suggests a more creative and pliable form of quotation, in which the voice of a past writer might be heard in the present.

III

Woolf continues to claim past literature for herself and female readers and to celebrate its life-affirming properties in *Mrs Dalloway*. A diary note made whilst writing the novel suggests that the reappearance of the past in the present was central to her innovative technique. Woolf wrote that she had made a 'discovery': 'I dig out beautiful caves behind my characters; I think that gives exactly what I want; humanity, humour, depth. The idea is that the caves shall connect, & each comes to daylight at the present moment' (*D*, II. 263). It is generally accepted that the 'beautiful caves' consist of the characters' memories and that these form part of what would later be labelled her 'stream-of-consciousness' technique, but the method also brings the literary past into the present, for prominent among the memories and thoughts of these characters are phrases and images which had emerged from Woolf's own reading of both Greek literature and Shakespeare at the time.[27]

The idea of the cave is a classical echo reminiscent of Plato's cave: Woolf's image of coming out into daylight echoes Plato's likening of true education to being freed from the cave to turn round to see sunlight, symbolising goodness, truth and justice. Plato argued that the educated have a duty to go back to the other prisoners and encourage them to turn round and see goodness too, but this process is fraught with danger, for the initiated risk being unable to see when they return to the cave, or antagonising their fellows into turning on them and killing them.[28] Plato argues that art can play a part in this educative process, but, in Book X of *The Republic*, he makes a crucial distinction between virtuous art and work which aggrandises war: heroic poetry, notably that of Homer.[29] Woolf wrestles with similar problems concerning harmful and positive uses of art in the polarity of Septimus and Clarissa.

Woolf explores the harmful effects in her treatment of Septimus Warren Smith. We have already seen how he has become a victim of an ideological educational system, but his hallucinations after the war suggest that ironically he believes he has attained a level of illumination. Septimus hears a sparrow singing

> freshly and piercingly in Greek words how there is no crime and, joined by another sparrow, they sang in voices prolonged and piercing in Greek words, from trees in the meadow of life beyond a river where the dead walk, how there is no death. (*MD,* 31)

The message Septimus hears echoes the Greek trope of the immortality of heroes, and the sparrows' location resembles Elysium, the place beyond the stream of Ocean, to which human heroes were allowed to pass to enjoy an afterlife. The presence of birds echoes Plato's account of the myth of Er, in which certain heroes become birds after their death: thus Orpheus becomes a swan, Thamyras a nightingale and Agamemnon an eagle.[30] The fact that Septimus hears small common birds rather than the noble birds of legend suggests a pathetic reappearance of the classical in the present. Septimus is an example of one of the initiated who cannot return to his companions to educate them: his apparent experience of higher truth only isolates and destroys him.

In the figure of Septimus, Woolf qualifies her positive view of the animating imagination in *Jacob's Room* for classical ideas about immortality are replayed in a tragic mode. Septimus's mental illness dramatises the contemporary resistance to emotion – a sort of shell-shock experienced by an entire generation[31] – for the war has left him unable to feel emotion, even for the death of his close friend, Evans. The sparrows' message that there is no death is a torture to him, and the ghostly appearances of Evans as a dramatisation of that song only renew his sense of guilt. Septimus imagines that he sees Evans, or hears him talking or singing behind a screen. Evans sings that the dead are in Thessaly – the mythical land of magicians and heroes from whence the Argonauts set sail – thus linking him with the heroes of Greek legend and also conferring on him a sinister form of immortality, as he haunts Septimus's visions, driving him to suicide. This suggests that for Septimus's generation, the classical can impinge on the modern world only as nightmare or psychosis.

Woolf treats Septimus in a more sympathetic light than Jacob, perhaps because she had an affinity with his experience. She had recently written about having hallucinations similar to his during her own mental illness of 1904 (*MB,* 186). The conjunction does not simply suggest that Septimus's delusions had an autobiographical source; for it also implies that the image Woolf used to describe her illness was itself informed by her reading in Greek literature. By drawing, consciously or unconsciously, on that literature, Woolf found a way of describing Septimus's hallucinations and of framing her own experience in a way that enabled her to overcome the trauma of writing what she called 'the mad part' of the novel which 'tries me so much, makes my mind squint so badly that I can hardly face spending the next weeks at it' (*D*, II. 248). Thus Woolf's project of exploring literary heritage becomes entangled with one of dealing with her personal past.

Septimus's traumatic engagement with classical literature can also be seen as part of Woolf's attempt to undermine those of her contemporaries who had used classical literature. In 'On Not Knowing Greek', Woolf remarks upon the superiority of the war poetry of classical Greece over that of her contemporaries, such as Owen or Sassoon:

> In the vast catastrophe of the European war our emotions had to be broken up for us, and put at an angle from us, before we could allow ourselves to feel them in poetry or fiction. The only poets who spoke to the purpose spoke in the sidelong, satiric manner of Wilfred Owen and Siegfried Sassoon. It was not possible for them to be direct without being clumsy; or to speak simply of emotion without being sentimental. But the Greeks could say, as if for the first time, 'Yet being dead they have not died.' (*CE*, I. 10)

Woolf sees contemporary poets, like Septimus, as evading emotions and treating war satirically, but praises a line from Simonides' epigram 'On the Lacedaemonian Dead at Plataea' which does not address the subject of war and even negates the concept of death: 'Yet being dead they have not died'.[32] This quotation comes from the *Greek Anthology*: yet another example of Woolf using Greek literature for its suggestions of immortality. By pitting the classical against the contemporary in this way, Woolf ignores the classical references and allusions which pervaded writing on the First World War; Wilfred Owen, for example, used classical references in his work, such as in his satirical allusion to Horace's saying 'Dulce et Decorum Est' in his poem of that name.[33] The fact that Woolf sees Simonides as expressing the sentiment 'as if for the first time' underlines her view that Greek literature has originality which contemporary writing lacks. In undermining the classical allusions in First World War poetry, Woolf attempts to deny that these writers had true sympathy with classical writings, just as she had teased Thoby that he was not a 'true Shakespearian'.

By contrast, Woolf shows how the sensibilities of the past might live on in the present in positive ways in the figure of Clarissa, Septimus's double who survives where he perishes. The theme of haunting – the survival of the past into the present and the need to come to terms with it – is as central to her story as it is to Septimus's. Although Clarissa's mental life, like Septimus's, can be compared to Plato's cave, she seems initially less enlightened than he is: the ease with which her past memories impinge upon her present (such as when, on a morning in London, 'she could hear now' the squeaking hinges of the French windows at Bourton when she was young (*MD*, 3)) suggests that she is happy to watch shadows rather than seek enlightenment.

Woolf introduces classical echoes into Clarissa's story. Her party can be seen as a comic reprise of the ending of the *Odyssey*, where Peter Walsh's appearance echoes Odysseus's return to Penelope. Peter has to wait for her to finish entertaining politicians (like Penelope's suitors) before he can be alone with her. The party also brings together a number of people she has not seen for several years, as though they are returning from the dead – for example, Peter Walsh is shocked to see Clarissa's aunt, Helena Parry, because he had been convinced that she was dead – as Odysseus was assumed to be dead until he returned from his travels. These echoes from the *Odyssey* suggest the parallels between *Mrs Dalloway* and *Ulysses* which have been noted by Harvena Richter and Maria di Battista among others.[34] However, Woolf's response to Homer is more subtle, allusive – and partial – than Joyce's extended project of linking each chapter in *Ulysses* with an episode in the *Odyssey*. Woolf's imaginative response to the *Odyssey* is a riposte to the conscious erudition of Joyce, whom she had described as 'a queasy undergraduate scratching his pimples' (*D*, II. 188–9); the pattern of Woolf's novel suggests that a lighter, more allusive engagement with literary tradition is ultimately more positive.

Woolf's championing of a more optimistic, feminine way of reading can be seen at several points where she shows Clarissa and Septimus thinking of the same authors or texts, but taking a very different approach. Using Woolf's analogy of the 'beautiful caves', Clarissa and Septimus's common heritage may be seen as a cavern behind both characters, from which they take divergent paths. Septimus's reading is based on the deluded assumption that he has access to authoritative truth:

> he, Septimus, was alone, called forth in advance of the mass of men to know the truth, to learn the meaning, which now at last, after all the toils of civilization – Greeks, Romans, Shakespeare, Darwin, and now himself – was to be given whole to . . . 'To whom?' (*MD*, 87–8)

Like Jacob, Septimus here attempts to colonise literature for himself, believing that he is the sole inheritor of culture. He thinks that he has benefited from 'all the toils of civilization', just as Jacob and his friends believed that 'civilizations stood round them like flowers ready for picking' (*JR*, 101). Woolf's critique of that attitude is more poignant here, because Septimus is so obviously deluded and victimised. The final question shows that Septimus has no idea of what to do with the learning he has been given: his suggested answer, 'to the Prime Minister', is bathetic, but also signifies that he has given up everything to anonymous, powerful political forces.

Septimus's question 'To whom?' is an allusion to the last line of Shelley's 'The Question'. Shelley's poem is set in a dreamscape where the speaker gathers a bunch of wild flowers, but is at a loss to know whom to give them to; Septimus poses the same question in a similarly insubstantial world. Shelley is invoked again later in the same passage when Septimus feels as though his body is 'spread like a veil upon a rock' (*MD*, 88), recalling the captive Prometheus 'bound to the precipice' of 'icy rocks' in *Prometheus Unbound* (significantly a poem with a classical theme). The association is reiterated later when Septimus is described as being 'exposed on this bleak eminence' (*MD*, 190). There are parallels between Septimus's situation and Prometheus's initial predicament. Septimus believes he is a special messenger; Prometheus stole fire from the gods. Septimus thinks he hears the voice of nature; Prometheus converses with the earth. Septimus kills himself by jumping out of a window; Mercury tempts Prometheus to commit suicide, to 'plunge | Into Eternity'. However, Septimus's potential to be a hero is undermined, for, bathetically, we are told that he is 'not on a hill-top; not on a crag; on Mrs Filmer's sitting-room sofa' (*MD*, 190). Septimus's Shelleyan associations link him with a poet who died tragically young (a similar impression is conjured up when Isabel Pole associates him with Keats (*MD*, 112)).

Clarissa alludes to 'The Question' in a briefer, more positive way: she thinks of her party as 'an offering; to combine, to create; but to whom?' (*MD*, 159). While the allusion may seem to critique the purpose and value of social entertaining, Clarissa's party does become an offering of sorts to Septimus. If Septimus is cast as a Shelleyan hero or as a tragic Romantic poet, Clarissa gives literature a passing glance but turns it to better effect.

Clarissa and Septimus are juxtaposed in their response to *Hamlet*. We have seen that Septimus was led into war by his love for Shakespeare and his attraction for a woman, but he is ultimately disillusioned by both Shakespeare and sexuality and believes that Shakespeare shared his sense of disillusionment:

> That boy's business of the intoxication of language – *Antony and Cleopatra* – had shrivelled utterly. How Shakespeare loathed humanity – the putting on of clothes, the getting of children, the sordidity of the mouth and the belly! . . . Love between man and woman was repulsive to Shakespeare. The business of copulation was filth to him before the end. (*MD*, 115, 116)

This passage hints at Hamlet's descriptions of the world as 'weary, stale, flat and unprofitable' (I. ii. 133) and humankind as 'a quintessence of dust' (II. ii. 308); his rant against Ophelia to 'Get thee to a nunnery. Why, wouldst thou be a breeder of sinners?' (III. i. 121); and his pronouncement that 'we will have no mo marriage' (III. i. 149). Septimus makes the mistake of attributing the sentiments of a character to Shakespeare himself, and the allusions serve to remind us that Septimus, like Hamlet, is mentally unstable.

While Septimus conveys the sentiment of the 'nunnery' speech, it is Clarissa who actually paraphrases it:

> often now this body she wore . . . seemed nothing – nothing at all. She had the oddest sense of being herself invisible; unseen; unknown; there being *no more marrying*, no more having of children now. (*MD*, 12–13; emphasis added)

Clarissa echoes Hamlet's disregard for the body and paraphrases his declaration that there will be 'no more marriage'. The quotation is slightly re-contextualised, for whereas Hamlet wishes that the practice of marriage would come to an end, Clarissa is merely commenting on her own situation of having been married a long time and being past childbearing age. However, Clarissa has rejected heterosexual relations: she sleeps apart from her husband, and we are told that she 'could not dispel a virginity preserved through childbirth which clung to her like a sheet' (*MD*, 40). When Peter Walsh visits her, she recoils from him 'like a virgin protecting chastity' (*MD*, 51). Clarissa and Septimus's views here are polar opposites: Septimus (like Hamlet) decries sexuality and women, and imposes celibacy upon his wife; Clarissa has retreated from her husband, but her chastity becomes a position of strength.

Clarissa's retreat from sexuality incidentally offers Woolf a way of dealing with the courtship narrative which had proved so problematic in her first two novels. The novel insists that it is possible to exist in different states, that Clarissa may be a virgin, wife and mother. Although Clarissa in her present-day existence seems the perfect society wife for her successful husband, her memories offer the alternative potentialities of her attraction to Sally Seton (thus offering a same-sex challenge to the heterosexual imperative of the marriage narrative) and her interest in Peter Walsh before settling on Richard Dalloway as a marriage partner. The closure required by a traditional marriage narrative is challenged by the facts that Clarissa continues to think of Sally and Peter, and that both come to her party. The prominent position of courtship within the retrospective narrative of *Mrs Dalloway* suggests that Woolf was still haunted by the legacy of the courtship novel, but her break with the linear plot structure enables her to challenge its assumptions, particularly the 'catastrophe' (*MD*, 44) of the heroine's change of status from virgin to wife. Furthermore, there is an ironic reference to Jane Austen, for Clarissa mistakenly calls Richard 'Wickham' on their first meeting, aligning a socially acceptable partner with the rake from *Pride and Prejudice*.

The refrain from *Cymbeline* – 'Fear no more the heat o' the sun | Nor the furious winter's rages' (IV. ii. 258) – which echoes throughout *Mrs Dalloway*, provides a point of reconciliation between the viewpoints of Clarissa and Septimus, for they both think of these lines. The quotation speaks of renewal: it is taken from a speech which (like Ariel's song in *The Tempest*), is a dirge for someone who turns out to be alive. It is sung for Cymbeline's daughter, Imogen, who is thought to have taken a deadly poison, but has actually taken a strong sleeping draught and eventually wakes to be reunited with her family. Imogen is also a celibate wife, for she appears not to have consummated her marriage (her husband Posthumus complains that 'Me of my lawful pleasure she restrain'd, | And pray'd me oft forbearance' (II. iv. 161)). Imogen thus stands for the possibility of seeming dead but being alive; of appearing sexually active but being a virgin.

The dirge from *Cymbeline* has an important elegiac function within the novel. Imogen's recovery, which speaks of renewal and survival, is congruent with Simonides' epitaph, 'Yet being dead they have not died'. It is also relevant to Clarissa, who has survived, albeit with a damaged heart, the influenza virus which killed thousands of her contemporaries (*MD*, 4). Woolf's invocation of Shakespeare suggests that the hope for renewal does not lie with individuals but with society at large, for she persistently introduces the quotation in connection with the mortality of individuals. The refrain first occurs in the novel when Clarissa thinks about her own mortality while shopping on Bond Street and asks, 'Did it matter that she must inevitably cease completely; all this must go on without her . . . ?' The closest she can get to envisaging immortality is to imagine that her existence is bound up with that of others, that 'somehow in the streets of London, on the ebb and flow of things, here, there, she survived, Peter survived, lived in each other' (*MD*, 11). The words from *Cymbeline* suggest Clarissa's resigned acceptance of mortality, for to die is to 'fear no more'. The refrain bears out Clarissa's idea of living 'in each other': the possibility that our shared cultural heritage might make us part of one another.

This theme recurs the next time the lines are used. Clarissa finds that her husband has been invited to lunch without her, and again she is reminded that death will one day separate them for ever (*MD*, 38). The thought leaves her with a feeling of 'exquisite suspense', as though she is about to dive, plunging in the sea to undergo a sea-change as the waves 'gently split their surface, roll and conceal and encrust as they just turn over the weeds with pearl' (*MD*, 39). Here, the lines from *Cymbeline* are linked with echoes from Ariel's song from *The Tempest*, reinforcing the implications (in both Shakespeare plays) of separation from one's loved ones and of regeneration and the hope of cheating death. Woolf allows this image from *The Tempest* to inform the next allusion to *Cymbeline*: 'Fear no more, says the heart. Fear no more, says the heart, committing its burden to some sea' (*MD*, 51). As the refrain becomes associated with both the beating of the heart and the sound of the waves – acquiring a rhythmic pattern reminiscent of both as it does so – the combined allusion balances the end of individual life against the continuities of the natural order.

Woolf uses Shakespeare's words as a link between Clarissa and Septimus, for shortly before his suicide, Septimus thinks he hears Shakespeare's words being whispered by Nature: 'Fear no more, says the heart in the body; fear no more' (*MD*, 182). Although Septimus thinks that Shakespeare's message is intended for him alone,[35] the echo suggests that Shakespeare is a shared inheritance, which cannot be possessed or appropriated by any one individual. When Clarissa hears of Septimus's suicide from a guest at her party, she uses Shakespeare to connect her experience with that of the young man she has never known. At first she is horrified at bad news being relayed at her party, but she gradually comes to reflect that, by committing suicide, Septimus had preserved himself from corruption. She remembers empathising with Othello's words in her youth – 'If it were now to die, 'twere now to be most happy' (*MD*, 242; *Othello*, II. i. 189) – and she recites them now to align her own experience with that of Septimus.[36] While the quotations from Shakespeare function as a point of commonality between Septimus and Clarissa, they also serve as a vanishing-point for both characters as individuals, in that each finds expression in the words of an other. The echo from Shakespeare thus suggests, as Woolf implied in her description of the British Museum in *Jacob's Room*, that although individuals die, Shakespeare's words will continue. In her final repetition of the words from *Cymbeline*, Clarissa allays her own fears while laying Septimus to rest: 'the words came to her, Fear no more the heat of the sun' (*MD*, 244). The phrase signals the resolution of her crisis and her decision to return to her party: they suggest an awakening like Imogen's when the sleeping draught has worn off.

The allusions to *Cymbeline* function as an elegy, but they can also be located within the context of debates over war, nationalism and the canon. The refrain here is used to signal recovery and the return of peace, in direct contrast to those who have used Shakespeare's words as a battle-call. The pacifist purpose of Woolf's use of *Cymbeline* is best seen by setting the quotation in the context of the rest of the play. *Cymbeline* has an unwieldy plot which yokes together a drama over marital relationships, in which Imogen is a central figure, with a saga of war and national identity, in which Cymbeline, King of Britain, wages a successful campaign against Imperial Rome. By taking her quotations from the plot-line concerning Imogen, Woolf gives prominence to a female character and refuses to give war importance by ignoring the second narrative strand.

However, in Clarissa, Woolf presents a contrasting view of English national identity to that of Lady Bruton: by quoting Shakespeare accurately and lovingly Clarissa draws on a life-affirming literary tradition. Although her quotations from *Cymbeline* refuse to celebrate Shakespeare as the 'national bard', they suggest the continuity of English culture, emphasising its positive, life-affirming values, rather than negative, warmongering ones. Significantly, the dirge speaks of the natural world in the passing of the seasons, in contrast to Lady Bruton who is associated with statuary and whose misquotation from John of Gaunt's speech leaves out his image of England as a garden, an 'Eden' or 'blessèd plot' (*Richard II*, II. i. 42, 50). In associating Shakespeare with the natural world, Clarissa links him closely with her memories of her adolescence at Bourton, with its fresh air, waves, trees and flowers (*MD*, 3). The picture of Englishness suggested here anticipates Woolf's examination of national identity here in *Three Guineas*, whereby she criticises patriotism but values the emotional impact of place, personal memories, and verse:

> [T]he outsider will say, 'in fact, as a woman I have no country. As a woman I want no country. As a woman my country is the whole world.' And if, when reason has said its say, still some obstinate emotion remains, some love of England dropped into a child's ears by the cawing of the rooks in an elm tree, by the splash of waves on a beach, or by English voices murmuring nursery rhymes, this drop of pure, if irrational, emotion she will make serve her to give to England first what she desires of peace and freedom for the whole world. (*3G*, 125)

While Clarissa's early sense of relief that 'the King and Queen were at the Palace' (*MD*, 5) is treated satirically, her sense of Englishness in literature and landscape is valued within the book.[37]

In *Mrs Dalloway*, Woolf ultimately locates the spirit of the literary past in feminine and domestic realms: Penelope takes precedence over Odysseus, whose return is figured as a society party; Imogen is championed over Cymbeline; and Clarissa becomes the true custodian of literature by virtue of her love of place and her philosophy of life. It represents a further stage in the sibling rivalry over literature, for a man's education is shown to be worth less than a woman's experience of life.

IV

Woolf's treatment of canonical literature in *Jacob's Room* and *Mrs Dalloway* suggests a subversive attempt to liberate great literature from the grasp of educated men and from patriarchy, militant nationalism and egotism. The ease with which she allows echoes from past literature to inform and influence the texts suggests that she did not seek to appropriate that literature for herself but rather to absorb it into her own voice, and to give up her voice into a communal one. Woolf's response differs from the appropriation of literature by James Joyce, whose works she accused of being ruined by the 'damned egotistical self' (*D*, II. 14); or even by T. S. Eliot, who, notwithstanding his theories of impersonality, wanted to establish a place for his own poetry by inserting 'the new (the really new) work of art' into a great tradition of monolithic 'existing monuments'.[38] Eliot emphasises the 'necessity to conform': as Bonnie Kime Scott has noted, he used architectural metaphors to set up 'an aesthetic of control through tradition'.[39] Woolf, by contrast, seeks her own route into literature as an outsider. Instead of envying or even emulating the education which patriarchy grants to its sons, Woolf practises the more subversive strategy of absorbing literature by covert means.

Woolf suggests that women readers and writers might become the custodians of literary culture, for they have the power to foster survival and renewal. The idea reappears in *Three Guineas*, where Woolf argues that women could play a role in protecting culture and liberty and thereby help to prevent war 'not by advising their brothers how they shall protect culture and intellectual liberty, but simply by reading and writing their own tongue in such a way as to protect those rather abstract goddesses themselves' (*3G*, 103).

Unlike the Bloomian account of influence in which a poet fights for the posterity of his own work,[40] Woolf seeks reassurance of the survival of others: the survival of the 'great minds' of literature in spite of war; and the survival of the individual in other people after death. The two processes are deeply interconnected. In these novels, Woolf's incipient pantheism seeks some form of personal survival after death, in contrast to the organised religion symbolised by King's College Chapel, which purports to offer eternal life but ironically leads young men to their deaths. Literature becomes a space in which the living might both identify with and distance themselves from the dead, as Woolf remembers Thoby through the classics and Clarissa elegises Septimus in the words of Shakespeare. As the next chapter will show, the process of using literature as elegy continued and intensified in *To the Lighthouse*.

Notes

1. Fowler, 'Moments and Metamorphoses', p. 217.
2. Delgarno, *Woolf and the Visible World*, p. 56.
3. Fox, *Woolf and the Literature of the English Renaissance*, p. 130; Schlack, *Continuing Presences*, p. 57.
4. These pressures are illustrated in two famous wartime posters: one simply stating, 'The Women of Britain say "Go!"', the other depicting the embarrassment of a non-combatant when asked by his children, 'What did you do in the war, Daddy?'
5. Fussell, *The Great War and Modern Memory*, p. 157.
6. Quiller-Couch (ed.), *The Oxford Book of English Verse*, p. ix.
7. Fussell, *The Great War*, p. 158.
8. Bate, *The Genius of Shakespeare*, p. 194.
9. Mackail, *Shakespeare After Three Hundred Years*, pp. 19, 21.
10. Raleigh, *Shakespeare and England*, pp. 3, 5.
11. Woolf refers to Mackail in 'On Not Knowing Greek' (*CE*, I. 12). She describes Raleigh as 'disgusting' (*L*, III. 252) and criticises him as a warmonger in her review of his letters: 'When the guns fired in August 1914 no-one saluted them more rapturously than the Professor of English Literature at Oxford' (*E*, IV. 346).
12. Maitland, *Leslie Stephen*, p. 475.
13. Raleigh, *Shakespeare and England*, p. 3
14. Fowler, '"On Not Knowing Greek"', p. 339.
15. Fowler, 'Moments and Metamorphoses', pp. 218–19.
16. Woolf, 'A Dialogue upon Mount Pentelicus', p. 979.
17. Ruddick, 'Private Brother, Public World', p. 190.
18. Plato, *The Republic*, p. 113 (415a).
19. Sterling and Scott, introduction to Plato, *The Republic*, p. 16.
20. Plato: *Phaedrus*, p. 49 (245c).
21. Plato, *The Republic*, pp. 209–15 (514a–521c).
22. Delgarno, *Woolf and the Visible World*, pp. 56–7.
23. *De Rerum Natura*, III. Sue Roe editorial annotations to *Jacob's Room* (Penguin), p. 171.
24. Delgarno, *Woolf and the Visible World*, p. 7.
25. *Phaedrus*, p. 50 (246a–d).
26. Mackail, *Select Epigrams from the Greek Anthology*, p. 145.
27. Woolf was reading Elizabethan drama and Greek literature including Homer, Plato, Euripides, and Aeschylus in preparation for *The Common Reader* (*D*, II. 196).
28. *The Republic*, pp. 209–15 (514a–521c).
29. Ibid., pp. 289–90 (599a–600b).
30. Ibid., pp. 309–10 (620a–b).
31. Saunders suggested that the condition of shell-shock characterised the Modernist era in 'War, History, and Madness'. Tate similarly argues for the incidence of a civilian form of shell-shock, 'civilian war neuroses', analogous to the modern 'post-traumatic stress disorder' in 'HD's War Neurotics', pp. 241–4.

32. Mackail, *Select Epigrams*, p. 140.
33. See Fussell, *The Great War*, pp. 155–69.
34. Richter, 'The *Ulysses* Connection: Clarissa Dalloway's Bloomsday', 305–19; and di Battista, 'Joyce, Woolf and the Modern Mind'.
35. Fox, *Woolf and the Literature of the English Renaissance*, p. 118.
36. Ibid., pp. 116–17.
37. In this respect, *Mrs Dalloway* exemplifies the affinity that Briggs has noted between Woolf's sense of Englishness and that of Edward Thomas ('In Search of New Virginias', pp. 172–5).
38. Eliot, 'Tradition and the Individual Talent', in *Selected Essays*, p. 15.
39. Scott, *Refiguring Modernism*, p. xxvi.
40. Bloom, *The Anxiety of Influence*, p. 71.

Chapter 4

To the Lighthouse and the Ghost of Leslie Stephen

Father's birthday. He would have been . . . 96, yes, today; & could have been 96, like other people one has known; but mercifully was not. His life would have entirely ended mine. What would have happened? No writing, no books; – inconceivable. I used to think of him & mother daily; but writing The Lighthouse, laid them in my mind. And now he comes back sometimes, but differently. (I believe this to be true – that I was obsessed by them both, unhealthily; & writing of them was a necessary act.) He comes back now more as a contemporary. I must read him some day. I wonder if I can feel again, I hear his voice, I know this by heart? (*D*, III. 208)

Woolf wrote these words in her diary entry for 28 November 1928, almost two years after *To the Lighthouse* was completed. She records that, retrospectively, she regarded the novel as a turning-point in her relationship with both her parents: by writing this heavily autobiographical novel and by translating her parents into the fictional characters of Mr and Mrs Ramsay, Woolf readjusted her relationship with her past. It is tempting to use this diary entry, as Fogel does, to read *To the Lighthouse* as a process by which Woolf overcame parental influences and took control of her own writing.[1] However, the latter part of the passage suggests a different dynamic, for it articulates a process of loss and recovery: although Leslie Stephen's death had left Woolf free to write, her sense of freedom was compromised by an 'unhealthy obsession', a form of longing for him. The process of writing *To the Lighthouse* helped Woolf address this loss by enabling her to know her father (though not her mother) in a new way: as a writer.

As earlier chapters have demonstrated, Woolf's identification with Leslie Stephen as a reader had influenced her practice as a writer. His views on women writers inform *The Voyage Out* and *Night and Day*, where Woolf seeks to emulate the domestic environments and courtship narratives of Jane Austen's novels, which Stephen had praised, while his disparagement of Austen's 'limited' subject-matter contributes to Woolf's ambivalence towards her female role-models. Although Woolf invokes and tackles patriarchal ideas in all her early novels, she does not address Stephen directly in them: for example, in *Jacob's Room*, she invokes her brother Thoby (and men of his generation) to critique the patriarchal appropriation of literature. In *To the Lighthouse*, Woolf finally tackles Leslie Stephen's legacy directly, not only by bringing him to life in the character of Mr Ramsay but by exploring his writings in a series of allusions throughout the novel.[2] This chapter will argue that Woolf came to know her father through his works, to make a shift from a familial relationship towards the more intimate relationship that exists between reader and writer.[3] In quoting and alluding to Stephen, Woolf appropriated his works for her own time and her own purposes, coming to see him as a 'contemporary' whose writings were relevant to her own time rather than to the late Victorian world he inhabited. We will also see that, in doing this, Woolf readjusted her relationship with her intellectual and literary heritage more generally.

Three works in particular structure Woolf's attempt to recall her father and lay his ghost in *To the Lighthouse*: *The Mausoleum Book*, *History of English Thought in the Eighteenth Century* and *An Agnostic's Apology*. Woolf's starting point for recalling her father is his *Mausoleum Book*, which is a straightforward autobiographical work, partly a memoir and partly a diary (it was not written for publication, although an edition is now available). Woolf draws on and interrogates her father's account of her childhood years, particularly of her mother, Julia, in the opening section of the novel; she examines *how* he represented the past and questions how far it is possible to recall past events and people who have died. The novel is concerned with the nature of elegy and the problem of presence and absence, and Woolf draws on the *History of English Thought in the Eighteenth Century* to explore these issues. Central to Woolf's meditation is the question of whether anything exists outside of our perceptions of it, a theme which Stephen discusses in connection with the English empiricist philosophers, particularly Hume, and which Woolf alludes to in *To the Lighthouse* in Mr Ramsay's research on 'subject and object and the nature of reality' (*TL*, 33).

The *History* and *An Agnostic's Apology* articulate Stephen's own attempts to grapple with past ideas. For Stephen, the conflict centred on religious issues. As a young man, he was a don at Cambridge, and, according to the conventions of the time, had been ordained into the Church of England. Over the years, he became convinced that the views which the Church propagated as sacred truths were false. After a painful crisis of faith, he gave up his post as don and resigned from Holy Orders in the late 1870s with Thomas Hardy as a witness. Stephen used empiricist philosophy to defend his rejection of God intellectually, first in the *History* and then at greater length in *An Agnostic's Apology*; but he still retained a Romantic spirituality and an emotional attachment to religious imagery. As I will argue in this chapter, Woolf found resonances in Stephen's departure from the religious and educational establishment for her own attempts to reject patriarchy.

I

The relationship between *The Mausoleum Book* and *To the Lighthouse* is extremely complex. We cannot look at *The Mausoleum Book* as a source for the novel because we cannot be certain whether events recorded in both books are simply two accounts of the same incidents remembered by both writers, whether Stephen's account of them in *The Mausoleum Book* helped to shape Woolf's recollection of certain events, or indeed, whether his book enabled her to picture scenes she had not witnessed at first hand. Alan Bell discounts the importance of parallels between the two books:

> It is less the indirect quotation of Stephen's text which is important, more the 'transcription' of gestures of body and attitudes of mind. The loosely-quoted anecdotes as well as the portrayal of intellectual feeling owe most to an inevitable store of family memories so strong that a direct reference to the documents would have been superfluous. (*MBk*, xxix)

Even if Woolf and Stephen both drew on their common family memories in their writings, Stephen wrote about them first, and in doing so had begun the process of describing and ordering them, and placing them in a literary idiom. The book was not wholly spontaneous, for Stephen paid close attention to the presentation of material: he wrote it in manuscript before making a fair copy, for which he made 'a good many alterations', including 'correcting slovenly phrases and repetitions' (*MBk*, 97). Woolf continued the process of turning family memories into literature and responded to Stephen's version of events in *To the Lighthouse*. So, while Stephen's memoir was not the sole source of descriptions, characters and events which also find their way into Woolf's novel, her account none the less engages with and challenges his record of events. As we have seen, Woolf looked back to the pre-war years in three of her previous novels, and attested to the power of patriarchy in shaping and recording that world. In *To the Lighthouse*, Woolf addresses not simply a generically patriarchal view of those years, but her own father's account.

Woolf replicates Stephen's methods of arranging and recounting certain incidents in 'The Window'. The setting – the Ramsays' holiday home on a Scottish island – is based on the Stephens' holiday cottage, Talland House at St Ives, which Stephen makes the backdrop for his descriptions of Julia, his children and some family friends, and the three things he uses to set the scene – cricket on the lawn, the garden and Julia's visits to the sick – are all found in the first section of *To the Lighthouse*.

Additionally, Woolf echoes Stephen's opinions about several friends and family members in *To the Lighthouse*, suggesting adult views of people she had known as a child. Stephen tells an anecdote of Julia Stephen's success in promoting Kitty Lushington's engagement to Leo Maxse in 1890. 'My Julia was of course,' he concedes 'though with all due reserve, a bit of a matchmaker' (*MBk*, 75). Woolf echoes this assessment by making Mrs Ramsay instrumental in bringing together Paul Rayley and Minta Doyle. Since Woolf would have been only eight years old when the Maxses were engaged, the importance she attaches to Mrs Ramsay's role in it is possibly based on other people's views of her mother rather than on her own observations. Also, since she had already portrayed the character of Kitty Maxse as Mrs Dalloway (*QB*, II. 87), the picture here of Kitty as a young woman is a shift, which suggests that Woolf took the story from somewhere else.

Woolf similarly echoes Stephen's view of Worstenholme, a brilliant mathematician 'whose Bohemian tastes and heterodox opinions had made a Cambridge career unadvisable', in her picture of Augustus Carmichael. Since Woolf was a child when she knew Worstenholme, it is unlikely that she would have known about the problems which had stunted his career. It is even less likely that she would have been allowed to know the details of his marriage. Stephen described Worstenholme as practically a hermit, married to an 'uncongenial and rather vulgar Swiss girl'; he was 'despondent and dissatisfied and consoled himself with mathematics and opium'. Julia 'took him under her protection, encouraged him and petted him' and invited him every year to St Ives, where 'he could at least be without his wife' (*MBk*, 79). Woolf uses this verdict as a basis for her description of Carmichael, who also takes opium, and is the object of Mrs Ramsay's pity, for 'what was obvious to her was that the poor man was unhappy, came to them every year as an escape', and that this unhappiness was 'his wife's doing' (*TL*, 56).

Woolf may have turned to *The Mausoleum Book* not simply for the history it recalled, but because it was concerned, as she was, with loss and how to overcome it. Stephen composed his memoir as a way of mourning Woolf's mother, Julia, who died on 5 May 1895. He describes how they met and were married, recounts incidents from their time together, and expresses his desolation over her death. Stephen wrote the main part of the memoir in the two months after Julia's death, but continued to use the book as a journal chiefly for recording the deaths of friends, acquaintances and family members, including Virginia's half-sister, Stella. *To the Lighthouse* is similarly concerned with remembering the dead. While writing *To the Lighthouse* Woolf suggested that mourning deaths and giving expression to loss were important aspects of her own writing: 'I have an idea that I will invent a new name for my books to supplant "novel". A new ——— by Virginia Woolf. But what? Elegy?' (*D*, III. 34; 27 June 1925).[4] In the first section, 'The Window', Woolf recaptures her childhood and memories of her parents and siblings; the priority it gives to reminiscence makes it the section which most closely resembles *The Mausoleum Book*. In the second section, 'Time Passes', Woolf alludes to the deaths of her mother, Stella and her brother Thoby in the characters of Mrs Ramsay, Prue and Andrew, as Leslie Stephen used his journal to record the deaths of friends and relatives. The last section, 'The Lighthouse', is concerned with enacting memorials: Lily Briscoe completes her painting of Mrs Ramsay; while Mr Ramsay, James and Cam make a trip to the lighthouse to take the provisions which Mrs Ramsay had always wanted to send to the lighthouse-keepers.

The Mausoleum Book and *To the Lighthouse* have an important common focus in the figure of the lost mother – Julia Stephen or Mrs Ramsay – and the void created by her death. While some similarities between the works can be explained simply by the fact that they use the same person for their model, it is evident that Stephen's portrait of Julia was in Woolf's mind as she wrote her novel. In her presentation of Mrs Ramsay, Woolf does not simply record her own impressions, but attempts to deal with Leslie Stephen's image of Julia. This process can be seen in her treatment of two important and interrelated themes: woman as the object of reverence and woman as the object of art. *The Mausoleum Book* is largely a hagiography: Stephen writes that 'my love was blended with reverence. She is still my saint' (*MBk*, 54). Woolf explores the issue of reverence by showing the kind of adoration which Mrs Ramsay inspires in others. Lily Briscoe notices how Mr Bankes looks lovingly at Mrs Ramsay, and realises that her womanhood is the reason for this veneration: Lily feels 'the reverence which covered all women; she felt herself praised' (*TL*, 66). More importantly, Mrs Ramsay is held in honour for being a mother, and is frequently seen in the first part of the novel with her youngest, and favourite, son, James. As Mr Bankes observes, mother and child are 'objects of universal veneration' (*TL*, 72). This echoes Stephen's sentiments in *The Mausoleum Book*:

The love of a mother for her children is the most beautiful thing in the world; it is sometimes the redeeming quality in characters not otherwise attractive. [Julia] was a perfect mother, a very ideal type of mother; and in her the maternal instincts were, as it seemed, but the refined essence of the love which showed its strength in every other relation of life. (*MBk*, 83)

Ironically, what is missing from this description is Julia herself: we are told that she epitomises motherhood, one of the most beautiful states of human existence, but this makes her more mysterious, since it only tells us what she was, not who she was. Stephen's sense of mystery is portrayed in Woolf's account of Mr Ramsay worshipping his wife and son, seeing them from a distance and finding them 'lovely and unfamiliar'. Woolf's narrative draws attention to the almost religious impulse behind this feeling: 'who will blame him if he does homage to the beauty of the world?' (*TL*, 51). In the close connection between veneration and admiration of physical beauty in this scene, the theme of woman as the object of reverence intersects with that of woman as the object of art.

In both *The Mausoleum Book* and *To the Lighthouse*, these themes are explored through the image of the Madonna, which links physical beauty with the mystery of motherhood. Leslie Stephen invokes the image to describe his first impression of Julia when they met at a picnic in 1866: 'I do not remember that I spoke to her. I saw and remembered her, as I might have seen and remembered the Sistine Madonna or any other presentation of superlative beauty' (*MBk*, 31). The image is significant, for, as Stephen records, Julia was used by Edward Burne-Jones as a model for the Madonna in his painting 'The Annunciation'. This picture was painted in 1879, after Leslie and Julia Stephen were married and, appropriately, while Julia was pregnant with Vanessa, the first child of the marriage.[5] Thus Stephen recovers his first memory of Julia through this later image. Suggestions of religious painting also hover around Mrs Ramsay. Woolf's description of Mrs Ramsay knitting juxtaposes her against a Renaissance religious painting: 'with her head outlined absurdly by the gilt frame, the green shawl which she had tossed over the edge of the frame, and the authenticated masterpiece by Michael Angelo' (*TL*, 42). Although Woolf draws attention to this absurdity to question whether Mrs Ramsay should be worshipped as a religious icon, she none the less shows that other characters revere her as a Madonna. Chief amongst these is Mr Bankes, who has visited the 'Sistine Chapel; Michael Angelo; and Padua, with its Giottos' (*TL*, 98). His views on art are shared by Lily Briscoe: although she tries to paint Mrs Ramsay in an abstract and post-impressionist style, with colourful, geometrical shapes, she respects traditional ideas about art. Her painting is closely associated with Renaissance depictions of the Madonna and Child, for Lily twice defends herself for representing Mrs Ramsay and James as a purple shadow, because mother and child, 'objects of universal veneration, and in this case the mother was famous for her beauty – might be reduced . . . to a purple shadow *without irreverence*' (*TL*, 72; emphasis added). Later, she argues that 'she did not intend to disparage a subject which . . . Raphael had treated divinely' (*TL*, 136). Lily never dispels her sense of reverence for Mrs Ramsay. When she later has a vision of Mrs Ramsay sitting on the step, she treats it as a holy visitation, for her appearance is 'part of her perfect goodness to Lily' (*TL*, 272).[6]

Although Lily tries to see Mrs Ramsay differently, Woolf shows the power of these traditional images, for Lily's vision confirms that Mrs Ramsay is beautiful, possesses 'perfect goodness' and commands respect. Like Julia Stephen in *The Mausoleum Book*, Mrs Ramsay remains mysterious. As beautiful women, Mrs Ramsay and Julia Stephen are in danger of becoming objects which other people can contemplate and consume: their capacity to think or feel is ignored in favour of their capacity to give pleasure to the viewer.

As Phyllis Rose has suggested, Woolf's portrait of Mrs Ramsay bears many of the hallmarks of the Victorian ideal of womanhood she satirised in her 1931 lecture, 'Professions for Women'.[7] Woolf named the stereotypical woman the 'Angel in the House' after a poem by Coventry Patmore, and described her as 'intensely sympathetic', 'immensely charming' and so unselfish that 'she sacrificed herself daily . . . in short, she was so constituted that she never had a mind or a wish of her own, but preferred to sympathise always with the minds and wishes of others' (*CE*, II. 285). Woolf claimed that she had rejected this image by 1931, for 'had I not killed her she would have killed me' (p. 286). This claim may be set in parallel with her comment that, had her father lived, 'his life would have entirely ended mine', that there would have been 'no writing, no books' (*D*, III. 208), for he had endorsed the idea of the Angel in the House. Though Woolf could claim to have killed the angel by 1931, her portrait of Mrs Ramsay in 'The Window' suggests that in the late 1920s she had not entirely rejected this ideal. Woolf picked an easy target for satire in Coventry Patmore's sentimental poem: in *To the Lighthouse*, however, she was tackling images of women which were much more powerful and personally resonant.

Religious iconography was problematic for both Stephen and Woolf. They were seduced by the poetry of language to the extent that they were prepared to let images like the Madonna and Child intrude upon their respective concerns for empirical truth and women's equality. Where Stephen wrote as an agnostic in a language which was heavily inscribed by Christianity, Woolf wrote as a woman in a language which had been inscribed by patriarchy. Although Leslie Stephen was agnostic, the language he uses to describe Julia is religious: she is his 'saint' and he holds her in reverence. As someone who had lost his faith, religious language was a tricky issue for Stephen. On the one hand, he was aware of the difficulty of expressing truth when all the available terminology was tinctured with old beliefs, with the result that 'old conceptions are preserved to us in the very structure of language' (*History*, I. 5). On the other, he was reluctant to dispense with the language of fantasy and imagination, because he felt that the decline in religious belief meant that 'we have lost a mode of expressing our emotions. The old symbols have ceased to be interesting, and we have not gained a new set of symbols' (*History*, I. 15).

The process by which Leslie Stephen dispensed with old conventions had implications for Woolf's challenge to patriarchy. Stephen was reluctant to dismiss the moral dimensions of Christianity and was determined 'to live and die like a gentleman'.[8] He did not see himself as clinging to Christian morals out of sentiment, but because the morality was valid without the support of a religious infrastructure. The figure of the mother was central to his moral outlook: he saw a mother's love for her children as 'the most beautiful thing in the world' and suggested that motherhood could 'redeem' characters who were 'not otherwise attractive' (*MBk*, 83). By making motherhood the ideal state for women, Stephen confined them to the domestic sphere and to the traditional family unit. The moral and poetic vestiges of religion can be seen to work together in *The Mausoleum Book*: the image of the Madonna and Child as a poetic, emotive expression of the beauty of motherhood is underpinned by a moral and social ideology.

Virginia Hyman has pointed out that Auguste Comte was a key figure behind Stephen's thinking on the family.[9] Comte's work had played an important part in Stephen's rejection of much of the Bible because it could not be proved to be true: Stephen wrote that he read Comte and became convinced 'among other things that Noah's flood was a fiction (or rather convinced that I had never believed in it) and that it was wrong for me to read the story as if it were a sacred truth' (*MBk*, 6). As T. R. Wright points out, Comte's views were inconsistent because they espoused both Enlightenment ideas on empirical verification and Romantic ideas leading to highly subjective plans to reform society and religion.[10] Thus, Stephen would have found in Comte a philosophy which embraced two competing tendencies in his own thinking: a commitment to the rigorous pursuit of truth and more idealistic schemes for improving the quality of life. Comte's social theory of Positivism emphasised the mother and the traditional family as vehicles of social progress. Comte sought to counter the destructive potential of individualism by creating a sense of community modelled on that of primitive Catholicism. Positivism preserved traditional structures by translating Christianity into the 'Religion of Humanity': Comte replaced a transcendent God with 'le Grand Être', or the soul of humanity, which he saw as intrinsically female. Comte's ideas shed light on the veneration of women and the Victorian ideals of womanhood, for he transmuted Catholic veneration of the Madonna into reverence for womankind in general. As Noel Annan ironically glosses it:

> Womanhood was the source of love; Positivist saints might be worshipped provided they were women; and in order to develop compassionate propensities to the full, priests were to be compelled to marry and imbibe . . . rich draughts of female affection.[11]

These venerated women are seen only in relation to others, particularly men. A woman's value is located in what she does for others or what she means to them, or in what she can inspire others to be. Such selfless giving is central to the Comtean ideology. The power of a woman's love to bring others closer to an ideal state of being is reflected in Leslie Stephen's summary of Julia Stephen's life:

> its value was the outpouring of a most noble and loving nature, knitting together our little circle, spreading its influence to others, making one little fragment of the race happier and better and aware of a nobler ideal. (*MBk*, 96)

Julia is depicted as fulfilling the positivist ideal of bringing about social improvement through loving others, but her power is limited to the space accorded to her by traditional patriarchal society, for her influence affects only her 'little circle' which constitutes 'a little fragment of the race'.

The contours of Leslie Stephen's ideology of the family can be seen in Woolf's portrait of Mrs Ramsay. Although she does not engage with Comte directly, Woolf reflects the Comtean background to Stephen's thinking in her description of female altruism in Mrs Ramsay's ability to give to others – such as when she lets Mr Ramsay 'protect her', giving 'of her own free will what she knew he would never ask' (*TL*, 89). Though Lily Briscoe later draws attention to the problems of such altruism – 'Mrs Ramsay had given. Giving, giving, giving, she had died' (*TL*, 203) – the earlier part of the book suggests that, like the 'noble and loving' Julia Stephen, Mrs Ramsay inspires a love capable of improving the quality of life. Woolf uses Lily to explore these ideas. For example, Lily watches Mr Bankes gazing at Mrs Ramsay and thinks that it was

> love . . . distilled and filtered; love that never attempted to clutch its object; but, like the love which mathematicians bear their symbols, or poets their phrases, was meant to be spread over the world and become part of the human gain. (*TL*, 65–6)

This scene could be read as a gloss on the description of Julia Stephen in *The Mausoleum Book*. Rather than denying the spiritual power Leslie Stephen attributes to Julia, Woolf exaggerates it in Mrs Ramsay. Where Stephen limits Julia's achievement to making her own family happy, Woolf suggests that the love Mrs Ramsay inspires might be 'spread over the world'. Here, Woolf harnesses a positive side of the Comtean ideal of womanhood by suggesting that even if women cannot take public roles, they can make an impact on society by influencing others to act. This exaggeration makes Mrs Ramsay seem more powerful by granting her a wider sphere of influence, but it also makes her more mysterious.

Like Stephen's adoption of Comtean ideas, the passing allusions to Positivism in *To the Lighthouse* engender contradictions. Where Stephen's use of Comte is a function of his inability completely to reject traditional ideas and conceptions, Woolf's (perhaps unwitting) acceptance of the spiritual side of Positivism prevents her from overturning traditional ideas about the family. Woolf makes it clear that Mrs Ramsay's secret power works to preserve the status quo, for Mrs Ramsay influences others to obey the 'universal law' that 'they all must marry' (*TL*, 69, 68). The description of marriage as a precept of 'universal law' makes it a divine institution rather than simply a form of social organisation. Lily reveres Mr and Mrs Ramsay as 'symbols of marriage, husband and wife' (*TL*, 99). In the draft version of the novel, she sees their relationship in more powerfully Christian terms, as they take on 'gigantic ~~meaning~~ stature – Crucified & transcendent, ~~blessing the world~~ or ~~with gestures of blessing a~~ with symbolic meaning' (*OHD*, 120). This use of Christian images to sanctify marriage suggests that Woolf equated Christianity with the patriarchal family.

Woolf's description of Mrs Ramsay's dinner-party further links religious ideas with the status quo. Mrs Ramsay's success in bringing her disparate guests into union suggests that she single-handedly manages to preserve civilisation as it was known, particularly when she attempts to promote marriages among her guests. She hopes to persuade Lily to marry Mr Bankes and instigates the engagement of Paul and Minta, which is announced at this meal. As Lily notes, there is something terrifying about Mrs Ramsay's matchmaking, for she 'led her victims . . . to the altar' (*TL*, 137). The phrase has strong ritualistic significance: the altar is the traditional location for a wedding, but is also the site for ritual feasts and sacrifices.[12] When Mrs Ramsay learns of Paul and Minta's engagement, she thinks of her party as 'celebrating a festival'; but she recognises that the meal is also a sacrifice, because 'the love of man for woman' they are celebrating also bears 'in its bosom the seeds of death' (*TL*, 135). The comment presages later events in the novel, for Paul and

Minta sacrifice their happiness by marrying, and Prue Ramsay is sacrificed (*'given* in marriage') and literally gives up her life for motherhood when she dies from 'some illness connected with childbirth' (*TL*, 179, 180; emphasis added). Mrs Ramsay's role as matchmaker literally has life-and-death significance and the sense of power and mystery which surrounds her is enhanced rather than exploded. Positioned at the centre of this festival and 'presiding over destinies which she did not understand', she becomes the focus of anxieties about the future, about life and death, and about the survival of civilisation.

These deep-seated anxieties about Mrs Ramsay's power over life and death are reinforced by another influence on *The Mausoleum Book*, and ultimately on *To the Lighthouse*: the Romantic tradition, and Wordsworth in particular. In the memoir, Leslie Stephen uses two quotations from Wordsworth to express his thoughts about Julia. One comes from 'Tintern Abbey':

> . . . that best portion of a good man's life,
> His little, nameless, unremembered, acts
> Of kindness and of love (l.33; *MBk*, 82)

It is ironic that a book of remembrance should use this quotation, which talks about acts which are 'unremembered' – forgotten or ignored. At the same time it suggests that a person should be remembered chiefly for what she or he did for others. While trying to preserve Julia's legacy, Stephen effectively denies it. These problems are even more evident in his other quotation from Wordsworth, from *Poems of the Imagination*:

> She was a Phantom of delight . . .
> A perfect woman, nobly planned,
> To warn, to comfort, and command;
> And yet a Spirit still, and bright
> With something of angelic light! (VIII. 1, 27; *MBk*, 33)

This quotation, specifically about a woman, firmly locates her importance in what she does for others: warning, comforting and commanding are all done to other people. At the same time, Wordsworth casts the woman as an angel, stressing her negligibility. A line which Stephen does not quote takes this idea further by emphasising the woman's mortality: she is 'a Traveller between life and death' (VIII. 24). In this poem, the woman is a Wordsworthian 'border' figure – a person who is not important in herself, but because, in her apparent position on the borders between life and death, she inspires the poet to higher thoughts.

In reading Stephen's interpretation of Wordsworth, Woolf had to deal with the problem that in poems such as these, the woman is the object of the male poet's reverence and desires, and is marginalised because she is so closely linked to mortality. As a female reader, Woolf had to find a way around this objectification. This problem was intensified because Woolf had first encountered Wordsworth through listening to Stephen reciting his poems from memory:

> His recitation, or whatever it may be called, gained immensely from this fact, for as he lay back in his chair and spoke the beautiful words with closed eyes, we felt that he was speaking not merely the words of Tennyson or Wordsworth but what he himself felt and knew. Thus many of the great English poems now seem to me inseparable from my father; I hear in them not only his voice, but in some sort his teaching and belief.[13]

This childhood memory bound Stephen and Wordsworth together as a common site of authority. Stephen validated Wordsworth's sentiments and knowledge by expressing them as his own; and he validated his own feelings and knowledge through reference to Wordsworth. This mutual validation consolidated father and poet into a powerful figure – one that was authorised to know and feel and one that had its knowledge and feelings authorised. As the speaker, Stephen took upon him the subjectivity of the poet; as the listener, Woolf could only act as witness to that subjectivity. And as a female listener, she must address the border position which the text assigned to her. Thus, although Woolf mocked Coventry Patmore, she found it difficult to attack Wordsworth, not only because of his status a great writer, but because his greatness was sanctioned by her father.

Woolf's allusions to Wordsworth in *To the Lighthouse* grapple with the problem of how to establish female characters within discourses which cast them as border figures. This can be seen in Mrs Ramsay's Wordsworthian reverie as she contemplates the lighthouse across the bay. Once the children have gone to bed, Mrs Ramsay feels that she can 'be herself, by herself' (*TL*, 85). The process of discovering an inner self after being freed from the identity conferred on her by her roles as hostess, mother, and wife echoes Wordsworth's praise of solitude in *The Prelude*:

> When from our better selves we have too long
> Been parted by the hurrying world, and droop,
> Sick of its business, of its pleasures tired,
> How gracious, how benign, is Solitude. (IV. 354)

In solitary communion with nature, Wordsworth confirms a sense of self which emerges once he has escaped from the 'unnatural self', or the identity which the busy life of college and city impinge upon him. However, while Mrs Ramsay's meditation appears to affirm her sense of self in a way which echoes Wordsworth, Woolf develops the Wordsworthian allusions in ways which render that self elusive and unstable. In *The Prelude* Wordsworth uses a person at prayer and a lighthouse-keeper as images of solitude:

> Votary (in vast cathedral, where no foot
> Is treading, where no other face is seen)
> Kneeling at prayers; or watchman on the top
> Of lighthouse, beaten by Atlantic waves;
> Or as the soul of that great Power is met
> Sometimes embodied on a public road,
> When, for the night deserted, it assumes
> A character of quiet more profound
> Than pathless wastes. (IV. 362)

Images from this passage are echoed in Woolf's description of Mrs Ramsay: the votary in a cathedral appears in the picture of Mrs Ramsay's 'self', freed from her body 'pushing aside a thick leather curtain of a church in Rome'; while the lighthouse-keeper mutates into a lighthouse beam. Wordsworth uses the worshipper and the lighthouse/lighthouse-keeper as symbols of solitude: the lonely nature of their tasks illustrates the solitary condition. Neither of them stands as a cipher for the poet's self, but their solitariness describes his state; and, as 'human centres' of solitude (IV. 359), their humanity is important to him. By contrast, Woolf uses the visitor at a cathedral, the lighthouse beam, and – more radically – the core of darkness as symbols to stand for what Mrs Ramsay becomes once she is released from roles which impose identity. Unlike Wordsworth's simile, Woolf's symbol fuses subject and object – Mrs Ramsay is not like the light, she *is* that light: 'inanimate things . . . expressed one . . . became one . . . knew one, in a sense were one' (*TL*, 87).

Thus, while Woolf sets out on the Romantic project of finding Mrs Ramsay's true or inner self she finds an absence, an empty symbol. This emptiness confirms Mrs Ramsay's status as the angel or ghost: although she is alive in this section of the novel, there is a suggestion that she has no existence of her own when she is not the object of someone else's thoughts or vision. Reduced to a symbol, she is absent. As Makiko Minow-Pinkney argues from French feminist theory, 'language, the symbolic order, representation itself' is 'made possible by the repression of "woman"'. Presence and absence are 'organised around the phallus as the Signifier (what Cixous terms "hierarchised oppositions"): full presence-masculine-active-positive-coherent (superior), absence-feminine-passive-negative-incoherent (inferior)'. Femininity is the 'term which has been repressed into marginality and silence by the order of representation, this constituting the very condition for the functioning of the symbolic order'.[14] By representing Mrs Ramsay's 'self' as a core of darkness, Woolf does not realise that self, but permanently defers it, rendering it unknowable.

The problem of Mrs Ramsay's loss of subjectivity goes deeper than the question of the non-representation of women in patriarchal discourses. The question of whether a person exists when no one else can see them is connected with both the work of the empiricists and the elegiac theme of remembering the dead, with its attendant question of whether there is such a thing as personal survival after death. Mrs Ramsay's reverie has elegiac overtones: for example, there is an allusion to the Lady of the Lake from *Morte D'Arthur* in Mrs Ramsay's feeling of a ghostly stirring inside herself: 'there curled up off the floor of the mind, rose from the lake of one's being, a mist, a bride to meet her lover' (*TL*, 87).

Woolf draws on themes from Leslie Stephen's philosophical work, *The History of English Thought in the Eighteenth Century*, to develop these elegiac questions in *To the Lighthouse*. As Gillian Beer has pointed out, there are 'congruities' between the *History* and *To the Lighthouse* which suggest that 'Woolf's writing is meditating on problems raised in the father's text'.[15] One of the most important of these problems is that of 'presence and absence'. Ann Banfield likewise has noted that Woolf's 'terms of familiarity with the problem of knowledge in the British tradition' are traceable to the *History*.[16] The empiricist philosophers Stephen discusses in *History* argued that nothing could exist apart from our perceptions of it: when something was not being perceived, it could be said not to exist. Beer and Banfield point to the use of the figure of the table as a link between Woolf, Stephen and the empiricists.[17] The question of whether a table can be said to exist independently of a viewer is a popular example used by empiricists, such as Hume: 'That table, which just now appears to me, is only a perception, and all its qualities are qualities of a perception'.[18] Stephen, while debating Hume, remarks that 'it is a plain fact of consciousness that we think of a table or a house as somehow existing independently of our perception of it' (*History*, I. 46). And in *To the Lighthouse*, Andrew Ramsay explains his father's research topic to Lily Briscoe by telling her to 'think of a kitchen table . . . when you're not there' (*TL*, 33).

As Beer's article makes clear, the problem of presence and absence is not only a philosophical exercise, but lies at the heart of elegy and any form of writing. Elegy is a way of writing about a person when they are no longer there, but, since language is made up of symbols for things which are absent, all writing is concerned with absence and loss. If elegy is an attempt to recapture a dead person in writing, it is doomed to failure because language can only preserve absence. And, if the symbolic order of language inscribes the absence of women, then elegies for women are doubly problematic. In responding to *The Mausoleum Book*, Woolf had to negotiate her father's elegy: *his* attempt to perpetuate Julia's memory in *his* language. This problem was seen in Woolf's attempt to get beyond the symbolic and reclaim her mother's subjectivity and inner self in Mrs Ramsay's reverie, where she confirmed rather than challenged her mother's absence.

For Woolf, as for Stephen, the elegiac question of how to make sense of a person's non-existence was made more urgent by the absence of Christian consolations. Woolf invokes agnostic questions specifically in Mrs Ramsay's reverie. Mrs Ramsay finds herself thinking, 'We are in the hands of the Lord', but then feels annoyed for thinking it, for the 'insincerity slipping in among the truths roused her, annoyed her' (*TL*, 87). Mrs Ramsay's dismissing of God as an 'insincerity' among 'truths' alludes to Leslie Stephen's concern that he could only accept as truth what could be proven; and that the existence of God could not be proved. Mrs Ramsay's meditation echoes a specific problem raised by Leslie Stephen in his chapter on Hume in the *History*. She asks: 'How could any Lord have made this world?' when 'there is no reason, order, justice: but suffering, death, the poor. There was no treachery too base for the world to commit' (*TL*, 87). This invokes an argument which Stephen made from Hume that the existence of the universe is no proof that there is a God: an imperfect world cannot prove a perfect maker; a heterogeneous world cannot prove a unified maker (*History*, I. 324–6); and it is impossible to prove the existence of a supreme moral ruler when all the universe suggests to us is (he quotes from Hume) 'blind nature, impregnated by a great vivifying principle, and pouring forth from her lap, without discernment or parental care, her maimed and abortive children' (*History*, I. 328). Woolf refers to Hume specifically in this passage, when Mr Ramsay walks past, laughing to himself over an anecdote about Hume, as a fat old man, being stuck in a bog and rescued by an old lady on condition that he says the Lord's Prayer (*TL*, 88). Of all the philosophers Stephen considers in the *History*, he holds Hume in the highest esteem because he makes an 'unanswerable' case against eighteenth-century theology (*History*, I. 341). It is perplexing that Woolf should make Hume an object of ridicule and deride him as a hypocrite for saying a prayer even though his scholarly work constituted a radical attack on religion. The joke is in part a buried allusion to the *History*: Stephen himself remarked that Hume's quarrel with religion was academic and that Hume admitted that his doubts disappeared once he left his study

(*History*, I. 44). However, it also points to a central tension in Stephen's thinking. On the one hand, he endorsed the ideal of the Angel in the House, with all its spiritual and religious ramifications, and maintained a Romantic belief in the saving powers of love and altruism; on the other, he applauded Hume's attempts to undermine religion and endorsed his pessimistic vision of 'blind nature' meaninglessly producing 'maimed and abortive children'.

Woolf's ambivalence in her treatment of Mrs Ramsay's reverie suggests that she too had difficulty in resolving this tension. Her exploration of the 'inner self' makes her engagement with the empiricists problematic, because the concept was alien to Hume's ideas. It also illustrates her uncertain relations with Romanticism because, although her concern with the inner self is Romantic, her difficulty in supporting that concept owes something to the empiricists. Hume argued that human beings were no more than their faculties of perception: that without the capacity to see or to be seen, a person would no longer exist. The ultimate instance of the removal of perceptions is death: 'were all my perceptions remov'd by death, and cou'd I neither think, nor feel, nor see, nor love, nor hate . . . what is farther requisite to make me a perfect non-entity?'[19] Woolf thus enters into two very different discourses in her exploration of self-hood and existence: a sceptical–empiricist one which casts doubt on personal existence and survival after death and a Romantic one which foregrounds the subjective and spiritual. We need to add to Beer and Banfield's accounts of Woolf's engagement with empiricist ideas an appreciation of how she also responded to Romantic ones.

II

Woolf plays out the tensions between Romanticism and empiricism in 'Time Passes', where she engages closely with Stephen's ideas and those of his major influences, to explore the theme of absence. On the one hand, Woolf rehearses empiricist ideas about whether something exists only when it can be seen, by writing about the Ramsays' cottage when the holiday party is not there and raising questions about whether it still exists when it is not seen or inhabited; and whether people are still present in the house when they are away from it. The section begins with darkness falling, and the substantiality of even the most solid of household objects is questioned, as lamps are put out and the house is plunged into darkness: 'Nothing, it seemed, could survive the flood, the profusion of darkness' which 'swallowed up . . . the sharp edges and firm bulk of a chest of drawers' (*TL*, 171–2). As the characters go to sleep, Woolf rehearses the argument that the act of sleeping, which cuts off the senses from the stimuli of the outside world, might also disintegrate identity – 'there was scarcely anything left of body or mind by which one could say "This is he" or "This is she"' (*TL*, 172) – thus invoking an extension of the empiricist argument that the self is only a collection of perceptions. On the other hand, Woolf invokes more Romantic ideas to suggest that, although the Ramsay family and their guests are absent, there are presences in the cottage to perceive it. Anthropomorphic images are found throughout the section: for example, the draughts which blow around the house are endowed with the capacities to think and to see, for they 'entered the drawing-room, questioning and wondering' (*TL*, 172). These airs are endowed with human characteristics but also seem to be ghosts: they move around 'ghostlily', as they 'all sighed together; all together gave off an aimless gust of lamentation to which some door in the kitchen replied; swung wide; admitted nothing; and slammed to' (*TL*, 173). The existence of ghosts, the manifestation of human spirits, implies the possibility of an inner being or soul (something which was anathema to the empiricists) and the possibility of existence after death or at least *in absentia*. However, the tension continues, for the ghost-story element does not release the section from the shadow of the empiricists: if 'Time Passes' was an attempt to prove that the *cottage* continues to exist when it is not seen, then it has not succeeded. While it implies that things continue to exist when identifiable individuals are not looking, it cannot eliminate the perceiving human subject altogether, for it is impossible to imagine an empty house other than as the object of someone's gaze. Rather than refuting empiricism, this sequence endorses it by demonstrating the main issues of the empiricist argument in graphic terms. In turning these tensions about, Woolf allows her fictional and imaginative narrative to interplay with rational and philosophical ideas.

In the third chapter of 'Time Passes', Woolf plays with sceptical and Romantic ideas to test the concept of the existence of a deity. The anthropomorphic spirit which inhabits the island has now assumed a godlike form and Woolf suggests that there may be a deity which can both allow and deny human beings transcendent vision: 'divine goodness had parted the curtain . . . divine goodness, twitching the cord, draws the curtain' (*TL*, 174). The anthropomorphic form represents what Stephen saw as the charms of the 'old order' of religion; and he associated ideas such as pagan gods with Wordsworth, who, he says, 'expresses the familiar sentiment when he wishes that he could be "a pagan suckled in some creed outworn". The sight of Proteus and Triton might restore to the world the long-vanished charm' (*History*, I. 14). On the other hand, Woolf brings this divine figure to bear on the empiricist argument which greatly interested Leslie Stephen – the question of whether God can be said to exist if He cannot be seen. The presence of 'divine goodness' presents Berkeley's hypothesis – discussed by Stephen in the *History* – that things continue to exist when we do not see them because they still exist in the mind of God. Yet by making this divinity anthropomorphic, Woolf reflects the more sceptical arguments of Hume which oppose Berkeley. According to Hume, the tendency to endow God with human characteristics called His existence into question because it jeopardised the idea of a *super*-human supreme being. The image of 'divine goodness' in the homely act of drawing curtains seems to call into question the conception of such a super-human being. As Stephen argues from Hume in the *History*, human attempts to imagine God do not prove His existence, for they lead only to an anthropomorphic god. The human mind cannot conceive of anything beyond its own experience: if it cannot conceive of something, then it cannot prove that thing's existence (I. 324; 336–7). Thus, Woolf's conception of a divine being as a fictitious figure both invokes and calls into question the existence of a divinity.

Woolf continues to pit a sense of mystery against agnostic doubt in a second group of human subjects introduced in 'Time Passes': the unnamed people who keep watch on the beach. Variously described as the mystic, the visionary and the hopeful (*TL*, 178–9), the watchers' interests are spiritual. There is a strong correspondence between these figures and the group of believers Stephen casts as his theological opponents in *An Agnostic's Apology*, whom he names Gnostics. Stephen introduces the Gnostics by attesting to the power of the temptation to seek answers:

> A complete solution, as everyone admits, is beyond our power. But some answer may be given to the doubts which harass and perplex us when we try to frame any adequate conception of the vast order of which we form an insignificant portion. We cannot say why this or that arrangement is what it is; we can say, though obscurely, that some answer exists, and would be satisfactory, if we could only find it. Overpowered, as every honest and serious thinker is at times overpowered, by the sight of pain, folly, and helplessness, by the jarring discords which run through the vast harmony of the universe, we are yet enabled to hear at times a whisper that all is well, to trust to it as coming from the most authentic source, and to know that only the temporary bars of sense prevent us from recognising with certainty that the harmony beneath the discords is a reality and not a dream. This knowledge is embodied in the central dogma of theology. God is the name of the harmony; and God is knowable. Who would not be happy in accepting this belief, if he could accept it honestly? (*Apology*, 2–3)

This passage articulates a quandary between submitting to the attractions of faith and admitting that it is logically and morally impossible to defend faith. The passage builds up to a crescendo of hope about what might be achieved if only one could believe, before crashing into the recognition that it is not possible to hold these beliefs honestly. A similar tension runs through Woolf's portrayal of the watchers. Like Leslie Stephen's Gnostics, Woolf's watchers believe in the existence of answers and of an invisible order underlying the visible universe. They have the sense of assurance that 'all is well', which Stephen supposed the Gnostics to enjoy, in their perception of a 'strange intimation . . . that good triumphs, happiness prevails, order rules' (*TL*, 180). Like the Gnostics, who believe in the reality of a god despite the fact that it cannot be perceived in any way, hidden as it is by 'the temporary bars of sense', Woolf's searchers find an answer to their questions, but are not able to communicate it to others: 'suddenly an answer was vouchsafed them (what it was they could not say)' (*TL*, 179). Echoing Stephen's attack on the Gnostics, Woolf demonstrates that the watchers' beliefs could be neither proved nor communicated. Woolf further calls into question the watchers' sense of assurance by setting them against a climate of loss, for she juxtaposes their first appearance with the announcement of Mrs Ramsay's death and Mr Ramsay's desolation (*TL*, 175). Woolf suggests the limited usefulness and effectiveness of the watchers' contemplation of nature and sense of prayers answered in the face of the pain of human bereavement.

Stephen's Gnostics and Woolf's visionaries can be seen as parallel, sceptical responses to Romanticism. In their responsiveness to nature and their sense of an indefinite and expansive quest, Woolf's watchers are closely identified with the figure of the solitary wanderers in Wordsworth's poetry, who contemplate nature and seek answers for deep spiritual questions. Similarly, although Stephen lambasts his opponents, in the passage quoted above, for adhering to the 'central dogma of theology', the vocabulary and imagery in which he characterises the Gnostics' beliefs – the prevalence of images of nature in the passage, the musical imagery, the idea of an underlying harmony – suggest Romantic ideals rather than traditional Christian imagery. When Stephen writes of the attractions of believing that 'the harmony beneath the discords is a reality and not a dream', he is not describing the appeal of orthodox religious doctrines but the power of a Romantic ideal, such as Wordsworth's idea that 'the immortal spirit grows | Like harmony in music' and 'reconciles | Discordant elements' (*Prelude*, I. 340–4). In 'Time Passes', Woolf, like Stephen, invokes harmony as an ideal and, like him, suggests that such an ideal is difficult to maintain. The watchers on the beach see warships which are 'out of harmony' with 'the usual tokens of divine bounty' (*TL*, 182). Where in 'The Window' Woolf saw Wordsworth and her father as a common site of authority who sought to marginalise female experience, she now aligns herself with Stephen by taking up his sceptical position towards Romantic ideas.

Woolf's sense of the inadequacy of Romantic ideas when dealing with death and loss comes into focus most clearly in her representation of the relationship between the human subject and nature. This relationship is celebrated by Wordsworth, who describes his growth as a poet as a process of being nurtured by nature – the 'common face of Nature spake to me I Rememberable things' (*Prelude*, I. 587) – and of entering into a 'spirit of religious love' with nature (II. 357). 'Time Passes', by contrast, voices doubts about the possibility of a communion between the human subject and nature. The divorce between the viewer and nature is emphasised in Section 6, when Spring is said to be 'entirely careless of what was done or thought by the beholders' (*TL*, 179). Nature is not a benign force but a cruel one, a cruelty which is reinforced by Prue's death in childbirth. Though Wordsworth recognised mortality as integral to the natural world, he believed that death was part of the working-out of a higher purpose: for example, he describes a dead child as having been 'checked I By special privilege of Nature's love' (*Prelude*, VII. 374). By contrast, Woolf views nature as a morally neutral, uncaring force: denying that death is the working of a higher purpose, and questioning the sanctity of the dead implied by the 'phantom of delight' and the 'angelic woman' celebrated by Wordsworth in 'Poems of the Imagination', and by the idea of the Angel in the House. Yet, here Woolf also draws on Stephen's interests, for her view of nature draws on Hume's argument (which Stephen endorsed) that nature is a 'blind' force which generates ugly creatures 'without discernment or parental care' (*History*, I. 328). She thus brings the two sides of Stephen's thought into direct conflict, by using sceptical ideas to undercut the Victorian ideals of womanhood he endorsed.

Woolf also challenges Wordsworth's aesthetic that poetry is formed from a process of opening up the mind to nature while allowing the imagination to augment what it sees, for her account of the watchers' struggle pours doubt on the capacity of the human mind to receive inspiration. Woolf sees the mind as 'a murky pool' and 'a cracked mirror', which is therefore an imperfect means of reflecting what it sees, while nature is an uncaring force which does not offer good:

> That dream, then, of sharing, completing, finding in solitude on the beach an answer, was but a reflection in a mirror, and the mirror itself was but the surface glassiness which forms in quiescence when the nobler powers sleep beneath? . . . contemplation was unendurable; the mirror was broken. (*TL*, 182–3)

The divide between humankind and nature is reinforced by the wartime setting of 'Time Passes'. The 'tokens of divine bounty – the sunset on the sea, the pallor of dawn, the moon rising, fishing-boats against the moon, and children pelting each other with handfuls of grass' cannot be appreciated when grey warships in the bay make it difficult 'to marvel how beauty outside mirrored beauty within' (*TL*, 182). The watchers on the beach discover that it is almost impossible to sustain a belief in the healing powers of nature in the shadow of war. Woolf dismissively lists natural features – along with the Romantic assumption that they can offer the viewer intimations of something more spiritual – as being of little worth in a time of war. She dismisses the characteristically Romantic responsiveness to the natural environment and the concept of 'divine bounty'; implying that belief in the power of nature is even less feasible during war than in peacetime.

Woolf further rebuffs Wordsworth by implying that the love of nature is inappropriate in wartime; for Wordsworth, writing against a background of the French Revolution and the Napoleonic Wars, suggested that a belief in nature was essential for humanity to survive the conflict. Like Woolf's observation about the warship in the bay, Wordsworth describes the shocking contrast between natural beauty and the evidence of war, for example, in his encounter with a soldier in the Lake District who appeared 'ghastly in the moonlight' (*Prelude*, IV. 396); whereas the warships in 'Time Passes' intrude upon the viewer's attempt to appreciate nature, war in *The Prelude* renders a love of nature even more important to the individual. Wordsworth wrote that while war disrupts humankind's capacity to commune with nature, peace can be restored if only people would listen to nature again: 'If new strength be not given nor old restored, | The blame is ours, not Nature's' (*Prelude*, X. 469). He described the end of the Reign of Terror in France (*Prelude*, XI. 31–4) as a chance for nature to help humankind to rebuild as the political system had collapsed and 'left an interregnum's open space | For *her* to move about in, uncontrolled'. Woolf, by contrast, finds the triumph of nature deeply sinister, something to be feared because it threatens to exterminate humanity. Nature's fecundity (like Prue's pregnancy) carries the threat of extinction as much as the promise of new life: 'What power could now prevent the fertility, the insensibility of nature?' (*TL*, 187). Eric Warner and Margaret Beede have noted that Woolf's Romanticism was essentially social,[20] but neither does justice to the strength of Woolf's desire to preserve the human and the social from the ravages of nature.

In Woolf's final anti-Romantic statement in 'Time Passes', she rejects the Romantic image of the ruin (celebrated in poems such as Wordsworth's 'The Ruined Cottage'), by playing it off against empiricist arguments about presence and absence. Woolf describes the ruination of the Ramsays' cottage not as a fruitful return to nature but as a fear that the lives led there will be obliterated:

> In the ruined room, picnickers would have lit their kettles; lovers sought shelter there, lying on the bare boards; and the shepherd stored his dinner on the bricks; and the tramp slept with his coat round him to ward off the cold . . . some trespasser, losing his way, could have told only by a red-hot poker among the nettles, or a scrap of china in the hemlock, that here once someone had lived; there had been a house. (*TL*, 188–9)

Gillian Beer reads the ruination of the cottage as an attempt to sever the building from its associations with domesticity by portraying the 'decaying humanism of the concept "house" – an object constructed for human use and so now, without function, present only as lexical play' (p. 49). This process might be seen as a challenge to Hume by suggesting that it is possible to get beyond the human-centred view which he thought was essential to all perception. In fact, the opposite happens, for human existence is cherished against all odds. Even at its most deserted, the cottage is not uninhabited: the lovers, tramps and picnickers will occupy the site and find tokens of the lives of the Ramsays and their friends. This passage suggests that it is impossible to imagine a world without humans; and, while it is possible to imagine a world without oneself, it is difficult emotionally to contemplate a world from which even the *memory* of oneself has been expunged. Rather than challenging Hume to show that it *is* possible to think beyond the human, Woolf agrees with him, for her picture of the empty house demonstrates the emotional impossibility of giving up the human viewpoint.

The dynamic of 'Time Passes', even as it contemplates loss and ruination, is towards the social, the human and the everyday, and away from the other-worldly, the spiritual and Romantic ideas about Nature. This means a rejection of the Angel in the House in favour of a more solid and practical definition of the female role. The resolution of 'Time Passes' lies in a restoration of the house by an old charwoman, Mrs McNab, in preparation for the return of some members of the Ramsay party; but Woolf also appropriates the Romantic figure of the borderer in Mrs McNab. Although Mrs McNab is treated with the full force of Woolf's class prejudices – she is described as toothless and witless, lurching and leering – and although she is oblivious to the watchers and continues to 'drink and gossip as before' (*TL*, 179), she is not simply a pitiable, comic, antithesis to them. A clue to her role is found in a draft, where she is given a mystic or visionary dimension of her own:

as if her message . . . were somehow transmitted – rather by the lurch of the body & the leer of her smile . . . & in them were the broken syllables of a revelation more . . . confused, but more profound, than any accorded to solitary watchers, pacers on the beach at midnight. (*OHD*, 216)

The picture of Mrs McNab as a lower-class figure capable of inspiring the viewer to deeper thoughts accords very strongly with figures like Wordsworth's 'Old Cumberland Beggar' or his leech-gatherer in 'Resolution and Independence'. Like the Cumberland beggar who can 'prompt the unlettered villagers I To tender offices and pensive thoughts' (l. 169), and the leech-gatherer who is 'like a man from some far region sent, I To give me human strength, by apt admonishment' (l. 111), Mrs McNab seems to transmit a profound message to those who see her.[21]

However, Woolf also revises the Wordsworthian figure of the borderer who inspires the viewer with thoughts of other worlds, for Mrs McNab is an agent for restoring the domestic and the ordinary. She is responsible for reclaiming the home of the Ramsay family, not simply from disuse but from oblivion. Where darkness had earlier caused a chest of drawers to cease to exist, Mrs McNab 'rescued from the pool of Time . . . now a basin, now a cupboard' (*TL*, 189). So, Mrs McNab represents both a revision of the borderer and an adjustment of empiricist views: she proves the solidity of objects against the suggestion that they are mere perceptions. Her handling of domestic artefacts is perhaps equivalent to the famous anecdote in which Samuel Johnson retorted to the empiricist idea that nothing exists outside of perception by kicking a stone and saying 'I refute it thus'.

The adjustments Woolf makes in her relationship to Romanticism and empiricism lead her towards new ways of memorialising the dead, beyond the stereotypical images of Wordsworth's 'phantom of delight' or Patmore's 'Angel in the House'. One way is to assert the importance of literary posterity – and the role played by the living in preserving the currency of the work of dead authors. In the process of restoring the cottage, Mrs McNab 'fetched up from oblivion all the Waverley novels' (*TL*, 189). This is an allusion to an incident at the end of 'The Window', when Mr Ramsay reads one of Sir Walter Scott's novels and Mrs Ramsay recalls a conversation in which Charles Tansley had said that 'people don't read Scott any more. Then her husband thought, "That's what they'll say of me"' (*TL*, 159). Sir Walter Scott was one of Stephen's favourite authors: Woolf recalled 'the thirty-two volumes of the Waverley novels, which provided reading for many years of evenings'.[22] The full significance of Scott for Stephen is seen in his essay 'Some Words about Sir Walter Scott', in which he reflects on the short life-span of literary fame. Writing less than fifty years after Scott's death, Stephen remarks that fewer people are reading him and that many consider his works to be dull. Stephen uses physical decay as a metaphor for fading literary fame – Scott's novels 'are rapidly converting themselves into mere debris of plaster of Paris' and asks, 'will they all sink into the dust together, and the outlines of what once charmed the world be traced only by Dryasdust and historians of literature?' Although Stephen points out weaknesses in Scott's writing – some of his characters lack depth, his history is not scholarly – he finds Scott's fall from popularity a *memento mori* for other writers, for, 'If Scott is to be called dull, what reputation is to be pronounced safe?'[23] Stephen was troubled by doubts about the durability of his work: he knew that, for a writer, immortality is the state of being read and appreciated by future generations. At the end of *The Mausoleum Book*, he expressed doubts that he would be remembered, that his name would 'only be mentioned in small type and footnotes' in a history of English thought in the nineteenth century. He speculates that 'had my energies been wisely directed, I might have had the honour of a paragraph in full sized type or even a section in a chapter all to myself' (*MBk*, 93). Mrs McNab rescues Scott for posterity by making his novels fit to be read again: like the Fates whom she resembles with her 'ball of memories' (*TL*, 191), Mrs McNab has the power to grant life and death. By making Mrs McNab save Scott, Woolf implies that the reputation of Mr Ramsay – and Leslie Stephen whom he represents – might also survive to a future generation. It suggests, furthermore, that the power to perpetuate Leslie Stephen's memory now resides with Woolf.

Woolf also uses Mrs McNab to address the more difficult question of how to preserve the memory of someone, like Mrs Ramsay, who did not write. Mrs McNab is the only human figure to be identified in 'Time Passes' outside square brackets, except for the opening section in which the Ramsays and their guests fall asleep, and the closing section, in which they wake up. Her conversation about the Ramsay family with her helper Mrs Bast is the point at which the family re-enters the narrative. Although Mrs McNab's verbal recollections are inexact – 'Some said he was dead; some said she was dead. Which was it?' (*TL*, 190) – her visual memories are powerful. She has the ability to see the past, as if through a telescope:

> She could see her [Mrs Ramsay] now, stooping over her flowers; (and faint and flickering, like a yellow beam or the circle at the end of a telescope, a lady in a grey cloak, stooping over her flowers, went wandering over the bedroom wall, up the dressing-table, across the washstand . . .) (*TL*, 186)

A telescope enables a person to see something which exists in the distance, rather than something which existed in the past; it suggests that the past still exists – but in a different place. The image elides the difference between something which is absent and something which does not exist: it suggests an objection to the empiricists' argument by implying that we cannot disprove the existence of something which is absent.

The flickering image of Mrs Ramsay which 'went wandering over the bedroom wall', and the moving picture of Mr Ramsay 'in a ring of light . . . wagging his head' (*TL*, 190), seen through an artificial lens and in a yellow beam, also suggest cinema projection. While writing 'Time Passes', Woolf analysed her early impressions of seeing a film reel in her essay 'The Cinema'. As Suzanne Raitt has pointed out, the echoes between the two pieces suggest that they were part of the same project.[24] 'The Cinema' deals with the sort of philosophical concerns raised in 'Time Passes'. Woolf saw the cinematic form as a way of preserving the past and making it exist in the present: past events can be recorded and brought to life again when the film is shown. She writes that the images on film are seen 'as they are when we are not there':

> We see life as it is when we have no part in it. As we gaze we seem to be removed from the pettiness of actual existence . . . we have time to open our minds wide to beauty and register on top of it the queer sensation – this beauty will continue, and this beauty will flourish whether we behold it or not. Further, all this happened ten years ago, we are told. We are beholding a world which has gone beneath the waves. (*CE*, II. 269)

This passage shares imagery with 'Time Passes': the events which Woolf sees on screen have now 'gone beneath the waves', just as the 'pool of Time' closed over the contents of the cottage (*TL*, 189); and Woolf was perhaps thinking of the ten-year time-span of 'Time Passes' when she remarked that the events captured on film took place ten years earlier. The passage also alludes to the central problem of the empiricists. Woolf is interested in how the concept of film contributes to the discussion about what exists 'when we are not there': film gives the impression that things do exist when they are not viewed by offering viewers a lifelike record of a world they have not seen in the flesh.

Although Woolf presented the cinema as an answer to the empiricists' problem in the essay, it does not provide a suitable answer in *To the Lighthouse*. Woolf sees the cinema camera as confirming a viewer's lack of involvement in what is seen: 'this beauty will flourish whether we behold it or not'. The camera cuts off the human subject's direct response to the natural world, like the force of nature in 'Time Passes' which takes no heed of human feelings or wishes, or like the cracked mirror which confirms the divorce between the human subject and nature. Human responses and perceptions become important again with the entry of Mrs

McNab: it is her imagination which makes the Ramsays live on. Her agency is what finally distinguishes her from a Wordsworthian borderer: she is not simply an object for other people's contemplation, but has the power to think and remember, and to re-create other people in her own imagination. Instead of the artificial lens of the cinema projector, this sequence suggests the creative eye of human imagination, and its power to project its own reality on the world. In other words, Mrs McNab's power to project her memories is closely related to Wordsworth's metaphor for his imagination: 'An auxiliar light I Came from my mind, which on the setting sun I Bestowed new splendour' (*Prelude*, II. 368). Mrs McNab's imagination, stirred by her surroundings, creates a vision of Mr and Mrs Ramsay. As with her role in granting Mr Ramsay posterity, this passage suggests that the past is in the control of the thinking subject (that is, the woman writer) in the present. Mrs McNab's vision, in which scenes and images thrown up by the memory have a power which renders them believable and real, echoes Stephen's challenge to Hume, using a logical proposition on the concept of 'fiction'. In the *History*, Stephen states Hume's case as: 'The belief that anything exists outside our mind, when not actually perceived, is a "fiction". The belief in a continuous subject which perceives the feelings is another fiction' (*History*, I. 44). He points to a logical flaw in this formulation, to argue that: 'If all reason is fiction, fiction is reason' (I. 49). In other words, fiction can have its own internal consistency which gives it plausibility.

Over the course of 'Time Passes', Woolf can be seen to be coming to terms with two traditions which form important parts of the literary and intellectual background to her writing. She provides an answer to the question of whether someone continues to exist when they are no longer there, by making Mrs McNab's mind the site of Mr and Mrs Ramsay's continued existence. This solution is reached through two complementary processes: first, Woolf counters the empiricists' idea that nothing exists outside human perception to suggest that something can still exist if it is perceived by the imagination; and second, she uses the empiricist idea that nothing exists outside of perception to modify the Romantic paradigm of the mind being open to inspiration from nature, by defending a space for the mind to create its own reality. In negotiating a position for herself within the two traditions that informed Stephen's work, she follows the same path as he took. As we have seen, Stephen tempered his Romantic sympathies by drawing on empiricist arguments, but he was also reluctant to follow Hume to the sceptical conclusion that nothing exists outside our perceptions of it. By the close of 'Time Passes', therefore, Woolf has achieved a balance between two important influences, but she has done so through engaging with her father's texts and has reached remarkably similar conclusions to his. Both Woolf and Stephen defend the freedom of the individual mind and conscience, by questioning assumptions about an external, transcendent reality and implying that the individual must seek and defend her/his own definition of truth.

However, an important contradiction has not been fully resolved. Although Leslie Stephen defended the freedom of the individual conscience, we have seen earlier that his treatment of Julia Stephen in *The Mausoleum Book* suggests a reluctance to recognise the subjectivity or agency of women. How does Woolf challenge the ideal of the Angel in the House when Leslie Stephen's texts continue to inform *To the Lighthouse*? 'Time Passes' goes part-way towards a solution: there is a challenge to authority implicit in the conception of nature worked out in the section. The impulse in 'Time Passes' towards the everyday and the domestic, culminating in the very practical restoration of the cottage, emphasises the importance of solidity and practicality over ideas about Nature and spirituality which underlie the concept of the Angel in the House. More importantly, by working out a series of objections to Romantic ideals by drawing on Stephen's work, Woolf begins to divide the double father/authority figure of Wordsworth and Stephen against itself. However, Woolf develops these issues more explicitly in 'The Lighthouse', where she brings Stephen's ideas to bear on the issue of representing women in art and literature.

III

Woolf continues to work out her reaction against the concept of the Angel in the House, or idealised versions of womanhood, in her description of Lily Briscoe's attempt to finish her painting of Mrs Ramsay in 'The Lighthouse'.[25] She articulates the inhibiting influences on Lily to point to the marginal position of women artists (or writers) which she had found frustrating, but did not fully voice, while writing *The Voyage Out* and *Night and Day*. Lily is discouraged by her awareness of the cynical attitude of her companions towards her work, especially Charles Tansley's notion that 'Women can't paint, women can't write' (*TL*, 67); Mrs Ramsay's patronising attitude that painting is only a hobby and can conflict with a woman's duty to be a wife and mother; and Mr Ramsay's demands for sympathy which impinge upon her consciousness as she tries to paint. In Lily's reaction to Mrs Ramsay's attitude, Woolf interrogates and dismantles the courtship narrative which she had battled with in her first two novels, for Lily sets her artistic creativity in direct opposition to social pressures to get married. This conflict originally surfaces in 'The Window', when Lily simultaneously makes a personal resolution to resist marriage and an aesthetic decision to change the position of a tree in her painting, thereby resisting pressure from Mrs Ramsay to pity William Bankes, 'in a flash she saw her picture and thought, Yes, I shall put the tree further in the middle; then I shall avoid that awkward space' (*TL*, 115). Later in the dinner-party, Lily's decision not to pity Mr Bankes becomes strengthened into a resolution to resist Mrs Ramsay's plans that she should marry him, and the decision to move the tree becomes a symbol (for her) of her resolution: 'at any rate, she said to herself, catching sight of the salt cellar on the pattern, she need not marry' (*TL*, 138). While the decision to move the tree carries personal meanings for Lily, the problem of space takes on a wider significance within the novel itself, for it becomes a way of dealing with women's marginalisation within patriarchal discourses. Lily feels that her resolution not to marry, like her decision to avoid an awkward space in her picture, saves her from 'dilution' (*TL*, 138). For Lily, marriage – and the wider manmade culture it sustains and represents – threatens her with a loss of self, for to get married would be to accept a role which would confer an alien identity on her. Thus Lily addresses the problem of women's marginalisation as she tackles the problem of space.

In 'The Lighthouse' Woolf tackles the marginalisation of women artists (or writers) on two levels: she investigates how women can practise art in opposition to social pressures to fulfil other roles; and the problem (raised in 'The Window' in relation to Renaissance painting) that art might be overdetermined by patriarchal conventions which do not allow women to be represented honestly. The first of these issues is evaded rather than overcome. Lily is unable to paint until Mr Ramsay has left, when she is alone except for Mr Carmichael who, 'rubicund, drowsy, entirely contented' (*TL*, 206), does not interfere with her work. When Lily exchanges the 'fluidity of life for the concentration of painting', she feels a sense of release from the role she is expected to play, as she subdues 'the impertinences and irrelevances that plucked her attention and made her remember how she was such and such a person, had such and such relations to people' (*TL*, 214, 213). Yet, while this leaves her free to concentrate on her art, the price is loss of personality. The implication is that Lily can paint only by denying her womanhood: 'myself, thought Lily, girding at herself bitterly, who am not a woman, but a peevish, ill-tempered, dried-up old maid presumably' (*TL*, 205). Her denial suggests that the meaning of the very word 'woman' has been colonised by society: by renouncing the role of the angel, Lily has to cope with a more derogatory identity. Almost immediately after remembering her decision to move the tree and resist marriage, Lily is confronted by Mr Ramsay who makes it impossible for her to work by demanding from her sympathy she cannot give. Her decision not to take on the role of a wife has not exempted her from the expectation that she should reassure men. Although the novel ends with Lily having 'her vision' and succeeding in completing her painting despite all odds, albeit after a hiatus of ten years, the end of the novel is ambiguous about what she has really achieved. Lily is pessimistic that anything will become of her picture once it is finished: she is convinced that it will be 'hung in attics' or destroyed (*TL*, 281). There is no indication that completing the painting has changed her life: her seemingly triumphant declaration, 'I have had my vision' (*TL*, 281), in the past tense, suggests that she has gained something that is only fleeting, which she has now lost. The painting of the final brush-stroke only continues the pattern of Lily's creative process as a whole: the experience of achieving temporary resolutions which quickly subside into new difficulties.

The second problem is worked out more thoroughly in 'The Lighthouse', for Woolf brings her meditation on questions of elegy and absence to bear on the question of the representation of women in art. Writing and painting carry conventions of representation, and, as we have seen, the images clustering around the Angel in the House informed popular ways of representing women in art. The issue Woolf addresses in 'The Lighthouse' is only partly to do with her personal battle against Victorian ideals of womanhood. The problem faced by both Lily painting Mrs Ramsay and Woolf writing about her mother as Mrs Ramsay lies in dealing with the image of the Angel, a fictitious figure which was difficult to subvert because it is 'far harder to kill a phantom than a reality' (*CE*, II. 286). Woolf's frustration with the Angel is not that it represents, but that it *fails* to represent, her mother: the angel is a symbol which underlines the fact that her mother is lost. Similarly, Lily's attempt to finish her painting of Mrs Ramsay is in part an attempt to grapple with symbols such as the Angel and the Madonna, which fail to represent Mrs Ramsay and have obscured the truth about her. Lily attempts to look beyond the symbols and recover her lost feelings for and memories of Mrs Ramsay.

Woolf draws on Leslie Stephen's writings and the philosophical traditions she invoked earlier in the novel to describe how Lily sets about dealing with these feelings, for the problems of how we can lay claim to any knowledge of the world or of other people and how we can convey that knowledge to others are central to Lily's attempt to finish her painting of Mrs Ramsay. Lily is preoccupied with questions of meaning, truth and reality. She asks herself, 'What does it mean?' She wants to get at 'the truth of things' and she seeks antidotes to her prevailing impressions of the cottage as 'aimless', 'chaotic' and 'unreal' (*TL*, 197–9). Her search for reality and truth is frustrated by the problem of change over time: Woolf stresses that Lily has returned to the island 'after all these years', with 'Mrs Ramsay dead; Andrew killed; Prue dead too' (*TL*, 198). If the dominant question at the start of 'Time Passes' was whether things continue to exist when there is no one to see them, 'The Lighthouse' takes up a related concern: whether there is a continuing reality which underlies apparent changes. This question picks up on a concern expressed by Leslie Stephen in the *History*:

> All things, as the old sceptics said, are in ceaseless flux . . . To find reality is to find the permanent thing which remains when all qualities of a perceived object are changed. To find truth must be to find a proposition which remains in spite of all changes in the perceiving subject. (I. 27, 28)

Lily's quest for reality and truth amid change reflects Stephen's concern that 'reality' is the permanent thing which remains despite changes in the perceived object; and truth is what remains once the perceiving subject has changed. Lily seeks reality as something permanent which remains now that Mrs Ramsay – the perceived object – has gone; and she seeks truth, as something which remains despite changes in herself over the ten-year interval. When she starts applying paint to her canvas, she finds the 'space' left between the brush-strokes most 'formidable'. Lily's technical difficulty in dealing with the spaces on her canvas is a function of these issues of absence and change: the space represents her struggle to depict someone who is now absent and to express reality which neither words nor paint can convey. Lily's 'formidable ancient enemy' is 'this other thing, this truth, this reality' which 'emerged stark at the back of appearances and commanded her attention' (*TL*, 214).

In her description of how Lily sets about discovering and describing the 'truth' about Mrs Ramsay, Woolf develops a compromise between sceptical and Romantic points of view which accommodates Leslie Stephen's views. Woolf initially seems to support Lily's search for transcendent reality, a desire to go beyond 'appearances' which is comparable with the Romantic aim of overcoming the 'tyranny of the eye'. Lily attributes to Mrs Ramsay a seemingly mystical power to create permanence, order and stability: she remembers sitting on a beach with Charles Tansley when Mrs Ramsay seemed to make time stand still, 'making of the moment something permanent'. This had the 'nature of a revelation. In the midst of chaos there was shape; this external passing and flowing . . . was stuck into stability' (*TL*, 218). However, Mrs

Ramsay's power to create stability is actually an imaginative demonstration of Stephen's (sceptical) proposition that to find truth we must find something permanent amid the flux. Woolf even tempers Lily's sense of revelation with scepticism, for she is not sure that transcendence has been achieved: 'The great revelation had never come. The great revelation perhaps never did come. Instead there were little daily miracles, illuminations, matches struck unexpectedly in the dark; here was one' (*TL*, 218). This pessimistic approach similarly accommodates Stephen's view, for the concepts of miracle and revelation were particularly anathema to him: in *An Agnostic's Apology* he argued that theologians could not both claim to know all about God and defend revelation as a source of knowledge, because the need for revelation would demonstrate that humankind could not know the truth. Revelation would suggest that 'it is all a mystery; and what is mystery but the theological phrase for Agnosticism?' (*Apology*, 35). Lily's 'little daily miracles' amount to the gradual stumbling towards truth which Stephen saw as part of the process of enlightenment:

> We are a company of ignorant beings, feeling our way through mists and darkness, learning only by incessantly-repeated blunders, obtaining a glimmering of truth by falling into every conceivable error, dimly discerning light enough for our daily needs, but hopelessly differing whenever we attempt to describe the ultimate origin or end of our paths. (*Apology*, 39–40)

Lily's belief in truth, reality and permanence, which she identifies with Mrs Ramsay, thus becomes tempered by a sceptical recognition of the limitations of the human mind. The truth she aspires to can at best be known only in part, but can never be declaimed with any authority.

In this manoeuvre, Woolf does not reject Stephen's views, but justifies her own work by making it consonant with his, for she uses this compromise to return to the problem of representing women in art. Woolf shows that Lily's attempt to capture the essence of Mrs Ramsay in paint is frustrated by the fact that art deals in symbols which have no connection with reality. Although Lily is a painter, Woolf explores this problem in an analogy with language. Lily overhears Mr Ramsay reciting Cowper's 'The Castaway': the quotation ends with the line, 'We perished each alone', and the words 'perished' and 'alone' impinge upon her thoughts, becoming detached from meaning and taking on a visual form to implant themselves on empty space: 'the words became symbols, wrote themselves all over the grey-green walls'. Lily feels that the words could lead her towards reality: if she could put them into a sentence, 'then she would have got at the truth of things' (*TL*, 199). Lily's wish to find truth through language resembles Leslie Stephen's exploration of the problem of how to find truth in a changing world. In the *History*, he suggests that the 'difficulty of reconciling change and permanence' is 'roughly' solved by the 'assumption that the name corresponds to some persistent entity'. Language could provide a framework for finding what is constant, because things continue to be known by the same name even if they change. But almost as soon as he raises this possibility, he dismisses it. Although we need to assume, in order to speak at all, that language has an ability to represent truth, this carries with it 'some, however infinitesimal, inaccuracy. If language is taken to be more than an approximation, we have at once a source of error' (I. 27). For Lily, too, the words do not lead to truth, but take on a kind of materiality as they become visual symbols detached from meaning: she finds that '*Words* fluttered sideways and struck the object inches too low', and asks 'how could one express in *words* these emotions of the body?' (*TL*, 240, 241; emphasis added). Woolf shows that no symbol (whether a visual image or verbal metaphor) can make an authoritative representation, but only gesture towards something which cannot be expressed directly.

Woolf brings these (agnostic) questions to bear on the problem of the pseudo-religious image of the Angel in the House. By playing with the disjuncture between symbols and reality, Woolf undermines any authority which may be claimed for language as a form of representation. Although Lily seems to aim for a representative form of painting – by responding to something outside herself, following 'some rhythm which was dictated to her . . . by what she saw' (*TL*, 215) – the activity of her mind becomes more important than what she sees. She begins to 'lose consciousness of outer things', with her mind working 'like a fountain', throwing up ideas, schemes, memories, phrases and names (*TL*, 215–16). The image of the fountain recalls Wordsworth's 'Intimations Ode':

> . . . those first affections,
> Those shadowy recollections,
> Which, be they what they may,
> Are yet the fountain-light of all our day (l. 152)

Lily's memories, like Wordsworth's 'shadowy recollections', become a source of inspiration into which she 'dipped' in order to create her picture. Echoing Wordsworth's image of the intimations as a 'fountain light', Lily finds that her memories of Mrs Ramsay are 'like a drop of silver in which one dipped and illuminated the darkness of the past . . . as she dipped into the blue paint, she dipped too into the past there' (*TL*, 232). The reference to paint changes Wordsworth's image significantly. The fountain is not, as Wordsworth uses it, a symbol for immortality, part of that 'immortal sea | Which brought us hither' (l. 167), but a literal substance – paint – which becomes the medium for Mrs Ramsay's continued existence. Like Mrs McNab's telescopic eye, Lily's memories and her painting provide the medium and conditions for Mrs Ramsay's existence in the present.

Lily revives Mrs Ramsay through fiction, for she makes up stories about the people she had met at the cottage as she paints. Lily remarks that 'this making up scenes about them, is what we call "knowing" people, "thinking" of them, "being fond" of them! Not a word of it was true; she had made it up; but it was what she knew them by all the same' (*TL*, 234). Lily cannot use fiction to reach transcendent truth, but to express what is true for her. The implication is that, while no one has access to absolute, authoritative truth, all people have experiences which are true for themselves and which they assume others will also recognise as true. The idea that there is some truth – but no absolute truth – in everyone's perceptions again ties in with an idea of Leslie Stephen's:

> What remains after Hume's scepticism has been allowed full play is the objective fact of the regularity of the external world, and the subjective faculty which corresponds to it, in virtue of which we assert, not that this or that truth, revealed by experience, is universally true, but that every experience implicitly contains a universal truth. (*History*, 53–4)

In 'The Lighthouse', Woolf plays with distance and perspective in order to explore the kinds of truth which emerge from different experiences. The account of Lily completing her painting is presented in counterpoint to the story of the voyage to the lighthouse made by Mr Ramsay, Cam and James. Woolf uses the contrast between the two narratives to show how definitions of reality change with angles of vision. Cam, viewing the island from the boat, thinks that it appears 'unreal' and the lives they had lived there 'were gone: were rubbed out; were past; were unreal, and now this was real; the boat and the sail with its patch' (*TL*, 225). Lily, on the other hand, looks across the bay and thinks that Mr Ramsay, Cam and James have been 'swallowed up' in the distance: 'they were gone for ever, they had become part of the nature of things' (*TL*, 253–4). Woolf uses the opposing viewpoints of Cam and Lily to suggest that the concepts of reality and unreality can be relative: what is perceived as real depends on point of view. Her description of James's first sight of the lighthouse at close range examines this further. He asks whether the lighthouse is the tall, whitewashed tower, or whether it is the distant shape he had seen from the island: 'No, the other was also the Lighthouse. For nothing was simply one thing. The other was the Lighthouse too. It was sometimes hardly to be seen across the bay' (*TL*, 251). The lighthouse does not simply appear to be one thing or another – it *is* both; it exists both as a distant light and as a close-up tower. The conclusion that 'nothing was simply one thing' leaves room to accommodate differing perspectives.

This compromise helps Lily recapture Mrs Ramsay from the images which have surrounded her: she finally succeeds in finishing her painting by accommodating both an empirical view of Mrs Ramsay and a mystical, Romantic one. She feels the need 'to be on a level with ordinary experience, to feel simply, that's a chair, that's a table' – the table alluding back to Mr Ramsay's research, and thus to Leslie Stephen and the empiricists – 'and yet at the same time, it's a miracle, it's an ecstasy'. Lily is enabled to see Mrs Ramsay as an ordinary woman: 'Mrs Ramsay . . . sat there quite simply, in the chair, flicked her needles to and fro, knitted her reddish-brown stocking', though, at the same time, she preserves her feeling that Mrs Ramsay has mysterious powers, for her ghost-like reappearance is 'part of her perfect goodness to Lily' (*TL*, 272). Although Leslie Stephen appears in the novel as Mr Ramsay, his views are more effectively represented by Mrs as well as Mr Ramsay, and by Romantic as well as empiricist ideas. The balance between these pairs which Woolf attains by the end of the novel suggests a reconciliation of the two tendencies in Stephen's thinking; it enables Woolf to put her memories of her father in proportion.

To the Lighthouse was a pivotal stage in Woolf's negotiation of her personal and literary pasts: she confronted Leslie Stephen's influence on her in a direct way, but she also drew on his ideas, using them for her own purposes. As she re-made her father as a 'contemporary', she also re-made herself as a writer. During the process of negotiation, especially in 'Time Passes', Woolf's dialogue with her father becomes a three-way conversation, between the two of them and some of his influences, notably Hume and Wordsworth, who represent the empiricist and Romantic traditions respectively. This wider conversation shows Woolf finding her own place within those traditions: though the ground she occupies within them is essentially that which was occupied by her father. In other words, Woolf claims her inheritance as Stephen's literary (and not just as his biological) daughter.

In 'The Lighthouse', Woolf uses Stephen's texts less explicitly and brings them to bear on preoccupations of her own: the woman artist going through her creative process and the problem of representing women in art. She applies his agnostic questions about how we can know God or the world directly to the question of how we can know other people, particularly women. Woolf came to think of her father as a contemporary by imbibing his ideas, exploring them for herself and then applying them to concerns of her own. Or rather, having taken on board his questions and his questioning, she applied them to new situations: where Leslie Stephen questioned the tenets of religion, Woolf questioned the values and 'certainties' of the Victorian patriarchal world. In doing so, she detached some of his ideas from their underlying patriarchal implications, and reconstructed Leslie Stephen the agnostic outsider as a model for herself as a feminist outsider.

Notes

1. Fogel, *Covert Relations*, p. 61.
2. Woolf's stated intention to read Stephen's works does not preclude the possibility that she had read them already. As Beer suggests, she is planning to read him not for the first time but thoroughly, 'that act of intimacy, homage and appraisal in which we subject ourselves to a writer's complete work' ('Hume, Stephen, and Elegy in *To the Lighthouse*', p. 54).
3. The distinction between the writer father and actual father is also suggested by Fisher in 'The Seduction of the Father', and Hyman in 'Reflections in the Looking-Glass'.
4. Lee notes that *To the Lighthouse* has affinities with the Victorian pastoral elegy (*Virginia Woolf*, p. 482). Davies demonstrates how the novel may be classified as an elegy in *Virginia Woolf: To the Lighthouse*.
5. Gillespie and Steele, intro. to *Julia Duckworth Stephen: Stories for Children, Essays for Adults*, p. xv.
6. I discuss Woolf's allusions to the Madonna and Her representation in Renaissance and Pre-Raphaelite painting in greater detail in 'Behind the Purple Triangle'.
7. Rose, *Woman of Letters*, p. 158.
8. Quoted in Annan, *Leslie Stephen*, p. 2.
9. Hyman, 'The Metamorphosis of Leslie Stephen'.
10. Wright, 'George Eliot and Positivism', p. 260.
11. Annan, *Leslie Stephen*, p. 271.
12. For example, Lilienfeld has noted that the meal evokes ritual festivals of the Great and Terrible Mother in '"The Deceptiveness of Beauty"'.
13. Maitland, *Leslie Stephen*, p. 476.
14. Minow-Pinkney, *Woolf and the Problem of the Subject*, pp. 16–17.
15. Beer, 'Hume, Stephen, and Elegy', pp. 39–42.
16. Banfield, *The Phantom Table*, p. 37.
17. Beer, 'Hume, Stephen, and Elegy', pp. 43–5; Banfield, *The Phantom Table*, p. 67.
18. Hume, *A Treatise on Human Nature*, I. 523.
19. Ibid., I. 534.
20. Warner, 'Some Aspects of Romanticism in the Work of Virginia Woolf', p. 54; Beede, 'Woolf – Romantic', p. 22.
21. Mrs McNab 'turning over scraps in her drawers' (*TL*, 178), echoes the Old Cumberland Beggar who 'from a bag . . . drew his scraps and fragments, one by one' (ll. 8, 10).

22. Maitland, *Leslie Stephen*, p. 474.
23. Stephen, *Hours in a Library*, I. 222, 220.
24. Raitt, *Woolf's To the Lighthouse*, p. 61.
25. Lilienfeld, "'The Deceptiveness of Beauty'", p. 347; Rose, *Woman of Letters*, p. 158.

Chapter 5

Rewriting Literary History in *Orlando*

Orlando is often taken on Woolf's own estimation as 'an escapade' (*D*, III. 131) and viewed as a lighthearted comic piece. However, when read in the context of Woolf's engagement with the literary past, it can be seen to serve the serious purpose of critiquing the assumptions of patriarchal literary history and developing feminist perspectives to replace them. Although Woolf's use of parody in *Orlando* is undoubtedly comic, it is also layered and strategic. On the one hand, her parody of academic conceptions is satirical: she mocks conventional approaches to literary history (as well as biography and history) by mimicking them in the voice of the narrator and the mock scholarly apparatus of preface, footnotes and index, all of which are shown to be inadequate frameworks for addressing the complex subject-matter of a character who lives for 350 years and changes sexes part-way through. She also attacks the literary-critical establishment through the heavily satirised figure of Nick Greene who sets himself up as an arbiter of taste, but is merely a self-publicist seeking financial gain (as a Renaissance and Restoration hack) and society's esteem (as a Victorian knighted professor). On the other hand, Woolf's parodies of English literary styles and her allusions to a wide range of texts and authors from the Renaissance to the present are more subtle and complex. Although there is some evidence of an ironic disdain for the weight of tradition – such as when she makes light of literary influence in her joke Preface ('no one can read or write without being perpetually in the debt of Defoe, Sir Thomas Browne, Sterne, Sir Walter Scott, Lord Macaulay, Emily Brontë, De Quincey, and Walter Pater' (*O*, 5)) she also conveys a sense of intimacy with past literature, bringing earlier writings to life in order to reclaim them from critics and historians. This chapter will focus on the ways Woolf rethought literary history by seeking to uncover a congenial and sympathetic past.

Orlando can be seen as a parallel project to *A Room of One's Own*, which Woolf was writing at the same time, where she urged her audience to 'rewrite history' by thinking 'back through our mothers' (*Room*, 72–3) in order to trace the development of women's writing, seeking out figures neglected by conventional (patriarchal) histories. *Orlando* rewrites literary history in a slightly different way, not by tracing lost female figures, but by following the fortunes of an aspiring writer who is female from the seventeenth century onwards, thereby posing questions about the relationship between women writers and the literary canon and considering how the conditions in which women writers live might affect their work.

A Room of One's Own laments the lost origins of a female tradition: Woolf notes that there was no female Shakespeare because conditions in the Renaissance would have made it impossible for a woman to write for the theatre. She creates an imaginary starting-point for her alternative history in the fictional character of Shakespeare's sister, Judith, whose life could only have ended in failure and suicide. Woolf concludes by urging her audience to reclaim these lost origins imaginatively in their own writings:

> Now my belief is that this poet who never wrote a word and was buried at the cross-roads still lives. She lives in you and in me . . . for great poets do not die; they are continuing presences; they need only the opportunity to walk among us in the flesh. This opportunity, as I think, it is now coming within your power to give her. (*Room*, 107, 108)

Woolf does not attempt to revive Judith Shakespeare in *Orlando*, for the protagonist is male during the Elizabethan era, but instead shows a modern woman writer who began life as a Renaissance man, thus claiming an imaginative starting-point for a history of writing by women. As we will see, in *Orlando* Woolf adopts a strategy of identifying elements in past literature which are conducive to feminist and lesbian agendas. Although the Renaissance is a highly significant focus for this process, we will start by exploring Woolf's first plans for *Orlando*, where she looked back to the eighteenth century and two of the first English novelists: Daniel Defoe and Laurence Sterne.

I

Defoe is the only precedessor mentioned in Woolf's first sketch for the novel (provisionally titled 'The Jessamy Brides') written in March 1927. She ponders writing a 'Defoe narrative for fun' in which 'sapphism is to be suggested' between two female protagonists, possibly the Ladies of Llangollen (*D*, III. 131).[1] At the time, Woolf was writing about Defoe for 'Phases of Fiction' and the particular intimacy between reader and writer she sought to capture in that essay – a concern with 'how to read all fiction as if it were one book one had written oneself' (*L*, III. 325) – is an apt description of her engagement with Defoe in the planning stages of novel. The sense of intimacy, combined with the flippant aim of writing one of his narratives 'for fun' and the dismissive take on his influence in the Preface, all suggest a particular ease with Defoe as a precursor.

Woolf's responses to Defoe are not determined simply by her own reading, for her reception of his work was closely bound up with her view of her upbringing and education and her attitudes towards Leslie Stephen. In an essay written in 1919, which appeared in the first *Common Reader*, Woolf described Defoe as an integral part of her upbringing and heritage, for 'we have all had *Robinson Crusoe* read aloud to us as children', and the 'impressions of childhood are those that last longest and cut deepest' (*CE*, I. 62). This statement makes light of Woolf's personal introduction to Defoe by suggesting that all children are introduced to *Robinson Crusoe*, but since we know that Stephen had read books aloud, these childhood memories of Defoe take on a special resonance. Furthermore, Woolf's understanding of Defoe's position in English literature was also conditioned by Stephen as a critic: in the *Common Reader* essay, Woolf describes Defoe as 'the founder and master' of an English school of writing (*CE*, I. 68), which is precisely the view that Stephen puts forward in *English Literature and Society in the Eighteenth Century* where, as Susan Squier notes, he claims Defoe for his own 'patrilineal tradition of English literature'.[2] In writing about Defoe in 'Phases of Fiction', Woolf seeks to detach Defoe's work from these deeply embedded associations by suggesting that she is choosing her reading matter at random to suit a particular mood. In planning 'The Jessamy Brides' as a comic take on Defoe's work, she denies the serious nature of her engagement with him but also detaches him from any lingering patriarchal associations by focusing specifically on the lives of women, and lesbians in particular.

There are several reasons why Woolf might have found Defoe congenial to her thinking as she planned 'The Jessamy Brides'. Woolf noted that the novel would be written at great speed, that 'wildness' would be a keynote for the story, and that 'no attempt is to be made to realise the character' (*D*, III. 131). Woolf's comments on Defoe in her notes for 'Phases of Fiction' suggest that she detected these qualities in his work: 'Adventure must carry a slight burden of psychology . . . You must keep moving if you are to have adventures.'[3] Significantly, this is precisely the opposite view of Defoe from the one Woolf had put forward in her 1919 essay, where she had defended him from Stephen's criticism (in *Hours in a Library*) that his characters lack psychological depth. Her change of opinion suggests that she was reading Defoe in 1927 in the light of what *she* wanted to achieve in her own writing.

Woolf's choice of Defoe as a model was underpinned by her feminist reading of his work: her admiration of his strong female characters and his ideas on women's rights, which were well in advance of his time (*CE*, I. 64–5). She liked his ability to elicit sympathy for notorious women and for those on the margins of society – such as the thief, Moll Flanders – and so his manner would provide a sympathetic way of voicing sapphism. Woolf also praised the way in which Defoe depicted his female characters' fortitude in the face of hardship, especially poverty. This again accorded with the plan for 'The Jessamy Brides', for Woolf originally toyed with ideas of having 'an unattractive woman, penniless, alone' as the main protagonist, or of focusing on 'two women, poor, solitary at the top of a house' (*D*, III. 131).

A background of poverty was abandoned when Woolf decided to base the novel upon the life and family history of her lover, Vita Sackville-West, when she began to write *Orlando* in October 1927 (*L*, III. 428–9). As a result, the theme of hardship became commuted into the narrative of an aristocrat grappling with loss of privilege on becoming a woman. Woolf's decision to base her novel on Sackville-West brought about a transmutation of her original idea of writing a pastiche of Defoe. Elements of Defoe remain: as Squier has suggested, certain details of *Orlando* echo *Moll Flanders*, for both characters describe themselves as men, consort with gipsies and prostitutes, are experienced travellers, become mothers and explore different strata of London life.[4] However, whilst Orlando's life follows a hectic course worthy of a Defoe heroine, these details also reflect elements of Sackville-West's life, for she often took on a male persona in her writings and sometimes wore men's clothes; she was a seasoned traveller and travel writer; and she became a mother. Although she did not actually mix with gipsies, Sackville-West was fascinated by their lifestyle and described her first lover, Violet Trefusis, as one several times.[5] The parallels suggest that a fusion took place, as Woolf retold Sackville-West's story along the lines of a Defoe novel.

Defoe's influence goes deeper than congruencies of subject-matter, for *Orlando* treads very similar ground to Defoe in terms of its concerns about dealing with truth in fiction. On the surface, their approaches seem quite different: Defoe presented his novels as factual works – *Robinson Crusoe*, *Moll Flanders* and *Roxana* are described in their prefaces as 'true histories' not 'stories' – while *Orlando* is overtly a fantasy. However, *Orlando* is a reappropriation of Defoe rather than a complete subversion of his work for it is a fictional rendering of Sackville-West's real-life story, much as *Robinson Crusoe* was an appropriation of the story of a stranded sailor, Alexander Selkirk: notwithstanding Woolf's jocular references to research in the Preface, she really did seek out information for the book, including exploring the Sackville family history, visiting Knole and selecting portraits from its gallery to use as illustrations (*L*, III, 435, 442).

On a deeper level, both Woolf and Defoe were aware of the possibilities and the dangers of revealing truth through the medium of fiction. Woolf notes in her 1919 essay that Defoe's 'truth of insight' is 'rarer and more enduring' than his adherence to facts (*CE*, I. 67). This can be seen in the preface to *Roxana*, where Defoe claims that he had to present his subject-matter in fictional form because it was dangerous to reveal the full details, 'lest what cannot be yet entirely forgot in the Part of the Town, shou'd be remember'd'. While this statement is partly a ruse to overcome contemporary suspicions about fiction by presenting his novel as a true account of actual events, it also alerts the reader to the fact that the social conditions determining Roxana's situation reflect those of real life and so Defoe's fiction can be read as social comment. In Woolf's case, the social issues addressed in *Orlando* include the unequal status of women and the precarious position of lesbians, being at once legally invisible (unlike homosexuality, lesbianism was not banned by law) and illicit (Radclyffe Hall's lesbian novel, *The Well of Loneliness*, was banned for obscenity as Woolf was writing *Orlando*). Woolf's sense of the dangers inherent in telling the truth are seen in her thinly veiled threat to Sackville-West when telling her of her plans for *Orlando*:

> But listen; suppose Orlando turns out to be Vita; and its all about you and the lusts of your flesh and the lure of your mind (heart you have none, who go gallivanting down the lanes with Campbell) . . . suppose, I say, that Sibyl next October says 'Theres Virginia gone and written a book about Vita' and Ozzie chaws with his great chaps and Byard guffaws, Shall you mind? (*L*, III. 428–9)

Jealous of Sackville-West's growing attraction to Mary Campbell, Woolf threatens to expose her and her sexual preferences in *Orlando*, but she also seeks to explore truths about sapphism at a time when they would have been dangerous to reveal. In this way, Woolf's fantastic novel may be seen to contain a 'truth of insight' worthy of Defoe.

Although Sterne is not mentioned in Woolf's plans for *Orlando*, he played a vital role in her thinking about fiction at the time. She read his work before, during and after writing the novel; she wrote about him at that time in a series of contemporary essays, 'The Narrow Bridge of Art',

'Phases of Fiction' and 'The Sentimental Journey', and mentions him in the mock preface. Woolf read *Tristram Shandy* as part of a process of thinking about the direction her own fiction might take. The process had begun as early as June 1925 when she discussed Sterne with Lytton Strachey, who had just read *Mrs Dalloway*. She recorded Strachey's advice in her diary: 'You should take something wilder & more fantastic, a frame work that admits of anything, like Tristram Shandy. But then I should lose touch with emotions, I said. Yes, he agreed, there must be reality for you to start from' (*D*, III. 32). When Woolf re-read *Tristram Shandy* the following year, she may have been considering Sterne as a possible model, for she became aware of his effect on her prose style: 'But reading Yeats turns my sentences one way: reading Sterne turns them another' (*D*, III. 119).

In 'The Narrow Bridge of Art', written during the gestation of *Orlando*, Woolf argues that the novel would become the key genre of the future, having taken on the mantle of poetry and drama; she cites *Tristram Shandy* as a model for this futuristic novel because it is written in an elastic style which incorporates poetry into its prose. Read in the context of Woolf's reading of Sterne, the essay can be seen less as a prediction for literature in general and more as a reflection on a process she herself was already undertaking.

Woolf's response to *Tristram Shandy* provides further evidence that she saw it necessary to look back to the literary past in order to move forward. Indeed, Woolf's predictions in 'The Narrow Bridge of Art' centre upon a dissatisfaction with current literature. She makes an unfavourable comparison between T. S. Eliot's 'The Waste Land' and Keats's 'Ode to the Nightingale' (*CE*, II. 223) and describes verse drama since Dryden as a failure, noting that the Elizabethans had a flexibility of thought that the modern age had lost (significantly making that age a touchstone for values she sought to recapture). When Woolf suggests that novelists should attempt to incorporate poetry and drama in the novel of the future (*CE*, II. 227), she is perhaps seeking to gain an advantage over her contemporaries by claiming access to a past she accuses them of neglecting.

Sterne thus partly inspired Woolf's meditations on genre, and these in turn had an impact on the final form of the novel. As J. J. Wilson has noted, *Orlando* is written in the spirit of *Tristram Shandy*. Wilson sees the similarity in terms of classification, placing both novels in the sub-genre of the 'anti-novel', a metafictional style which invokes and satirises novelistic convention.[6] Sterne's joke dedication of *Tristram Shandy* and Woolf's mock preface to *Orlando* are characteristic of the sub-genre, as are their addresses to the reader and their open endings. Wilson cites

Woolf's original notion of ending *Orlando* with ellipsis to illustrate the latter, but the actual ending of *Orlando* can itself be read as a direct allusion to *Tristram Shandy*. *Orlando* ends with the arrival of the 'wild goose'; Sterne's novel ends with the revelation that the story we have just heard is about 'A COCK and a BULL'. Woolf jokes that if *Shandy* is a cock-and-bull story, then *Orlando* is a wild-goose chase.[7] This allusion to Sterne invites the reader to place *Orlando* in a tradition of the anti-novel, as Sterne himself does in his references to his own model, Cervantes.

As with Defoe, Woolf's interest in Sterne led her to renegotiate Leslie Stephen's ideas. The process can be traced to her early essay on Sterne: in *Hours in a Library*, Stephen explores how far Sterne's scurrilous behaviour might impact on his work and decides that, although Sterne is 'perhaps the greatest artist in the language' (III. 142), his works lack moral seriousness and depth of feeling. Woolf similarly asks whether Sterne was a good man, and suspects him of hypocrisy in *A Sentimental Journey*. However, she detects an element of tragi-comedy which Stephen categorically denied was there:

> *The Journal to Eliza* in which the most secret passions of his heart are laid bare is but the notebook for passages in the *Sentimental Journey* which *all the world may read*. Sterne himself, no doubt, scarcely knew at what point his own pain was dissolved in the joy of the artist. (*CE*, III. 92–3; emphasis added)

The sublimation of life into art, which may be both a disguise and a revelation, is a key element in *Orlando*, a public document reflecting Woolf's private relations with Sackville-West. Woolf's analysis of *A Sentimental Journey* seems to foreshadow one of the impulses behind *Orlando*. Writing to Vita Sackville-West in a fit of jealousy, Woolf warned: 'If you've given yourself to Campbell, I'll have no more to do with you, and so it shall be written, plainly, for *all the world to read* in Orlando' (*L*, III. 431; emphasis added).

Woolf's feminist response to Stephen informs the novel at the deepest level. Woolf's treatment of both Defoe and Sterne can be read in terms of a construction of a myth of origins. In her attempt to develop the novel as a form, Woolf revisits the work of two of the first novelists, uncovers the elements of their style which are potentially useful for feminist fiction, and seeks to draw on them to point the way forward for her own novel-writing. In doing so, she sought to reclaim them from Leslie Stephen, who had written extensively about both.

II

Woolf confronts her intellectual heritage from Stephen directly in the published version of *Orlando*, where she critiques his ideas and also those of his contemporary, John Ruskin. Woolf makes a direct riposte to Stephen by satiring his best-known work when she argues that the 'true length of a person's life, whatever the *Dictionary of National Biography* may say, is always a matter of dispute' (*O*, 291) and she publicly distances herself from Stephen's approach by giving her fantastic novel the subtitle 'A Biography'. Woolf planned to 'revolutionise biography in a night' in *Orlando* (*L*, III. 429), and the novel departs from Stephen's principles of biography in several respects: she uses fantasy as a means of conveying truths about people; her subject, Sackville-West, was alive (whereas biographies were generally written about the dead); and her subject had an unconventional lifestyle, rather than the exemplary career deemed necessary for a Victorian biography, or indeed for inclusion in the *DNB* as Stephen and his colleagues had devised it.[8]

However, it is Woolf's challenge to Stephen's views on literary history which is most significant in terms of her negotiation of his accounts of the literary past, and it is here that she finally confronts his influence on her as a reader. *Orlando* reflects Woolf's profound ambivalence about prevalent models of literary history. This is most evident in her treatment of periodisation which, as Sally Greene has noted, had been a key organising feature of Victorian historical discourse.[9] On the surface, *Orlando* is organised along the lines of clearly demarcated literary periods – the Renaissance, the Restoration, the Enlightenment, the Romantic era, the Victorian period and the present – but these categories become unstable for they are frequently treated ironically. Woolf's narrator often attempts to characterise the literature of a particular period, but the method is rendered ridiculous by the sheer excess of connections made, as in the hyperbolic examination of the Orlando's writing style during the Restoration period:

> For it is for the historian of letters to remark that he had changed his style amazingly. His floridity was chastened; his abundance curbed; the age of prose was congealing those warm fountains. The very landscape outside was less struck about with garlands and the briars themselves were less thorned and intricate. Perhaps the senses were a little duller and honey and cream less seductive to the palate. Also that the streets were better drained and the houses better lit had its effect upon the style, it cannot be doubted. (*O*, 108–9)

This passage can be read more narrowly as a critique of Leslie Stephen's sociological approach to literary history. Stephen's method is seen in its most systematic form in *English Literature and Society in the Eighteenth*

Century, in which he argues that great writers reflect the concerns of their time, and that past writings must be approached through an attempt to deduce what contemporary tastes may have been (*English*, 5). He proposes a model of literary history developing in a series of reactive changes, with audiences influencing literary production (*English*, 151): for example, he sees Swift and Pope as expressing prevalent upper-class disaffection with the Walpole government, and Defoe as writing for the emerging middle class. Stephen's conclusion expresses the holistic approach at its most extreme by using the Romantic notion of each generation advocating a 'Return to Nature', advocating that writers needed to be 'sincere and spontaneous; to utter the emotions natural . . . in the forms which are also natural' and that literature should be 'produced by the class which embodies the really vital and powerful currents of thought which are moulding society' (*English*, 218). Woolf's suggestion that *Orlando*'s changing style bears the direct impress of the changing countryside and successive gastronomic tastes can be read as a *reductio ad absurdam* of this argument.

Although Woolf's own method was essentially sociological – *A Room of One's Own*, after all, considers the effect of the conditions of production on the quality of writing – her satire of Stephen's views arises from a perception that his focus on the influential classes was deeply ideological. Questions of gender are central to this for, while Stephen neglects gender entirely, Woolf shows that it is a significant factor in determining how people write and whether they can be arbiters of taste. So, where Stephen was interested in male writers who both expressed and helped to influence the ideas of their time, Woolf presents a counter-history of a woman writer who tries to retain artistic integrity by resisting the mood of her time. Stephen focuses on mainstream, influential writers, dividing the century into a series of 'schools' gathered under key male figures such as Pope (whom he claims as a 'leading figure' (*English*, 109)); Defoe; Johnson and Boswell; Crabbe and Cowper; and the Romantics. *Orlando*, by contrast, depicts an aspiring writer (female from the seventeenth century onwards), who does not achieve any recognition in her own right until the twentieth century, when her poem *The Oak Tree* is published and wins a prize. Canonical writers are viewed through Orlando's eyes and this perspective is often used to cut them down to size: quite literally so in the case of Pope, who (perhaps in a direct riposte to Stephen) is described as a 'little gentleman' (*O*, 193).

Woolf's quarrel with Stephen's approach is at its most cutting in her treatment of the concept of 'the spirit of the age' which reverberates throughout his work. Stephen opens his work on eighteenth-century literature with the statement that literature is valuable as 'one manifestation of what is called "the spirit of the age"' (*English*, 2), and it quickly emerges that this statement applies specifically to the work of the great male writers. Indeed, in a slightly tautological argument, expressing the 'spirit of the age' becomes the mark of a great writer: thus, he sees Pope as pre-eminent because he 'reflects so clearly and completely the spirit of his own day' (*English*, 109). Stephen's gender bias is seen in *Hours in a Library*, where he praises Sir Walter Scott for expressing the spirit of his age, but criticises Charlotte Brontë for being out of tune with hers, arguing that if she had read Hegel or Sir William Hamilton, 'her characters would have embodied more fully the dominating ideas of the time'.[10] Brontë is criticised both for neglecting the works of two male writers and for not submitting to the 'dominating' ideas of her time.

Woolf satirises the idea of the 'spirit of the age' by repeating the phrase *ad nauseam*, and by attacking the idea as a regulatory ideological force. Significantly, the satire is at its strongest in the nineteenth-century section of the novel where the 'spirit of the age' persistently affects Orlando's behaviour; making her embarrassed at the idea of pregnancy, censoring her writing and compelling her 'to yield completely and submissively to the spirit of the age and take a husband' (*O*, 225, 252–3, 232). Since marriage has never appealed to Orlando, this development may be seen as a violent coercion.

Woolf's satire is double-edged, for although she mocks Stephen's method of characterising literary periods, she also uses periodisation to dismiss Victorian ideas as outmoded products of their time. She alludes to John Ruskin in a very similar way when she uses *The Storm Cloud of the Nineteenth Century* to characterise that period. Ruskin had claimed that a 'storm-cloud' or 'plague-cloud' was 'peculiar to our own times',[11] and Woolf parodies this by describing the arrival of the nineteenth century as the descent of a fog influencing every aspect of life: 'A turbulent welter of cloud covered the city. All was darkness; all was doubt; all was confusion . . . the Nineteenth century had begun' (*O*, 216). She mocks Ruskin's model of sweeping change again when she distinguishes the Edwardian from the Victorian era, by linking the change in monarch improbably with changes in the weather, a celebration of the lifting of the Ruskinian storm-cloud: 'The sky itself, she could not help thinking, had changed. It was no longer so thick, so watery, so prismatic now that King Edward . . . had succeeded Queen Victoria. The clouds had shrunk to a thin gauze' (*O*, 282–3). This frivolous and comic indication of a change in era is underwritten by a sense that the quality of life *had* changed for the better by the twentieth century, for modernity is welcomed in the form of the motor car and electric lighting, and celebrated for breaking through the gloom of Victoriana. Thus whilst mocking

Ruskin, Woolf uses his approach to periodisation to separate her own age from his.

Woolf's attitude towards Victorian periodisation can thus be seen as profoundly ambivalent. Although she used it as a method of distancing herself from the Victorians, she also distrusted the way in which their formulations of history threatened to make the past inaccessible to later generations. The latter impulse can be seen in the closing section of the novel where Woolf attacks history as a discourse that kills off the past: we are told that Orlando's house, now a tourist attraction, 'belonged . . . to history; was past the touch and control of the living'. Orlando's vivid memories counteract this by looking down a gallery and seeing it 'as a tunnel bored deep into the past. As her eyes peered down it she could see people laughing and talking' (O, 304) Here the past is represented spatially rather than temporally, so that it still exists to be viewed from the present.

Woolf's suspicions about moralistic and schematic approaches to literary and cultural history are at their strongest in her treatment of the Renaissance. Significantly, Leslie Stephen had not contributed to this debate, for he wrote little on Elizabethan literature and so, by entering this discussion, Woolf was able to move on to literary territory that her father had not already claimed. The Renaissance forms the emotional backbone for *Orlando*: first, because the narrative begins in the late sixteenth century, and this starting-point becomes a frequent point of reference for what follows; and second, because proportionately more of the text is allocated to the Elizabethan and Jacobean eras, with more than half the book covering the period from the late sixteenth century to the Restoration. Yet, in engaging with this movement, Woolf had to grapple with Victorian ideas and conceptualisations for, as Sally Greene points out, Victorian scholars were influential in shaping the idea of the Renaissance: the term was brought into English from the French, and the Renaissance period was identified during the Victorian era, and its character and meaning were fiercely contested by critics.[12] A close reading of Woolf's treatment of the Renaissance in *Orlando* reveals that she engaged with Victorian debates over the nature of the period in submerged allusions to the views of John Ruskin, Walter Pater, John Addington Symonds and Vernon Lee (Violet Paget).

Ruskin, who made one of the first attempts to demarcate the Renaissance period in *The Stones of Venice*, attacked it on moral and aesthetic grounds which were closely linked to questions of gender. He argued that the dawn of the Renaissance saw the 'first corruptions introduced into the Gothic schools', which manifested themselves as 'over-luxuriance and over-refinement' or, tellingly from a gender point of view, as a 'decline, into luxury and effeminacy as the strength of the school expires'.[13] Ruskin criticised the high point of the Renaissance for demonstrating a lack of religious faith by giving classical mythology and Christian symbolism equal prominence in art. He saw the seeds of the fall of Venice being sown in this period, diagnosing the symptoms in biblical terms as the sin of pride in science, state and system.[14] Ruskin's third and final phase was the 'corruption of the Renaissance itself', which he characterised by a 'grotesque' spirit of 'idiotic mockery'.[15] Having established that art and architecture were corrupted by the Renaissance, Ruskin concludes by urging a return to the Gothic forms of the more pious Middle Ages.

As Sally Greene has suggested, Woolf's account of the Great Frost in the seventeenth-century section of *Orlando* can be read as a satire of Ruskin's view of the Renaissance as a frost that swept away the values of the Middle Ages: 'the Renaissance frosts came, and all perished'.[16] Although Woolf partly agrees with Ruskin by criticising the decadence of the courtiers who celebrate even while countryfolk lose their livelihoods, she none the less detects an inner spark which Ruskin had categorically denied: she notes that the 'moon and stars blazed with the hard fixity of diamonds' and describes a bumboat woman who appears full of life although frozen beneath the Thames (*O*, 35). Orlando, in the first throes of love for Sasha, comes to life inside: 'the ice turned to wine in his veins; he heard the waters flowing and the birds singing' (*O*, 39). Ruskin's devastating Renaissance frosts are thus rewritten as the start of revival and reawakening, so that his linear historical model is replaced with a cyclical one of natural renewal.

Woolf's depiction of the Renaissance as a fire beneath the ice echoes the view of a critic of a different school from Ruskin: Pater, who noted 'how deeply the human mind was moved, when, at the Renaissance, in the midst of a frozen world, the buried fire of ancient art rose up from under the soil'.[17] As Perry Meisel has pointed out, Woolf knew Pater's work and frequently adopted his metaphors in her own criticism, but masked her indebtedness to him by rarely referring to him directly in her essays.[18] The dynamic in *Orlando* is slightly different, for Woolf ironically acknowledges herself and all writers to be 'perpetually in the debt' of Pater in the Preface, making light of his legacy whilst also signalling that his ideas play a part in the book's argument.

Pater, together with J. A. Symonds and Vernon Lee, countered Ruskin's moralistic attack on the Renaissance by arguing that it initiated the advance of personal and political freedoms. Pater celebrated the Renaissance for the very reasons that Ruskin deplored it, seeing it as a movement which brought intellectual and sensual enjoyment and a healthy liberalisation of thought and broadening of perspectives. He detected the earliest signs of the Renaissance in the Middle Ages, evidenced in a 'spirit of rebellion and revolt against the moral and religious ideas of the time. In their search after the pleasures of the senses and the imagination, in their care for beauty, in their worship of the body, people were impelled beyond the bounds of the Christian ideal.'[19] Orlando's discovery of sexuality with Sasha is a moment of joyful liberation of the sort that Pater associated with the Renaissance.

Pater, Symonds and Lee also offered Woolf (like Lytton Strachey) an antidote to conventional models of history. As Hilary Fraser has noted, all three were criticised in their time for being 'unhistorical' and for writing history as literature, and all three have been largely ignored by historiographers.[20] They offered Woolf a more helpful approach to periodisation than either Stephen or Ruskin. Rather than seeing the Renaissance as arriving suddenly to sweep away the Middle Ages and destroy its values, as Ruskin would have it, Pater and Symonds saw it as originating in the Middle Ages and continuing into their own time: Symonds argued that 'we still participate' in 'the onward progress of the Renaissance';[21] Pater saw the Renaissance continuing in the work of William Blake, Victor Hugo and the eighteenth-century German art critic Johann Joachim Wincklemann. Woolf's sense of the past as alive and active, seen in Orlando's long memory, particularly in her musings at the end of the novel, reflects this spirit. Woolf may have used Pater to support her belief that one can resist the spirit of the age: Pater described Wincklemann as possessing 'the key to the understanding of the Greek spirit' in his own nature, 'like a relic of classical antiquity, laid open by accident to our alien, modern atmosphere';[22] Woolf's description of Orlando's inability to accommodate herself to the nineteenth century because 'the lines of her character were fixed, and to bend them the wrong way was intolerable' (O, 233) follows very similar lines.

These critics proved helpful to Woolf by suggesting that the Renaissance spirit was not only alive in the present but also played a vital role in modernity: Pater, for example, defined the Renaissance quite literally as a rebirth, where classical learning went alongside 'the coming of what is called the "modern spirit"'.[23] Meisel argues that Woolf's 'greatest anxiety about Pater is that she had inherited modernism rather than created it herself',[24] but it is more accurate to say that Woolf found Pater congenial because he confirmed her view that one must tap into the past in order to discover the modern. As Juliet Dusinberre has argued, the idea of the Renaissance had two resonances for Woolf: 'her affinity on many different levels with the early modern period, and her own sense of being reborn through the creation of an alternative tradition of reading and writing whose roots go back to the Elizabethans and beyond'.[25] This second dimension inclines towards Pater, for, as Sally Greene notes, he helped Woolf see the Renaissance as a process of discovery that could happen at any time, a 'founding yet also renewable movement'; and as a result she used 'its liberating spirit' to support her feminism and modernist aesthetic.[26]

Vernon Lee set a precedent for Woolf and Strachey by taking an impressionistic approach to the past, privileging subjective responses to art and literature over objective, scholarly analyses. Lee distinguished her work from that of an historian:

> I have seen . . . what I might call the concrete realities of thought and feeling left behind by the Renaissance, and then tried to obtain from books some notion of the original shape and manner of wearing these relics, rags and tatters of a past civilisation.[27]

Having spent most of her life in Italy, Lee first formed her conception of the Renaissance from the art and architecture she saw around her, then used book learning to bolster these ideas.

Woolf's conception of the past – and of the Renaissance in particular – was similarly subjective and, in the case of *Orlando*, rooted in a sense of place. She conceived the central historical idea of the novel on a trip with Vita Sackville-West to her ancestral home of Knole in Kent. In a diary entry, Woolf recalls seeing a cart bringing wood to be chopped and Sackville-West saying that 'she saw it as something that had gone on for hundreds of years'. Woolf goes on to fantasise about Knole's history:

> All the centuries seemed lit up, the past expressive, articulate; not dumb & forgotten; but a crowd of people stood behind, not dead at all; not remarkable; fair faced, long limbed; affable; & so we reach the days of Elizabeth quite easily. (*D*, III. 125)

Here Woolf gives history a voice and revives long-dead people in her imagination to create an intimate link between herself and the Elizabethan age. The diary entry also reveals Woolf's fascination with Sackville-West's personal connections with literary history. One of her ancestors, Thomas Sackville, was an Elizabethan author and another, Charles Sackville, was a literary patron commemorated in the literature of the Augustan age; both figures are reflected in details of Orlando's biography. Woolf describes Sackville-West finding a love-letter and a lock of hair from a seventeenth-century ancestor, Lord Dorset, and Woolf remarks that 'one had a sense of links fished up into the light which are usually submerged.' (*D*, III. 125)

Woolf attempts to express this sense of intimacy with the past by basing the character of Orlando on Sackville-West, by drawing details of his/her life from Sackville ancestors and by basing her description of Orlando's estate on Knole. Woolf's fictional history places her in the tradition of Pater and Lee, but it also draws on Sackville-West's own history of her family, *Knole and the Sackvilles*, which itself follows this tradition. In *Knole and the Sackvilles*, Sackville-West presents herself as a central figure in, and a summation of, her family history by frequently positioning herself within the narrative as a descendant and spectator, looking at paintings and imagining the characters of the people depicted, or handling historical artefacts and empathising with their former owners. Woolf reflects Sackville-West's sense of being an active participant in family history both in the fantasy of Orlando's longevity and in the compression of the family history into the life of one figure, based on the character of Vita, manipulating history to present her as the summation of family history.[28]

If Pater, Lee and Symonds offered Woolf models for resisting dominant Victorian patriarchal approaches to history, Sackville-West's position drew her attention to the necessity for a woman to find access to history. As a female, Sackville-West could not inherit Knole: her father died while Woolf was writing *Orlando* and the estate passed to an uncle. Sackville-West had sought consolation for her disinherited position by presenting alternatives to the legal process of inheritance and emphasising the importance of embracing the past imaginatively. This fantasy is worked out most fully in her novel *The Heir: A Love Story* (1922). Peregrine Chase, an insurance clerk, inherits from his aunt an estate very similar to Knole. The estate is heavily in debt and his solicitors persuade him to put it up for auction, but Chase falls in love with the house and the land, and Sackville-West makes it clear that his emotional ties to the estate are much more important than the legal rights which have been conferred upon him as heir. In the closing pages, Chase attends the auction and buys the house for himself, thus effectively bypassing and rejecting the legal process by which he would have inherited it.

In *Orlando*, Woolf goes further in setting up economies of love and empathy, as opposed to economies of the market: she fulfils Sackville-West's wishes by writing a book which, as Nigel Nicolson wrote, 'identified her with Knole for ever. Virginia by her genius had provided Vita with a unique consolation for having been born a girl, for her exclusion from her inheritance, for her father's death earlier that year'.[29] Woolf thus demonstrates that imagination and empathy are more powerful ways of staking a claim to the past than either inheritance laws or conventional models of history can offer.

Orlando, therefore, enacts the imaginative search to rediscover lost origins which Woolf had advocated in *A Room of One's Own*, by using Orlando's long life to trace a heritage for a twentieth-century woman writer back to the Renaissance. In satirising the methods of Stephen and Ruskin, she rejected Victorian patriarchal metanarratives which had left out the history of women writers and had attempted to package the past in ways which reinforced patriarchal ideologies. Instead she inclines to a school of critics who sought to tap into the past and release its energies, and who used the strategies of fiction to bring history alive and see it at work in the present.

III

We can now see that Woolf uses literary parody and allusion in *Orlando* as strategies for putting her alternative model of history into practice. These devices enable her to express intimacy with the literary past in order to forge alternative chains of inheritance based on affinity, and help her to resist patriarchal configurations of literary history by allowing literature to tell its own story. As Linda Hutcheon has pointed out, parody is not always satirical but can be an expression of accord, and Woolf's technique of free indirect discourse can be seen as a way folding the voices of past writers into her own. For example, summarising themes of sixteenth-century poetry, Woolf notes that 'the poets sang beautifully how roses fade and petals fall. The moment is brief they say; the moment is over; one long night is then to be slept by all' (*O*, 26). The statement moves rapidly from reportage ('the poets sang', 'they say') to direct statement ('the moment is over; one long night is then to be slept by all'), the last phrase paraphrasing Hamlet's image of the 'sleep of death' (III. i. 66–8).

    Orlando presents an impressionistic history of English literature after the manner of Pater and Lee, for Woolf does not present a painstaking imitation of particular linguistic or literary styles and *Orlando* shows none of the linguistic dexterity or scholarly knowledge of the history of the English language that James Joyce, for example, demonstrates in the 'Oxen of the Sun' episode of *Ulysses*. She uses language to create some historical colour, especially in the earlier parts of the novel, by using archaisms such as ''twas', 'sennight' or 'trolling their ditties', but Woolf often uses these words outside of the historical contexts given them in the *Oxford English Dictionary*: thus the word 'hodden', which appears in the Elizabethan sequence of the novel, was not recorded until 1792, 'bumboat', which is used in the account of the Great Frost of 1608, was not recorded until 1671, and 'phantasmagoria', used in the eighteenth-century sequence, was not coined until 1802. Such infelicities reflect

Woolf's suspicion of official scholarly accounts of the history of the English language (doubts about whether dictionary accounts of etymology reflect actual word usage at any given time) and draw attention to the imaginative and suggestive ways in which Woolf evokes literary periods.

The anachronisms help Woolf undercut accepted approaches to periodisation, for they are essential to the novel's representation of literary history as a complex tissue of interconnections which should not be broken down into discrete eras. Thus the sex-change scene, presented in the seventeenth-century genre of the masque, ends with allusions to the work of Jane Austen. The narrator dismisses the subject by saying 'let other pens treat of sex and sexuality' (*O*, 134), a phrase which alludes to the opening sentence in the last chapter of *Mansfield Park* ('Let other pens dwell on guilt and misery'), while playing on the title of *Sense and Sensibility*. This anachronism attempts to rewrite literary history in several ways: it introduces the words of a woman into an era when female writers were not recognised, and it reverses the chain of influence by suggesting that later writings may influence past ones in that earlier literature can only be seen through the lenses of writing which has taken place in the meantime.[30]

Woolf laces the novel with allusions to the Renaissance to show its ideas persisting into the present day. The process is epitomised by recurrent cameo appearances of Shakespeare, who is first encountered in his historical setting of the Elizabethan period when Orlando encounters 'a rather fat, shabby man, whose ruff was a thought dirty, and whose clothes were of hodden brown' (*O*, 21), an image which resurfaces in Orlando's mind three times during the novel as 'that earliest, most persistent memory' (*O*, 157). In Orlando's first encounter with Shakespeare, he wants advice but is too shy to ask (*O*, 21). The second time Shakespeare appears, Orlando is not so much inspired to write as filled with ambition and the desire for fame, leading to despair as he tries to 'win immortality against the English language' (*O*, 79). The final time Orlando recalls him, she is a published author and prize-winner, but still declares herself '"Haunted! Ever since I was a child"' (*O*, 299). These allusions testify to ways in which Shakespeare's formidable reputation can have an inhibiting influence on writers: Orlando the aspiring writer can be seen in this respect as an allegory for English authors *en masse* who are both inspired by Shakespeare and struggle to deal with his legacy.

However, overt and buried allusions to Shakespeare in *Orlando*, along with a pervasion of his ideas, suggest that Woolf sought to write *with* him rather than attack him as a canonical male writer. Orlando watches a production of *Othello* as he anticipates eloping with Sasha. Woolf sets the scene for the play by engaging with Shakespeare's own paradox that 'all the world's a stage' (*As You Like It*, II. vii. 138): that 'real' life is theatre but that theatrical performances have their own reality, not least because they stir up real emotions. Woolf describes the audience at this performance as though they are in costume: 'variously rigged out as their purse or stations allowed; here in fur and broadcloth; there in tatters with their feet kept from the ice only by a dishclout bound about them' (*O*, 54). These costumes signify rank in theatrical terms, but Woolf shows that there is more to clothing than the conventions of representation, because we are also told that the way these people dress has been determined by economic forces and social structures ('as their purse or stations allowed') and so clothing is indeed the visible manifestation of underlying economic realities. This recognition of the dynamic relationship between art and life sets the scene for Orlando's empathy with Othello, which is so intense that the 'frenzy of the Moor seemed to him his own frenzy, and when the Moor suffocated the woman in her bed it was Sasha he killed with his own hands'. Orlando temporarily thinks that Sasha has already betrayed him, and recites lines from *Othello* in which the hero realises the full implications of his murder of Desdemona and the loss of her love: 'Methinks it should be now a huge eclipse | Of sun and moon, and that the affrighted globe | Should yawn – ' (*O*, 55; *Othello*, V. ii. 100). Orlando goes on temporarily and wilfully to misread these words believing that the darkness of the night that has just come on will give him the cover he needs to escape with Sasha, but the quotation is quickly revealed to be prophetic as Orlando discovers that Sasha has deserted him and departed for Russia. Thus, Woolf alludes to Shakespeare's idea that the world is a stage first to suggest that Orlando's empathy with Othello stirs up real-life emotions which influence his actions, but then, as if by sleight of hand, leads her protagonist to a state of desolation which is closer to Othello's than he had bargained for.

Orlando continues to play the part of a Shakespearean tragic hero in his period of dejection after losing Sasha. He visits the crypt where his ancestors are buried and asks, 'Whose hand was it? . . . The hand of man or woman, of age or youth? Had it urged the war horse, or plied the needle? Had it plucked the rose or grasped cold steel?' (*O*, 69). The ruminations are those of Hamlet in the grave-digging scene at the opening of Act V, where he speculates whether a skull (which turns out to be Yorick's) had belonged to a politician, a courtier or a lawyer (though even the male Orlando supplements Hamlet's speculations with the recognition that the bones may be those of a woman). The Shakespearean allusions also spill over into the thoughts of other characters, for example, Orlando's housekeeper is relieved to find that he has not been 'foully murdered' in the crypt (O, 70), echoing Old Hamlet's revelation that he has been the victim of a 'murder most foul' (I. v. 27).

In the eighteenth-century sequence of the novel, a sighting of Shakespeare is again seen alongside a covert allusion to his work, as Orlando imagines his lost love Sasha 'mopping and mowing and making all sorts of disrespectful gestures towards the cliffs' of Dover (O, 157). The description recalls *King Lear*, where Edgar, offering to lead his father to Dover cliffs, describes how he has been inhabited by demons including 'Flibbertigibbet, of mopping and mowing' (IV. i. 60–1). The appearance of Shakespeare, this time in the form of a cliff-like 'dome of smooth white marble', not only brings these covert references to the surface but leads to a meditation on the monolithic power of tradition, for Orlando goes on thinking about 'the glory of poetry, the great lines of Marlowe, Shakespeare, Ben Jonson, Milton' (O, 157).

Shakespeare's appearance in the present-day section of the novel serves to raise questions about the nature of the self. Orlando summons up her various selves: the different incarnations she has taken during her lifetime and over history, and the different roles she fulfils in relation to various people in the present. Each 'self' enters as though fulfilling a stage direction (one is clumsy, one comes 'skipping'), and each expresses a different point of view, as if contributing to a choral poem (O, 296–8), before Shakespeare's actual appearance prompts Orlando's integration into 'a single self, a real self' (O, 299). Although the scene may be read as a sketch for a modern theatrical performance, it is also a Renaissance moment, an enactment of Jacob Burckhardt's suggestion that the individual came into being in Renaissance Italy as a 'many-sided man'.[31]

The sequence associates Shakespeare with two contradictory views of the self: one fragmentary and divided, for the idea that each person plays many different parts during a life-time echoes Jaques' 'seven ages of man' speech in *As You Like It* (II. vii. 138–65); the other integrated and whole, for Shakespeare's appearance is linked to Orlando's becoming a 'single self'. Recent studies of the Renaissance have suggested that many writers of the era were exercised by this very contradiction and that it found particular expression in Shakespeare's plays. Stephen Greenblatt has argued that the early modern period saw 'a change in the intellectual, social, psychological and aesthetic structures that govern the generation of identities', which resulted, paradoxically, in both a new emphasis on the power of the will and a renewed assault upon the will; in a heightened awareness of alternatives and an effort to control alternatives.[32] Greenblatt argues that Hamlet's soliloquies are one place in which this contradiction is acted out;[33] Anthony B. Dawson similarly notes that *Hamlet* delineates

> the unfolding of one man's mind, the assailable but uniquely independent spirit forming itself in opposition to, but also in conjunction with, the forms and pressures of the time and its deeply entrenched structures of power. Out of this struggle comes a sense of a fragmented and subjected self, but one which is also improvisatory and questing, very much its own.[34]

The appearance of Shakespeare in the present-day sequence suggests that Orlando's twentieth-century crisis of selfhood and rediscovery of herself is a Renaissance 'moment', again drawing on the Paterian idea that 'renaissance' or rebirth can happen at any time.

In drawing Shakespeare into her narrative and voice, Woolf also subtly makes him an ally in her own concern to question patriarchal world-views. Woolf uses Shakespeare and Renaissance theatre as touchstones for questioning sexual identity throughout the novel in order to criticise society's differential treatment of men and women and, by extension, to defend same-sex attraction. This strategy can be read as a challenge to nineteenth-century critics such as Matthew Arnold who had used Shakespeare to uphold conventional morality ('To understand Shakespeare aright the clue is to seize the morality of Shakespeare'),[35] and to the generations of critics who either disregarded the sonnets or wilfully ignored the same-sex attraction expressed within them. The use of boy actors to play female roles in the Renaissance period enabled playwrights to make much of gender ambiguity, and Woolf picks up on this when she questions Orlando's sexual identity from the first sentence of the novel, 'He – for there could be no doubt of his sex, though the fashion of the time did something to disguise it' (O, 13). Here the protagonist is described as 'really' male, but he borders on being a female impersonator because his clothing 'disguises' his sex. This description is ambivalent, for the insistence that there can be 'no doubt' about Orlando's gender implies that there is indeed reason for doubt. The narrator's description of Orlando as male but wearing an effeminate costume can be compared with those moments in Shakespeare's plays when the boy actor calls attention to his biological sex, as in the epilogue to *As You Like It*. (Sasha's gender is similarly ambiguous and the narrator's pronouncement that she is female because 'no boy ever had a mouth like that; no boy had those breasts; no boy had those eyes which looked as if they had been fished from the bottom of the sea' (O, 36–7) uses equivocation comparable with that of Viola in *Twelfth Night* when she deflects Olivia's advances by arguing that 'I have one heart, one bosom, and one truth, I And that no woman has; nor never none I Shall be mistress of it' (III. i. 160).)

Shakespearean allusions persist into the Restoration episode where Orlando's sex-change is narrated as a masque. The personified virtues of Purity, Chastity and Modesty, who try to cover up what is happening to Orlando, are described as 'Horrid Sisters', echoing the three witches, or 'Weird Sisters', from *Macbeth*, whose sex is ambiguous: as Banquo comments: 'you should be women, I And yet your beards forbid me to interpret I That you are so' (I. iii. 45). Like the masque as a whole, this allusion satirises the three figures who seek to uphold establishment values on behalf of capitalists, lawyers and doctors by suppressing those who refuse to conform to gender roles or who are attracted to members of their own sex. The 'Truth' they wish to suppress is that there may be no difference between men and women, but the hint at the witches of *Macbeth* suggests that they themselves may be transgressing the very boundaries they are trying to police.

Woolf minimises the process of change and blurs the boundaries between the genders when her narrator insists that little visible change has occurred although Orlando has changed sex: 'their faces remained, as their portraits prove, practically the same'. (The portraits referred to are illustrations of different people – plate 4 of the novel, depicting one of Vita Sackville-West's ancestors and plate 5, a portrait of Sackville-West herself posing as Orlando.) We are also told that masculine and feminine traits can be found in the same person, for 'his form combined in one the strength of a man and a woman's grace' (O, 132–3). Shakespeare remains a touchstone for this ambiguity, for the narrator's claim recalls the identical twins Viola and Sebastian in *Twelfth Night*, who are described as 'One face, one voice, one habit, and two persons' (V. i. 214).

The motif of cross-dressing persists into the eighteenth-century sequence of the novel where it serves to undercut the emergence of separate spheres to which Orlando is subjected in that era. Cross-dressing provides a respite from misogyny when Orlando, incensed by a comment by Pope, dresses as a man and goes out to look for women. Moreover, as on the Renaissance stage, cross-dressing enables same-sex encounters to be presented under the cover of their appearing heterosexual. *Twelfth Night* exploits cross-dressing where Viola dresses as a boy and attracts the attention of Olivia, thus evoking same-sex attraction between the two male actors and the two female characters under the guise of one actor wearing male and the other female attire. Woolf's Orlando harnesses its subversive power when she dresses as a man and meets a prostitute: the narrator notes ironically that Orlando experiences 'all the feelings which become a man' (O, 207) – in other words, a moment of lesbian attraction. Thus, the gender ambiguities of the Renaissance stage allow Woolf to validate same-sex attraction whilst escaping the attention of the censors.

Woolf also uses gender ambiguity to subvert eighteenth-century attempts to invoke binary oppositions. The narrator attempts to set up a thesis–antithesis argument for separate spheres, to argue first that clothes construct a person's gender and then that clothes are an expression of inner reality, until the theme of gender ambiguity rises to the surface to prevent synthesis and subvert the argument: 'In every human being a vacillation from one sex to the other takes place, and often it is only the clothes that keep the male or female likeness, while underneath the sex is the very opposite of what it is above' (O, 181).

Where Woolf allows Renaissance ideas to permeate her narrative, she uses parody and caricature to distance herself from certain elements of the literature of the eighteenth and nineteenth centuries. Although Woolf silently draws upon Defoe and Sterne throughout the novel (as we have seen), she satirises Stephen's idea of the eighteenth century as the age of Addison, Dryden, Pope and Swift, whose names become Orlando's mantra. Where Woolf incorporated echoes of Renaissance texts into her own discourse, she distances herself from Pope, Addison and Swift by using clearly demarcated long quotations from their work ('The Rape of the Lock', an essay denouncing hooped petticoats and *Gulliver's Travels*). Academic conventions here help the distancing process, for each quotation is introduced formally and then followed by a piece of analysis. Two of the quotations are particularly misogynistic: Pope satirises the vanity of a woman who can 'stain her Honour, or her new Brocade' (O, 200) with equanimity and Addison describes woman as 'a beautiful, romantic animal that may be adorned with furs and features, pearls and diamonds, ores and silks' (O, 201), and so Woolf's strategy of setting these quotations apart from her text helps to keep the misogyny at a disdainful distance.

Woolf also responds in kind to these writers' dismissive views of women by silencing them, for example when she excises Pope's words:

> Then the little gentleman said,
> He said next,
> He said finally, *
>
> * These sayings are too well known to require repetition, and besides, they are all to be found in his published works. (O, 193)

It is also seen when we are told that the notebook Orlando keeps to record memorable sayings by Addison, Pope and Swift is empty (O, 199), implying their inability to say anything of significance. Johnson and Boswell, two other famous writers whom Stephen had valued, are denied a voice as Orlando passes the house where they are talking 'without hearing a word' of their conversation (O, 213). Woolf thus redresses the balance of literary history by giving short shrift to writers whom Stephen had deemed central.

Woolf attempts to set the nineteenth century at a distance by creating a caricature – from motifs and allusions drawn from a variety of its writers – which is easy to attack. The form of parody found in this section is made at the expense of the source text rather than as an expression of intimacy. In particular, Woolf revisits the courtship narrative which had troubled her earlier in her career by treating it comically in Orlando's marriage to Shelmerdine and denying its universalising power by contextualising it as a concern of late Romantic and Victorian literature. The scene in which Orlando meets Shelmerdine ridicules courtship and marriage in a pastiche: the setting is Brontëan, as Orlando runs wild on the moors as 'nature's bride' (O, 237), echoing the rugged country and love of nature which Woolf admired in *Wuthering Heights* (CE, I. 90); Orlando falls and injures her ankle, a cliché found in countless earlier novels; and then is rescued by Shel who becomes engaged to her on the spot. The comic timing denigrates the institution of marriage by suggesting that no time for deliberation is either desired or required. Shelmerdine himself is something of a Romantic hero, his name evokes Shelley (whose poetry he later reads), and he is depicted in a Byronic stance 'towering dark against the yellow-slashed sky of dawn' (O, 239). Although Orlando and Shelmerdine's relationship is eventually depicted as a partnership of equals, this is achieved in spite of their being married rather than because of it, for Shel continues his travels around the world, and Orlando uses the cover of her marriage to write poetry about 'Egyptian girls', escaping censure because she has a husband and can 'pass' as heterosexual (O, 253). The way that Shel and Orlando continue to live their lives thus frustrates the submission of wife to husband which Woolf satirically identifies as central to the stereotypical Victorian concept of marriage.

This satire also represents an important stage in Woolf's rejection of the Victorian 'Angel in the House'. Besides demonstrating alternatives to submissiveness in marriage, she also mocks the deathly associations of the image of the angel. Coventry Patmore's poem 'The Angel in the House' celebrated the ideal wife as someone closer to death than life by being closer to heaven than earth: 'a woman deck'd with saintly honours | Whose her eyes express her heavenly mood!' This ideology is mocked in a series of spoof death scenes in the nineteenth-century chapter:

Orlando contemplates death as she lies injured before meeting Shelmerdine, and comically declares herself dead when they meet: '"Madam," the man cried, leaping to the ground, "you're hurt!" "I'm dead, sir!" she replied' (O, 239). During their time together, Orlando continues to experience periods when she seeks solitude and death:

> 'Bonthrop,' she would say, 'I'm off,' and when she called him by his second name, 'Bonthrop', it should signify to the reader that she was in a solitary mood, felt them both as specks on a desert, was desirous only of meeting death by herself, for people die daily, die at dinner tables, or like this, out of doors in the autumn woods. (O, 247)

Here, Woolf reduces to a racy summary the deathbed scene which was a set-piece of Victorian fiction, and renders death as comic because it is not a final condition (Orlando has, after all, cheated it for three centuries). The term effectively becomes a by-word for a state of personal contemplation, thus rebutting vacuous notions of saintliness.

By continuing the narrative of *Orlando* up to the publication date of 11 October 1928, Woolf is able to articulate the differences between past and present in certain respects – particularly distinguishing modernity from the Victorian era – whilst also demonstrating continuities between selected past writers and herself. The former strategy, marked by irony, comic treatment and parody, enables her to put the past in perspective; the latter strategy helps her to lay claim to the past without being inhibited by it. The process of absorbing echoes of past writings into her own work, through repeated themes, scenarios or phrases, enables Woolf to achieve an intimacy with congenial spirits from the literary past. The notion is reinforced by Orlando's final vision of looking at the past through a tunnel demonstrates that that past is still alive and has a place in the present.

Orlando's poem, 'The Oak Tree', epitomises the element of continuity in literary history, for she continues to work on it over the 350 years scanned by the novel. When the work is eventually published and wins a prize in the twentieth century, it bears the impress of the developments of English literature over that time. 'The Oak Tree' also represents Vita Sackville-West's long poem, *The Land*, which won the Hawthornden Prize in 1927 (Woolf includes a short extract from this poem as an example of what Orlando is writing (O, 252)). The allusion suggests that Sackville-West herself might represent an accumulation of literary history, just as she represented an accumulation of family history. Yet Woolf can also be seen to identify herself with Orlando as a writer, for the progress of 'The Oak Tree' runs in parallel with that of the novel: this is comparable to Woolf's identification of herself with Lily Briscoe, whose attempt to paint Mrs Ramsay runs concurrently with *To the Lighthouse*, or with Miss La Trobe, whose play runs parallel with *Between the Acts*. In identifying herself with Orlando, Woolf seeks to claim her character's long literary history for herself.

Woolf further binds herself to literary history through a process of self-parody or self-inscription. This can be seen when she alludes to her own work in the Renaissance episode of the novel, in a witty summary of 'Time Passes':

> things remain much as they are for two or three hundred years or so, except for a little dust and a few cobwebs which one old woman can sweep up in half an hour; a conclusion which, one cannot help feeling, might have been reached more quickly by the simple statement that 'Time passed' (here the exact amount could be indicated in brackets) and nothing whatever happened. (*O*, 94)

Stuart Clarke has suggested that this is a riposte to Arnold Bennett's denouncement of 'Time Passes' as pointless,[36] but the passage goes further than this, for it develops into an exploration of themes of time by digressing on the need to distinguish between 'time on the clock and time in the mind' (*O*, 95). The digression justifies Woolf's concern to look closely at concepts of time, and in turn it gives a rationale for temporal manipulation in *Orlando*. In her original plan, she noted that her 'own lyric vein is to be satirised' (*D*, III. 131). The self-portrait is a device often found in metafiction, and the satirical element suggests that Woolf did not want to take her work too seriously, yet the overall effect is that she literally inscribes herself into literary history by alluding to her own earlier works alongside those of other writers. By alluding to her own work in the context of the Renaissance, Woolf plants her intellectual roots in that movement: presenting herself in Paterian terms as a Renaissance spirit and thereby laying claim to a Renaissance of her own.

A diary entry Woolf made after *Orlando* was published suggests that she had internalised this history, for she traced her own intellectual inheritance from the Elizabethan age:

> It was the Elizabethan prose writers I loved first & most wildly, stirred by Hakluyt, which father lugged home for me – I think of it with some sentiment – father tramping over the Library with his little girl sitting at HPG in mind. . . . I used to read it & dream of those obscure adventurers, & no doubt practised their style in my copy books. I was then writing a long picturesque essay upon the Christian religion, I think . . . & I also wrote a history of Women; & a history of my own family – all very longwinded & El[izabe]than in style. (*D*, III. 271)

Woolf had always had a passionate interest in Elizabethan literature (two of the essays in the first *Common Reader* are 'The Elizabethan Lumber

Room' and 'Notes on an Elizabethan Play'), but this diary entry gives the era special emphasis in that she locates her origins as reader and writer in the Elizabethan age. She cites her encounter with Elizabethan prose as a formative reading experience and remembers her earliest attempts at writing as imitations of the work of Hakluyt and his contemporaries. We can see how Woolf's account of her own history has shifted in emphasis if we compare this piece with a diary entry of 1924 where Woolf described her youthful literary tastes and listed Richard Hakluyt, along with later writers, Prosper Merimée, Thomas Carlyle and Edward Gibbon, as a favourite prose writer rather than as an Elizabethan (*D*, II. 310). The personal emphasis in this diary entry thus attempts to establish an intimate contact with the Elizabethan age. (As such, *Orlando* can be seen to represent a significant development of Woolf's attempt to claim Shakespeare as a forebear in a tradition of women's writing in *Night and Day*; and her quest to reclaim him from educated men in *Jacob's Room* and *Mrs Dalloway*.)

The account also demonstrates a shift in Woolf's attitude towards her father's memory for, having satirised his methods, she can now paint an affectionate picture of him bringing her volumes of Hakluyt. The anecdote suggests that she is staking a claim to an inheritance of literature in her description of him bestowing books on her. This expands upon a comment Woolf made in a letter to Sackville-West on beginning *Orlando*: 'my fortune gilds the future for me – if my father didn't leave me pearls, this was by way of a makeshift' (*L*, III. 344). Woolf's 'makeshift' inheritance of books, especially Renaissance books, is offered as a substitute for Sackville-West's inheritance of pearls and upbringing in an Elizabethan mansion. Woolf attempted to forge her own connections with history and establish an intellectual pedigree by seeking to engage closely with and to embody the literary past in *Orlando*. Where Sackville-West had presented history in *Knole and the Sackvilles* through the lives and activities of her own ancestors, Woolf constructs a history of the same period through reference to writers and themes in English literary history: her own literary heritage.

IV

Orlando is the first novel in which Woolf most wholeheartedly turns to the past and embraces it, but while doing so she also places herself very carefully in relation to that past. As we saw in previous chapters, Woolf's earlier novels often looked back to past writings, but her relationship to them was often made problematic by an awareness of the ideologies and assumptions which had accrued to those earlier texts. In *Orlando*, Woolf begins to ease some of those difficulties by critiquing the scholarly discourses which structured her relationship with the past, attacking their inherent assumptions, particularly regarding gender. By ridiculing the attempts of patriarchal scholars to gain a hold on the past, she exposes the shallowness of their methods and ideologies. Having done so she paves the way for the construction of an alternative history: *Orlando* attempts to show that by constructing our own history, we can find our way forward. As we have seen, Woolf uses reference, parody and allusion strategically to place herself in relation to the literary past by choosing where her affinities lie. She reinvents tradition by refusing to accept the account of the past that had been handed to her and seeking out allegiances of her own.

Woolf in *Orlando* can therefore be seen to answer her own call in *A Room of One's Own* to 'rewrite history' imaginatively. Her methods of using fiction – even fantasy – and of using allusions so that literature is made to tell its own story, represent significant departures from the patriarchal methods she satirises in the novel. However, *Orlando* does not seek out the alternative history of neglected women writers she advocated in *Room* because, as we have seen, the literary allusions are generally to the work of the canonical male writers. Rather, Orlando reflects upon women writers' relationship with the canon, not only through the story of Orlando the aspiring writer but by claiming the work of canonical male writers Defoe and Sterne, but chiefly Shakespeare, the most celebrated English writer, as conducive to feminist and lesbian concerns (thereby parallelling her claiming of Shakespeare as an androgynous writer in *Room*). Thus Woolf rewrites literary history in *Orlando*, not to present an alternative account of women writers as a separate group, but to reshape the history of canonical literature to find lost origins of women's writing within it.

Notes

1. Lady Eleanor Butler and Miss Sarah Ponsonby, who eloped from Ireland in 1778 and set up home together at Plasnewydd in Llangollen, Wales.
2. Squier, 'Tradition and Revision in Woolf's *Orlando*', p. 168.
3. *Reading Notebooks*, p. 14.
4. Squier, 'Tradition and Revision', p. 168.
5. Nicolson, *Portrait of a Marriage*, p. 138.
6. Wilson, 'Why is *Orlando* Difficult?'
7. Little describes *Orlando* as a wild-goose chase in which truth constantly collapses in '(En)gendering Laughter'.

8. See Raitt, *Vita and Virginia*, pp. 17–40 for a full account of Woolf's treatment of biography in *Orlando*.

9. Greene (ed.), *Woolf: Reading the Renaissance*, p. 19.

10. Stephen, *Hours in a Library*, III. 332.

11. Ruskin, *The Storm Cloud of the Nineteenth Century*, p. 1.

12. Greene, *Woolf: Reading the Renaissance*, p. 19. Although Greene argues that the English term 'Renaissance' was coined around 1860, the earliest example cited by the OED is from Queen Victoria's journal of 1842, and Ruskin used it in *The Stones of Venice* (1851).

13. Ruskin, *The Stones of Venice*, III. 2–4, 7.

14. Ibid., III. 35.

15. Ibid., III. 3, 121.

16. Greene (ed.), *Woolf: Reading the Renaissance*, p. 20; Ruskin, *The Stones of Venice*, I. 225. The allusion is a compound one for, as Bowlby suggests, Woolf also draws on an account of the Great Frost reprinted in Edward Arber's *An English Garner*, by an anonymous seventeenth-century writer, who describes the hardships of the frozen winter and satirises the ruling classes ('The Great Frost: Cold Doings in London, except it be at the Lottery').

17. Pater, *The Renaissance*, p. 193.

18. Meisel, *The Absent Father*, p. xiii.

19. Pater, *The Renaissance*, p. 26.

20. Fraser, *The Victorians and Renaissance Italy*, pp. 213–15, 230.

21. Symonds, *A Short History of the Renaissance in Italy*, p. 3.

22. Pater, *The Renaissance*, p. 232.

23. Ibid., p. 113.

24. Meisel, *The Absent Father*, p. 52.

25. Dusinberre, *Woolf's Renaissance*, p. 5.

26. Greene (ed.), *Woolf: Reading the Renaissance*, p. 24.

27. Lee, *Euphorion*, p. 16.

28. Kellermann, 'A New Key to Virginia Woolf's *Orlando*'.

29. Nicolson, *Portrait of a Marriage*, p. 190.

30. Woolf's suggestion that later writings can change our perception of past works is comparable to T. S. Eliot's idea that 'the existing order' is changed by the introduction of a 'new work of art' ('Tradition and the Individual Talent', in *Selected Essays*, p. 15).

31. Burckhardt, *The Civilization of the Renaissance in Italy*, p. 85.

32. Greenblatt, *Renaissance Self-Fashioning*, pp. 1–2.

33. Ibid., p. 87.

34. Dawson: *Hamlet*, pp. 7–8.

35. Taylor, *Reinventing Shakespeare*, p. 166.

36. *Orlando: The Original Holograph Draft*, p. 80n.

Chapter 6

'Lives Together': Literary and Spiritual Autobiographies in *The Waves*

Woolf considered *The Waves* to be the novel which came closest to capturing her own ideas and establishing her own style. When exploring her earliest ideas for the work, she noted a desire to write a book which was 'made solely & with integrity of one's thoughts' (*D*, III. 102), and after finishing it, she noted, 'I think I am about to embody, at last, the exact shapes my brain holds. What a long toil to reach this beginning – if The Waves is my first work in my own style!' (*D*, IV. 53). Although these statements may appear to be declarations of originality or expressions of a Bloomian desire to overcome the anxiety of influence, the reverse is true. Woolf's comments on her style are couched in provisional, exploratory terms ('I think . . .'; 'if The Waves is . . .'), suggesting a writerly identity which was in process rather than achieved.[1] The novel itself is profoundly polyphonic, for its prose enfolds many earlier texts in a variety of subtle ways: quotations are absorbed very deeply into the fabric of the novel, with very few being offset or placed in quotation marks; there is much paraphrasing of famous texts; and well-known literary moments (like the mysterious laughter in *Jane Eyre* (*W*, 207)) are replayed as part of the characters' experiences. In other words, in expressing her thoughts or 'the shapes [her] brain holds' (not 'produces'), Woolf inevitably expressed the works which formed an important part of her mental landscape, for reading was integral to her intellectual life.

Woolf's diary notes during her stay at Rodmell in 1926, when she conceived her first ideas for the novel, testify to the intimate connection between her reading and writing at this time. An entry entitled 'My Own Brain' reveals how she recovered a sense of self through reading the work of others:

> Thought I could write, but resisted, or found it impossible. A desire to read poetry set in on Friday. This brings back a sense of my own individuality. Read some Dante & Bridges, without troubling to understand, but got pleasure from them. Now I begin to write notes, but not yet novel. (*D*, III. 103)

Here Woolf sees herself reflected in the work of others, and the act of reading releases her from an impasse to write some notes. This occurs partly because, as we have seen, Woolf saw reading as a creative process in which the reader helps to make the work 'compose'.[2] In the case of Dante, the process of self-discovery was also helped by the fact that she had read his work before (she read him in translation as early as 1917), so in re-reading his poetry she was also revisiting her past intellectual experience.

Woolf's exploratory approach to writerly identity is reflected in her diary notes on writing *The Waves*, which reveal that she took a highly reflexive approach to the creative process, attempting to deduce her own methods as though looking in from the outside. When sketching her initial ideas in September 1926 she noted: 'I want to watch & see how the idea at first occurs. I want to trace my own process' (*D*, III. 113). Three years later, while grappling with the first draft, she wrote that 'these premonitions of a book – states of soul in creating – are very queer & little apprehended' (*D*, III. 253), the word 'premonitions' implying that she saw writing as a process of uncovering something preordained rather than making it up or working to a self-imposed pattern. Writing *The Waves* therefore involved relinquishing control over her writing: this is seen even more strongly when she describes finishing the novel, 'having reeled across the last ten pages with some moments of such intensity & intoxication that I seemed only to stumble after my own voice, or almost, after some sort of speaker (as when I was mad)' (*D*, IV. 10). Woolf pictures herself as an amanuensis for her own voice and the voices of other speakers. Her attempts to look inwards therefore also involved a movement outwards to recognise the presence of other voices.[3]

This movement was bound up with an examination of spiritual questions which also emerges in the earliest notes for *The Waves*. Having reflected on her state of mind in a series of diary entries from July to September 1926, she noted: 'I wished to add some remarks to this, on the mystical side of this solitude; how it is not oneself but something in the universe that one's left with . . . One sees a fin passing far out' (*D*, III. 113). Introspection leads to a quest for something outside of the self, evoked in the symbol of the fin. Woolf's next diary entry elaborated upon the spiritual quest by suggesting a book which was to be 'an endeavour at something mystic, spiritual; the thing that exists when we aren't there' (*D*, III. 114). (Woolf subsequently noted in the margin that the first of these diary entries concerned *The Waves*, and later diary entries testify that her probing of the vision of the fin was a major concern in writing the novel (*D*, III. 302; *D*, IV. 10).) The finished novel explores the nature of individual and communal existence, addresses elegiac concerns (Woolf briefly thought of dedicating the novel to her brother Thoby, the model for Percival) and raises questions about the creation and end of the world.

Having its gestation in the closing stages of *To the Lighthouse*, *The Waves* extends that novel's intellectual project by considering what exists beyond the self: the 'thing that exists when we aren't there' is a version of Andrew Ramsay's image, 'think of a kitchen table, when you aren't there' (*TL*, 33). The six speakers of *The Waves* function like the ghostly presences and Mrs McNab in 'Time Passes', in that they witness the world – seeing, hearing and touching it – on behalf of an anonymous, impersonal narrator whose only function is to report their speeches; in Banfield's words, the novel attempts to 'correlate the third person perspectives via an impersonal style for the description of sensibilia'.[4] The effect of this, as in 'Time Passes', is to provide reassurance of the continuity of the world and human endeavour, although as we will see, it reaches more sceptical conclusions about the survival of the individual.

Woolf's diary notes, written in preparation for *The Waves*, suggest that the novel can be read as a version of the spiritual autobiography: a meditative work which, as G. A. Starr has defined it, reflects on its author's spiritual growth and development, and on questions of belief. Crucially, this often took place in close dialogue with reading material[5] and, as this chapter will show, Woolf's exploration of her themes was informed by the poetry she was reading – or, more importantly, re-reading – during the gestation of *The Waves*. The chapter will focus on the part played by Woolf's re-reading of Byron, Shelley, Wordsworth and Dante in her process of self-examination in *The Waves*.

The structure of *The Waves*, as it evolved over the drafts, facilitated her reflexive approach and helped her manage her relationship with the literary past in three important ways. First, the whole novel is set out as a series of speeches by other voices: the episodes are organised as a series of dramatic monologues by six speakers and the interludes are made 'other' by being set in italics. If, as Leonard Woolf suggested, the six protagonists represent 'different aspects of Virginia's personality'[6] then they can be seen as mirrors in which she explored facets of her vision and creativity. By projecting herself onto six characters, Woolf goes beyond the Romantic conception of the writer as a solitary genius, thus attacking what Jane Marcus has described as a 'still-living English Romantic quest for a self and definition of the (white male) self against the racial or sexual other'.[7] Since the literary echoes, paraphrases and quotations are part of the characters' speeches, the speakers can also be seen as mirrors for exploring her relationship with the literary past.

Second, *The Waves* is structured around repetition (a process which ties in closely with the process of re-reading Woolf was undertaking): the speakers echo literary works, restate things they have already said (particularly at the two key moments of reminiscence: the party for Percival and the reunion at Hampton Court) and quote one another. The repetitive pattern is taken to an extreme in the summing-up where Bernard recapitulates the entire narrative, repeating other characters' statements and their literary quotations. Woolf therefore gives priority to retelling rather than making up stories, offering a model for creativity which prioritises imitation and repetition over originality.

Third, in conceiving the novel as a 'poetic work' and a 'play-poem' (*D*, III. 131, 139), Woolf defied generic boundaries and thus freed her work from their conventions. This move distanced her work from the kinds of narrative pattern she had grappled with in her earlier novels and replayed ironically in *Orlando*, and it provided her with a structure which would embrace a wide variety of other writings. Her use of conflated cycles to structure the novel – the hours of a day, the seasons of a year, the stages of life and the existence of the world from Creation to Apocalypse – gave her a framework in which the many echoes could be gathered.

I

Woolf uses the characters to explore her response to writers she was re-reading and consider their impact on her creative process. This section will show how re-reading Byron, Shelley and Wordsworth helped Woolf explore aspects of her creativity.

Woolf treats Byron's works in a playful and ironic way which reflects her ambivalence about his writing: many years earlier, she had declared herself 'impressed by the extreme badness' of his poetry but admired the satire in his letters (*D*, I. 180). She reiterated these sentiments when re-reading *Childe Harold's Pilgrimage* whilst drafting *The Waves*. She listed five contradictory elements she saw in his work: 'something manufactured: a pose; silliness'; some strong rhetoric; something which 'rings truer to me, & is almost poetry'; some satire; and 'the inevitable half assumed half genuine tragic note' (*D*, III. 288).

Woolf distances herself from Byron in mocking parodies by ridiculing Bernard's admiration of his poetry. As a student, Bernard is a poseur who wears a cloak to imitate Byron, even though he is too clumsy and untidy to achieve the desired effect. He tries to write a love-letter in the style of his hero: 'It is the speed, the hot, molten effect, the laval flow of sentence into sentence that I need. Who am I thinking of? Byron of course. I am, in some ways, like Byron' (*W*, 61). Bernard's speech alludes to the volcanoes which appear with some frequency in Byron's poetry – both as features of the landscape and as metaphors, for example when he describes Don Juan feeling 'the blood's lava . . . the pulse a blaze' during a kiss.[8] The joke is against Bernard, for Byron also satirised the crassness of the device: later in *Don Juan* he mocked it as a 'common place' and a 'tired metaphor': 'Poor thing! How frequently by me and others, | It hath been stirred up till its smoke quite smothers!' (XIII, st. 36). Woolf articulates her ambivalence towards Byron and his followers by giving Bernard words and phrases which typify his style, rather than actual quotations, thus writing *about* Byron rather than with him.

Shelley's poetry is treated more seriously, for it is implicated more deeply in that Woolf associated him with her earliest ideas for *The Waves*. A year after her vision of the fin, she wrote:

> it is today the 4th Sept, a cold grey blowy day, made memorable by . . . being again visited by the 'spirit of delight'. 'Rarely comest thou, spirit of delight.' That was I singing this time last year; & sang so poignantly that I have never forgotten it, or my vision of a fin rising on a wide blank sea. No biographer could possibly guess this important fact about my life in the late summer of 1926. (*D*, III. 153)

Shelley's poetry becomes an *aide mémoire* of the formative moment of the novel in the vision of the fin and memories of Rodmell. Woolf quotes Shelley for similar reasons three years later, resuming *The Waves* after an illness while looking forward to visiting Rodmell (*D*, III. 295). Quoting his poetry also helps her reflect upon her own mood by setting it at a slight distance: in this entry, she uses his song of longing for a lost sense of delight to celebrate a brief moment of happiness amidst depression. A comment in 'The Pastons and Chaucer' throws light on how she used Shelley to sum up her own feelings, for there she suggests that his poetry could offer solace and protection against harmful experiences: 'Shelley, Wordsworth and Coleridge are among the priests: they give one text after text to be hung upon the wall, saying after saying to be laid upon the heart like an amulet against disaster' (*CE*, III. 13). Woolf echoes this idea in Rhoda who is insecure about her own identity and needs to borrow a protective front by copying others: 'I will attach myself only to names and faces; and hoard them like amulets against disaster' (*W*, 33).

Woolf dramatises her tendency to adopt Shelley's words when she describes Rhoda reading his poem 'The Question' in order to escape the torture of life at school:

> Here is a poem about a hedge. I will wander down it and pick flowers, *green cowbind* and the *moonlight-coloured May, wild roses* and *ivy serpentine*. . . . I will sit by the river's *trembling edge* and look at the *water-lilies, broad and*

bright, which lit the oak that overhung the hedge with moonlight beams of their own watery light. (W, 44; emphases added)

Rhoda retreats into the world of the poem, placing herself on its river-bank setting and fusing her own voice with that of the speaker, for the italicised phrases are direct quotations from the poem itself. She asks herself the speaker's question of what to do with the flowers: 'present them – Oh, to whom?' From this vision, Rhoda slips into a state of agony, which she describes using another phrase from Shelley: 'I faint, I fail', from 'The Indian Serenade' which, like 'The Question', is about pursuing an elusive lover. Finally, Rhoda seeks to give not just her bouquet but her whole self to another: 'To whom shall I give all that now flows through me, from my warm, my porous body?' (W, 44) The speech dramatises the loss of self which can follow from becoming engrossed in a poem; the shift reflects the novel's theme of exploring a world beyond the self.

Woolf reflects her own experience of revisiting a poem when she shows Rhoda recalling 'The Question' after hearing of Percival's death. She initially questions whether Shelley can offer solace, for Rhoda now reads the poem in a different light: the lush, colourful landscape of the poem is withered, for the oak tree is split by lightning, the wild flowers are ravaged and trampled by cattle, and the only ones she imagines picking are the deathly violets (mentioned in Shelley's poem, but not in Rhoda's first recitation) (W, 131, 135). However, Woolf also shows the consoling power of Shelley's work when Rhoda manages to answer her original question by throwing flowers into the sea as an 'offering to Percival' (W, 135).

Woolf's engagement with Wordsworth is more vexed than these two examples, for it involves exploring affinities but also continuing her long-running argument with his ideas. Woolf was re-reading *The Prelude* when she started writing *The Waves*, and six weeks into the first draft, she copied into her diary 'some lines I want to remember' from Book VII:

> The matter that detains us now may seem,
> To many, neither dignified enough
> Nor arduous, yet will not be scorned by them,
> Who, looking inward, have observed the ties
> That bind the perishable hours of life
> Each to the other, & the curious props
> By which the world of memory and thought
> Exists & is sustained. (D, III. 247; *Prelude*, VII. 458–65)

Significantly, Woolf revisits her own earlier reading here, for she had copied these lines into a notebook while writing *Mrs Dalloway*, adding 'good quotation for one of my books'.[9] This suggests a highly reflexive process whereby Woolf takes a second look at a piece which had already influenced her aesthetic. In these lines, as elsewhere in *The Prelude*, Wordsworth justifies using the ordinary events of his life as subjects for literature, and they sum up much that interested Woolf about representing 'an ordinary mind on an ordinary day' (*E*, III. 33). In the diary entry, Woolf describes the mundane activities of a day and attempts to capture her experiences of it: 'But my skeleton day needs reviving with all sorts of different colours.' The word 'reviving' is significant because it suggests the importance of the elegiac activity of rescuing something lasting from the ephemeral. The minutiae of the day have ceased to be important, but what can be 'revived' are the impressions they have made. The lines from *The Prelude* are emblematic of Woolf's concern to establish permanence within the ephemeral: to express the 'ties | That bind the perishable hours of life | Each to the other'.

Woolf's engagement with Wordsworth helped her articulate her concept of 'moments of being': experiences which stand out from the ordinary round of life by being fused symbolically in the memory. Woolf used this phrase as a working title for *The Waves* and writing the novel was an important stage in her development of the concept, as she explores the characteristically Romantic concern of the interactions between the outside world and the mind and memory.[10] Critics have pointed out that there are close parallels between Woolf's 'moments of being' and Wordsworth's 'spots of time',[11] but this is not mere imitation, for Woolf applies Wordsworth's concepts to analyse characters' experiences, which, in turn were based on incidents in her own life. These processes can be seen in her descriptions of the formative moments of Neville and Rhoda.

Neville's moment of being comes after overhearing talk of a violent death. The incident becomes fused with an apple-tree he seems to have been looking at when hearing the news:

> The apple-tree leaves became fixed in the sky; the moon glared; I was unable to lift my foot up the stair. . . . I shall call this stricture, this rigidity, "death among the apple trees" for ever. There were the floating, pale-grey clouds; and the immitigable tree; the implacable tree with its greaved silver bark. The ripple of my life was unavailing. I was unable to pass by. (*W*, 17–18)

The tree becomes a symbol of death and mortality but it also serves to crystallise and preserve the memory, for Neville uses the tree to help recall the scene and relive the feeling, to help him come to terms with it. This scenario is based on an incident from Woolf's own childhood, when she overheard that a man who had recently visited her family had killed himself:

The next thing I remember is being in the garden at night and walking on the path by the apple tree. It seemed to me that the apple tree was connected with the horror of Mr Valpy's suicide. I could not pass it. I stood there looking at the grey-green creases of the bark – it was a moonlit night – in a trance of horror. I seemed to be dragged down, hopelessly, into some pit of absolute despair from which I could not escape. My body seemed paralysed. (*MB*, 82–3)

Critics generally refer this to the account from 'A Sketch of the Past' to demonstrate that the scene in the novel had an autobiographical source, but while the *memory* described in 'Sketch' is a source for the incident in *The Waves*, Woolf wrote the memoir ten years later, in 1939, and so she had already rehearsed her account of the incident in fictional form before presenting it as a memoir. 'Sketch' thus becomes less important as a document for interpreting *The Waves*; rather, the novel can be seen as an important stage for Woolf in working out the analysis of her own creative process which later appeared in the memoir.

Woolf drew on Wordsworth's concept of 'spots of time' (*Prelude*, XII. 208–335) to provide a structure for describing and exploring these childhood experiences. Woolf's account of Neville's vision reflects a number of key themes from *The Prelude*. One of these is the power of the imagination to create associations: Wordsworth argues that poetry results from the active engagement of the mind with its surroundings, from 'observation of affinities | In objects where no brotherhood exists | To passive minds' (II. 384). Second, there is an emphasis on specific moments – 'spots of time' which are 'scattered everywhere' throughout life, but significantly date from 'our first childhood'. Third, these moments help to preserve a moment by making it memorable and become a focal point for future memories: they have 'a renovating virtue, whence . . . our minds | Are nourished and invisibly repaired'.

Like Neville's moment of being, Wordsworth's spots of time are formed in response to death. This is seen in *The Prelude* in the two childhood anecdotes used to illustrate spots of time. In the first, he describes becoming lost on a moor and passing the spot where a gibbet had stood. This initially leaves him with a sense of 'visionary dreariness' (XII. 256), so that even when he travels on to a more hopeful vista, it is tinged with gloom. Yet, while the mind had altered the perception of the scene in one way, memory gives it a different hue, for the event has invested the place with 'radiance more sublime' (XII. 267). In the second anecdote, memory changes a scene to make it bleak in retrospect. Wordsworth remembers looking out across a moor while waiting for a carriage to take him home from school for Christmas. His father died during the holiday, and the sight of the moor, with its sheep, 'one blasted tree', 'the bleak music' of a stone wall and the mist over the road, become imprinted with this memory: 'All these were kindred spectacles and sounds | To which I oft repaired, and thence would drink, | As at a fountain' (XII. 319–26). Events are stored in memory and become attached to perceptions, to be revived at a later date.

In presenting fleeting moments, then, the 'spots of time' attempt to fend off death and dissolution. This becomes a feature of Woolf's 'moments of being', for Neville's vision of 'death among the apple-trees' becomes a recurring image in his speeches. He recapitulates this scene when the six characters reunite for a dinner-party and share what is on their minds, using it as protection against the threat of being subsumed by the group. He uses the incident protectively again when he hears of the death of his friend Percival: 'I will stand for one moment beneath the immitigable tree, alone with the man whose throat is cut' (*W*, 125).

Woolf rehearses another experience of her own in Rhoda's formative moment of being. Rhoda finds that physical contact with solid objects can help regain a sense of self:

> I came to the puddle. I could not cross it. Identity failed me. We are nothing, I said, and fell. I was blown like a feather, I was wafted down tunnels. Then very gingerly, I pushed my foot across. I laid my hand against a brick wall. I returned very painfully, drawing myself back into my body over the grey, cadaverous space of the puddle. (*W*, 50)

This account also formed part of Woolf's examination of her own creativity in 'A Sketch of the Past', where she describes encountering a puddle in her way: 'everything suddenly became unreal; I was suspended; I could not step across the puddle; I tried to touch something . . . the whole world became unreal' (*MB*, 90; ellipsis in original). Although the puddle incident is based on a memory Woolf mentions in her diary when planning the novel ('couldn't step across a puddle once I remember, for thinking, how strange – what am I?' (*D*, III. 113)), her account in *The Waves* addresses the problem intellectually, through philosophy and poetry. First, Rhoda's touching of the wall recalls Samuel Johnson's challenge to idealism, by kicking a stone and saying 'I refute it thus'. Second, Woolf draws on Wordsworth to structure the accounts of the event in *The Waves* and 'Sketch', for, as Pines has suggested, the sequence has parallels with Wordsworth's description of a similar experience, in a note to his 'Ode: Intimations of Immortality from Recollections of Early Childhood':

> Nothing was more difficult for me in childhood than to admit the notion of death as a state applicable to my own being . . . With a feeling congenial to this I was often unable to think of external things as having external existence and I communed with all that I saw as something not apart from but inherent

in my own immaterial nature. Many times while going to school have I grasped at a wall of tree to recall myself from this abyss of idealism to the reality.[12]

The similarity suggests that Woolf drew on Wordsworth's note to help analyse Rhoda's moment of being, then based her later, analytical bio-graphical account on the passage in the novel.[13]

While Wordsworth's ideas helped Woolf find a framework for articu-lating her moments of being, she also questions his concepts through uneasy echoes of his poetry. These are found in the speeches of Bernard who invokes but falls short of Wordsworth's ideals. For example, at college Bernard finds solitude an uneasy experience: 'when I have left a room, and people talking, and the stone flags ring out with my solitary footsteps, and I behold the moon rising, sublimely, indifferently, over the ancient chapel – then it becomes clear that I am not one and single, but complex and many' (*W*, 61). The moment revisits Wordsworth's descrip-tion of escaping college society to enjoy nature in solitude, and find a pure and clearly defined sense of self: 'Gently did my soul | Put off her veil, and self-transmuted stood, | Naked, as in the presence of her God' (*Prelude* IV. 150–2). Bernard fails to find any spiritual sense of self in solitude (the moon is perfectly 'indifferent' to the chapel), and indeed challenges a Romantic concept of self by recognising that he has many selves and is bound inextricably with others. The passage denies Wordsworthian sub-limity, for the word 'sublime' is used in its more basic sense of 'high up' to refer to the moon and not to the elevation of thought or mood, found, for example, in the 'sense sublime | Of something far more deeply inter-fused' of 'Tintern Abbey' (l. 95–6). Bernard rebuts sublimity explicitly in his summing-up, when he describes a miserable holiday in Cumberland (Wordsworth's birthplace and the setting for many of his poems), where he 'felt grumpy under the eternal hills and not in the least sublime' (*W*, 215).

Although Bernard's failure to achieve sublimity could merely reflect his own inadequacies, his speeches contribute to a debate on Romanticism within the novel by articulating a resistance to such a state. Further light is thrown on this in Woolf's account of Bernard's arrival in London and the party to celebrate Percival's departure for India, where Woolf draws directly on her own recent reading. Bernard's view of London echoes Wordsworth's in the section of *The Prelude* from which Woolf quoted in her diary. Bernard describes London as an 'ant-heap' whereas Wordsworth describes it as an 'ant-hill', and both compare it favourably with Rome (*W*, 91; *Prelude* VII. 124). Additionally, as Gillian Beer and Kate Flint have both suggested, Bernard's description also contains echoes of Wordsworth's 'Sonnet

Composed Upon Westminster Bridge': both accounts see London as fair, majestic and sleeping; and Bernard's list of 'factories, cathedrals, glass domes, institutions, and theatres' nearly repeats Wordsworth's 'ships, towers, domes, theatres and temples' (*W*, 91, 'Westminster Bridge', l. 6). Since Woolf knew London well, it is curious that she would have drawn on Wordsworth's descriptions here. Although the passage could be a mockery of Bernard for needing other people's words to express himself, it dramatises the phenomenon which Woolf herself noted in a diary entry on 1919, of seeing London 'through the eyes of Defoe' (*D*, I. 263). It voices a recognition that, contrary to Romantic notions of the self communing with the world, our view of world is formed and conditioned by what we have read.

Woolf's resistance to sublimity emerges as the passage develops. Her account of Bernard's mental interactions with city scenes continues to engage with *The Prelude*: Bernard experiences city life as a stream, 'like one carried beneath the surface of a stream ... the stream of this crowded thoroughfare' (*W*, 93–4), then finds that the 'roar' of the street numbs the senses and 'drugs one into dreams' (*W*, 93). The images echo Wordsworth's description of the London crowd as 'an endless stream of men and moving things' (VII. 150–1); and his account of how the 'roar' produces a trance-like state where 'the shapes before my eyes became | A second-sight procession, such as . . . appears in dreams' (VII. 633–4). However, although both are stirred from reverie by the imagination, Wordsworth experiences a visionary moment, as he sees a blind beggar whom he takes as 'an apt type . . . of the utmost we can know, | Both of ourselves and of the universe', whereas, when Bernard's imagination is stimulated by the sight of a girl and a crane, he begins to make up stories which rapidly peter out: 'soliloquies in back streets soon pall' (*W*, 95). Although this curtailment partly reflects Bernard's inadequacy as an artist (Neville notes that Bernard often fails to end his stories), it also reflects Woolf's more sceptical perception that no moment of vision can last: a point expressed quite sympathetically in relation to Lily Briscoe at the end of *To the Lighthouse*. Furthermore, Bernard's preference for society over solitude – he finds soliloquies inadequate because he craves company – reflects Woolf's response to the Romantic idea of nature. As she had noted in 'The Pastons and Chaucer': 'There is something morbid, as if shrinking from human contact, in the nature worship of Wordsworth' (*CE*, III. 9).

Woolf continues to question Wordsworth's transcendent vision in her depiction of friendship and company, as she continues to engage more loosely with the *Prelude* in her description of Percival's farewell dinner. In Book VIII of *The Prelude*, Wordsworth articulates a theory of 'Love

of Nature Leading to Love of Man', by which Nature helped him overcome the self-destroying, transitory things of London in order to achieve
'composure and ennobling Harmony' with others. Again, Bernard represents a diminished form of this ideal: Neville notes that although
Bernard is sociable, he is pessimistic in some ways about the value of
caring for others, for he has a 'love of mankind (crossed with humour at
the futility of "loving mankind")' (*W*, 100).

The unity the friends achieve at the party pointedly resists the sort of
sublimity or transcendence Wordsworth associated with human society.
Instead of Wordsworth's notion of people uniting in 'one spirit over
ignorance and vice' (VIII. 669), Bernard pictures their coming together
as a momentary linking of different perspectives: 'We have come together
. . . to make one thing, not enduring – for what endures? – but seen by
many eyes simultaneously' (*W*, 104). Wordsworth pictured human unity
as stemming from, and leading to, God:

> The soul when smitten thus
> By a sublime idea, whencesoe'er
> Vouchsafed for union or communion feeds
> On the pure bliss, and takes her rest with God (VIII. 672–5)

Woolf's characters, on the other hand, see their unity as an artistic or
structural formation and not as a vision of the sublime: Susan notes that
'a chain is imposed'; while Louis says, 'see us fixed, see us displayed, see
us held in a vice' (*W*, 116). Both statements suggest that unity is imposed
on them from the outside rather than something achieved by the soul's
perception of some inner reality.

The seven friends create something by witnessing and taking part in
the same social event together, so that the single flower on the table
becomes 'a seven-sided flower . . . to which every eye brings its own contribution' (*W*, 104). Gillian Beer has suggested that the seven-sided
flower 'calls up Wordsworth's poem of continuance beyond death, "We
are seven"' (*W*, 104 n.), but *The Waves* resists this line of thinking. In
'We are seven', a little girl insists that she is one of seven siblings even
though two have died, but when the friends in *The Waves* meet years
after Percival's death, Bernard does not count him among the group but
sees them as 'a six-sided flower; made of six lives' (*W*, 190–1).

This episode does, however, suggest the power of art to achieve a state
of permanence. The party is a work of art: Louis comments that 'something is made', whilst Jinny speaks of making 'this moment out of one
man'. It is an example of Woolf's 'moments of being', as different elements are fused together in a totality. Bernard's last statement in the
section highlights the artistic and elegiac elements when he states that

'We are creators. We too have made something that will join the innumerable congregations of past time' (*W*, 119–20). The confidence in permanence expressed here is undermined as the triumphant ending to the party episode is followed immediately by the news that Percival has died. His death has destroyed all the party created, for not only is the circle of friends broken, but society itself seems less secure.

Woolf's engagement with Wordsworth also informs her examination of ideas about human existence, as she explores questions concerning the origins of the world and of the individual, and considers diverse understandings of the end of the world and the death of the individual. As we will see, Woolf pursues these ideas in her re-reading of Dante as well as Wordsworth, and these reflections contribute to an exploration of the nature and purpose of writing.

II

The start of the novel posits a variety of origins for self and world by presenting a collage of different interpretations of creation. The opening interlude is a creation story, for Woolf's description of a sunrise bringing the world into view contains passing glances at the creation story from Genesis, as Kate Flint has noted.[14] Both accounts begin with formlessness and darkness being transformed by the arrival of light; both continue with the sky (or heaven) being separated from the sea; and both describe the arrival of the sun, trees and birds. Biblical images ripple forwards into the novel as the six characters live out their early childhood (their innocent stage) in a garden, until experience intrudes in the form of Jinny kissing Louis and a version of the Fall occurs in Neville's vision of 'death among the apple trees', an idea reinforced by his perception that we are 'all doomed, all of us, by the apple trees' (*W*, 18).

Woolf revises the Genesis account, in that the world of *The Waves* takes shape through female agency, for light is introduced by a woman holding a lamp. Harvena Richter has suggested that the sequence evokes Eos or Aurora, the goddess of the dawn, in place of the Christian God; she argues that *The Waves* 'presents a displaced creation myth rendered in distinctly feminine terms and expressing particularly feminine ambitions'.[15] The passage alludes to arts which are traditionally female, for it uses the metaphor of appliqué work – the sea is a piece of 'grey cloth', the waves 'a thin veil of white water', the sun flames 'in red and yellow fibres', the sky is 'woollen grey' (*W*, 3). The image of a woman's arm rising above the sea also carries echoes of the Lady of the Lake in the *Morte d'Arthur*. The female figure is a vestige of the narrator Woolf had envisaged and experimented with in earlier drafts; this figure is in turn recalled in the woman whom Susan and Bernard see writing at Elvedon. These could be signatures of Woolf, the female creator of this textual world.

A further skein of the novel raises different ideas about origins by pointing back to classical mythology. Louis' dream of turning into a tree to hide from his friends – 'My hair is made of leaves. I am rooted to the middle of the earth' (*W*, 8) – evokes the story of the nymph Daphne in Ovid's *Metamorphoses*, who is turned into a laurel tree to escape from the amorous Apollo. Woolf extends this image to suggest that Louis' roots also go down to Ancient Egypt, for his eyes become 'the lidless eyes of a stone figure in a desert by the Nile' (*W*, 7). Ovidian images become a motif within the novel, as the characters frequently seem on the brink of becoming plants or animals: for example, shortly after Louis' speech, Jinny describes her hand as 'like a snake's skin', and Bernard's face as 'like an apple tree netted under' (*W*, 17). Bernard and Jinny's foray into the undergrowth bespeaks another narrative of origins, this time the scientific one of the prehistoric swamp.

Additionally, in the earliest draft of the novel, Woolf explored and challenged Wordsworth's ideas of origins in a series of buried allusions to his 'Immortality Ode'. The draft begins as the protagonists are literally born out of the sea:

> waves succeeding waves; endlessly sinking & falling; . . . waves that were ~~the forms~~ . . . of many mothers, & again of many mothers, & behind them many more, endlessly sinking & falling, & lying prostrate, & each holding up . . . as the wave pass its crest . . . a child. (*HD*, I. 9, 10; Ellipses indicate deletions in the original)

Woolf's description of the children arriving out of the sea echoes Wordsworth's vision of 'that immortal sea | Which brought us hither', a place to which one can travel in imagination and 'see the Children sport upon the shore, | And hear the mighty waters rolling evermore' (ll. 167–71). Where the sea in Wordsworth's poem is a metaphor for the traffic of the soul between heaven and earth, the image of the mothers in Woolf's draft suggests female creativity and physical birth. The passage could be read as a celebration of childbirth, where the children are carried on the amniotic waters out of the body of the sea while their mothers lie prostrate. Through this allusion, Woolf portrays birth as a physical as well as a spiritual event, revising Wordsworth's notion of birth as the moment when the body becomes a 'prison house' in which the soul is forced to reside.

Wordsworth argues that small children have recollections or 'intimations' of past existence and that this gives evidence of immortality. Woolf hints at a similar phenomenon in the first draft of *The Waves*, where the children have visions of life beyond the here and now, for 'moments of clairvoyance seize specially the young mind, which is not yet attached by fibres' to the mundane and ordinary. However, childhood for Woolf is not the blessed state which Wordsworth believes it to be, but an unhappy time, partly because of a child's openness to intimations, which are among the horrors of childhood: 'the terrible revelations; the faces that look out from behind leaves; ~~the surprises; the intimations; the beckonings; the sudden~~ shadows on the ceilings'. The two children who are especially open to this sort of experience are Susie, who is described as 'one of those ~~ancient prophetesses~~ . . . to whom the Lord spoke', echoing Wordsworth's eulogy of the child as 'Mighty Prophet! Seer blest!' (l. 114) and Louis who feels a calling to the Christian ministry (*HD*, I. 20).

References to Louis' calling and Susie's status as a prophet disappear after the earliest drafts; and Woolf reworks ideas from the 'Immortality Ode' to question Wordsworth's access to mystery by undermining the religious assumptions within his poem. Though Wordsworth's beliefs were not entirely orthodox,[16] the 'Ode' presupposes the existence of God as a transcendent being and creator: 'trailing clouds of glory do we come | From God, who is our home: | Heaven lies about us in our infancy!' (l. 64). Paradoxically, Woolf uses Louis to challenge this assumption: she paraphrases Wordsworth's image of life after birth as 'but a sleep and a forgetting', so that Louis thinks of life as 'a dream', but also as a 'stage of being; some long meditation', implying that life is not just a 'forgetting' but a conscious experience. Louis' visions are not of a past existence in heaven, but of life in other cultures at other times. His life is:

> some long meditation, begun when the pyramids were still building in Egyptian sands . . . For he had . . . existed endlessly; & now; on this . . . particular day was forced to state the result of those dreams, those ~~pre-natal meditations, charactered upon the walls of his mind~~ (*HD*, I. 11)

The suggestion here is that human consciousness may have a continuing existence, but on earth rather than in heaven.

In the published novel, Woolf re-works Wordsworth's image of the sea to present existence as collective rather than individual: the characters are like waves, shifting, changing, and merging with one another. Louis echoes Wordsworth's Ode when he has an intimation of the sea from which he emerged: 'I dash and sprinkle myself with the bright waters of childhood' (*W*, 53). The sea here is not a symbol of the glory experienced in childhood, but it shows that individual identity can be subsumed by collective existence: as Louis says when the friends meet at Hampton Court, 'our separate drops are dissolved; we are extinct' (*W*, 188), as

each group member loses a sense of individuality. The episode recapitulates the birth-scene from the earliest drafts, for, seeing his friends from
a distance, Louis finds that they appear not as people but as fish:

> The net is raised higher and higher. It comes to the top of the water. The water
> is broken by silver, by quivering little fish. Now leaping, now lashing, they are
> laid on shore. Life tumbles its catch upon the grass. There are figures coming
> towards us. Are they men or are they women? They still wear the ambiguous
> draperies of the flowing tide in which they have been immersed. (*W*, 193)

Seen from a distance, his companions lose humanity and individuality,
becoming an amorphous catch of fish. This scene invokes but subverts
Wordsworth's idea of the 'border experience', where he describes how
shepherds in the distance appear to be giants, ennobling humankind and
inspiring him with 'love and reverence | Of human nature' (*Prelude*, VIII.
278). Woolf presents a border experience in which the human form is pri-
mitivised: the Christian overtones of Wordsworth's poem are overwritten
with Darwinian implications that no form of life is exalted, because all
species ultimately evolved from sea creatures.[17] At the close of this episode,
Neville suggests that human life might return to the water, for 'we are
scarcely to be distinguished from the river' (*W*, 194). Woolf rewrites
Wordsworth's image of the persistence of individual existence before birth
and after death, to suggest that the individual may have a part in a wider
collective existence that persists beyond the life-span of one person.

In considering spiritual questions about death and the afterlife, Woolf
also turned to Dante's *Inferno*. She read *The Inferno* slowly and carefully
in Italian while drafting *The Waves*, taking in a canto a week (*D*, III.
320), so that her reading ran concurrently with her writing of the second
typescript.[18] She often records her progress with each side by side: for
example, she mentions Dante in the entries where she records the significant structural decisions of organising the narrative into dramatic
monologues and subsuming all the stories into Bernard's summing-up
(*D*, III. 312, 339). These decisions owe something to the structure of *The
Inferno*, for the poem is a dramatic monologue by Dante's pilgrim, which
subsumes other stories, as he meets both dead writers such as Virgil and
characters from literature, such as Cleopatra and Ulysses.

Woolf's experience of Dante clearly affected her views of her own
writing. On first mentioning him in her diary, she noted:

> I am reading Dante, & I say, yes, this makes all writing unnecessary. This sur-
> passes 'writing' as I say about Sh[akespea]re. I read the Inferno for half an
> hour at the end of my own page: & that is the place of honour; that is to put
> the page into the furnace – if I have a furnace. (*D*, III. 313)

Reading Dante side by side with her own work, Woolf's first response is awe, finding her own writing inferior and pointless – although she also alludes to his work, for she expresses her desire to burn her own page in a pun on the title of Dante's poem.

Woolf's decision to read Dante at this point in drafting *The Waves* is not coincidental. Although this was her first serious, systematic reading of his work in the Italian, she had read his work before, significantly during the formative period of *The Waves* at Rodmell in 1926. During this latter period, Dante's poetry had helped her out of a creative crisis and so her reading of his work had played a small but significant part in her early thinking about the novel (*D*, III. 103).

Images from *The Inferno* are present in portions of *The Waves* written before Woolf's intensive reading of 1930–31. In the first draft of the episode relating to the characters' middle age, Jinny descends into an underground station and experiences a moment of panic and fear, as she sees the downwards movement as a kind of descent into hell:

> the extraordinary descent, the flight of bodies, down the moving stairs, affects me . . . seemed like the descent <a winged avalanche> . . . the falling through the air of some winged, terrible, noiselessly . . . descent of winged, of silent, of doomed. (*HD*, I. 322)

The draft also includes animal imagery characteristic of Dante's style which survives into the published version of the novel: Jinny's desire to 'cower and run for shelter' at the vision, and her image of herself as a 'little animal . . . sucking my flanks in and out with fear' (*W*, 160–1), echoes *The Inferno*, where the pilgrim, momentarily wishing to end the expedition into hell before it begins, is described as 'a frightened beast that shies at his own shadow' (*Inferno* II. 37–42, 487).

In studying Dante while rewriting *The Waves*, then, Woolf returned to a text that had already made an impression upon her and that was already part of her mental landscape when she had begun the novel. On re-reading *The Inferno*, Woolf revised this passage to include further references to Dante's poem which serve to augment her earlier picture and bring her work closer to Dante's, parading his influence rather than editing it out. For example, in some new lines, Jinny remarks on how many people have died:

> Millions descend these stairs in a terrible descent. Great wheels churn inexorably urging them downwards. Millions have died. Percival died. I still move. I still live. (*W*, 160)

As the pilgrim Dante was the only living soul to visit hell, so Jinny feels alone as a living person amongst hordes of the dead. Her reaction is comparable to the pilgrim Dante's first view of hell:

And so I looked and saw a kind of banner
rushing ahead, whirling with aimless speed
as though it would not ever take a stand,
behind it an interminable train
of souls pressed on, so many that I wondered
how death could have undone so great a number.[19]

The published version of this scene also augments the military metaphor found in this quotation (and in several other places in *The Inferno*), as Jinny envisages the 'terrible descent of some army of the dead' (*W*, 161).

There are further Dantean echoes in the following speech by Neville, which Woolf added to the manuscript while studying *The Inferno*: 'here in a car comes Cleopatra, burning on her barge. Here are figures of the damned, too, noseless men by the police-court wall, standing with their feet in fire, howling' (*W*, 163). The passage is a dense compression of images from *The Inferno*: the damned passing judgement (V. 13–14), frequent instances of mutilation, most specifically the sower of discord with 'his throat slit, and his nose | cut off as far as where the eyebrows start (XVIII. 64–5) and burning feet: 'the soles of every sinner's feet were flaming' (XIX. 25). Cleopatra also has a place in Dante's inferno, in the second circle of hell reserved for the lustful – 'there is Cleopatra, who loved men's lusting' (V. 63) – although Neville's speech also alludes to Shakespeare's play (which he is reading), in particular Enobarbus' description: 'The barge she sat in, like a burnished throne burned on the water' (*Antony and Cleopatra* II. ii. 197–8).[20] Neville continues the image of hell by describing Louis and Rhoda as 'anguished souls'.

This sequence goes beyond alluding to Dante to hold a conversation with his ideas, for Jinny's speeches in particular issue a profound challenge to his world-view by locating hell and salvation in the everyday world. Jinny laments the lifeless existence of her fellow commuters, but gets her own feelings of life and comfort from make-up, clothes and home furnishings. In a direct inversion of Dante's image of the pilgrim following a banner into hell, Jinny declares: 'I am a native of this world, I follow its banners' (*W*, 162). Jinny's infernal vision is therefore temporary and easily covered up by the pleasures of consumerism, whereas Dante's pilgrim goes on a seven-day journey through hell, purgatory and paradise to replace his sights of torment with a vision of salvation. Jinny sums up her crisis and its resolution later, in the reunion at Hampton Court, in an allusion to the gates of Dante's *Inferno*:

'The iron gates have rolled back,' said Jinny. 'Time's fangs have ceased their devouring. We have triumphed over the abysses of space, with rouge, with powder, with flimsy pocket-handkerchiefs.' (*W*, 190)

Jinny's worldly view and celebration of the body is antithetical to the Christian ethos of *The Inferno*, where Epicurus and his followers, who sought earthly happiness as the greatest good, were punished in hell as heretics (X. 15).

Although these are Jinny's views, they reflect a sentiment found in Woolf's diaries. In the entry for 23 December 1930, Woolf domesticates *The Inferno* in a joking allusion when she describes herself as being 'admitted to the underworld' when her bag was stolen (*D*, III. 339). The previous day, she had copied into her diary some lines in Italian from *The Inferno*. Mark Musa translates these as follows:

> Not sweetness of a son, not reverence
> for an aging father, not the debt of love
> I owed Penelope to make her happy,
>
> could quench deep in myself the burning wish
> to know the world and have experience
> of all man's vices, of all human worth.
>
> So I set out on the deep and open sea
> with just one ship and with that group of men,
> not many, who had not deserted me. (*The Inferno* XXV. 94–102)

These lines are spoken by Ulysses, who is punished in hell for persuading his comrades to sail to the forbidden sea where they are shipwrecked. There is a tension between these lines and the adjacent diary entry, where Woolf records her decision to incorporate all the voices into Bernard's long summing-up: 'to show that the theme effort, effort dominates: not the waves: & personality: & defiance' (*D*, III. 339). Where Ulysses in *The Inferno* is punished for his adventurous nature, Woolf seeks to celebrate such adventurousness and defiance of rules. The words of Ulysses, the reckless mariner, are suitably emblematic for a novel which ends with a character flinging himself 'unvanquished and unyielding' against death.

Bernard's summing-up does not, however, pursue this defiant approach, for it develops into a fairly pessimistic meditation on two themes which are prominent in *The Inferno*, as well as Wordsworth's 'Intimations Ode' and *The Prelude*: the related concerns of life after death and literary posterity. The 'Immortality Ode', as we have seen, seeks to put forward a concept of the continuity of life before birth and after death; while Wordsworth sought literary posterity in the *Prelude* by writing it as a preamble to a 'literary work which might live'.[21] Dante's depiction of the pilgrim's journey through hell and purgatory to heaven, culminating in his reunion with his lover Beatrice, illustrates the continued existence of the dead, while his encounters with past writers, particularly Virgil, and with characters from classical works, also celebrate literary posterity. Woolf's meditations on these themes take a radically different approach, for her summing-up argues with Wordsworth and Dante by questioning the existence of the individual, denying the existence of God, questioning the authority of the author and undermining the power of the written word.

The summing-up completes a process that is evident throughout the novel, whereby collective existence is seen as more potent and durable than individual life. Bernard recapitulates and conflates the life-stories of himself and his friends, by using images associated with the other characters, such as Neville's apple tree, and describing scenes which had originally appeared as the imaginings of others. He takes on a composite identity in which the attributes and experiences of the others are collected in his body: 'Here on my brow is the blow I got when Percival fell. Here on the nape of my neck is the kiss Jinny gave Louis. My eyes fill with Susan's tears. I see far away, quivering like a gold thread, the pillar Rhoda saw, and feel the rush of the wind of her flight when she leapt' (*W*, 241). The other characters are lost in the figure of Bernard, but in the process they also continue as part of him.

Bernard's vision offers glimpses of a writer outside himself, whose whispers and fragmentary phrases hint towards, but can only barely offer assurance of, something permanent. Woolf explores the question of what might be permanent early on in the summing-up, when Bernard says that: 'On the outskirts of every agony sits some observant fellow who points; who whispers' (*W*, 208). Although the phrases he hears merely sketch out a scene from his childhood, Bernard suggests that the shadowy figure is important for indicating something beyond the personal perspective: 'he directed me to that which is beyond and outside our own predicament; to that which is symbolic, and thus perhaps permanent, if there is any permanence in our sleeping, eating, breathing, so animal, so spiritual and tumultuous lives' (ibid.).

Bernard's sense of something beyond the self is reminiscent of Wordsworth's account of crossing the Alps in *The Prelude*. Wordsworth describes the 'immeasurable height I Of woods decaying, never to be decayed, I The stationary blasts of waterfalls' (VI. 624), suggesting that there may be permanence in repetition, for constant change produces constant stasis. The passage goes on to argue that the features of the mountains

Were all like workings of one mind, the features
Of the same face, blossom upon one tree;
Characters of the great Apocalypse,
The types and symbols of Eternity,
Of first, and last, and midst, and without end. (VI. 636)

The monumental Alps are emblems of their creator and thus are symbols of an Eternity beyond the confines of self but, as Mary Jacobus has argued, this perception threatens the individual consciousness with extinction. In referring to the end of the world and to Eternity, Wordsworth voices awareness of his mortality both as person and as writer, and so, as Jacobus suggests, 'unless both face and writing can be redefined as transcendental, inscription undoes the autobiographer's imagined presence in the text to leave only dead letters'. In order to evade the idea of his own death, Wordsworth tries to substitute divine writing – that is, the mark of the creator on the mountains – for his own.[22]

Wordsworth suggests that the powerful figure of the Author-God lies behind the individual author. This concept was articulated in detail by Coleridge in *Biographia Literaria*, where he argues that the *will* of the poet is a form of self-consciousness (the 'SUM/I AM'), in which the will of the creator-poet is at one with the will of the Creator-God: 'We begin with the I KNOW MYSELF, in order to end with the absolute I AM. We proceed from the SELF, in order to lose and find all self in God.' Poetic imagination thus becomes 'a repetition in the finite mind of the eternal act of creation in the infinite I AM' (*Works*, VII. i. 283, 304).

Woolf is sceptical of the attempts of Wordsworth and Coleridge to conceive of a kind of writing which is authoritative and can gain posterity because it has access to God. This challenge is made most strongly in her account of Bernard's encounter with death which tests rigorously any ideas about the possibility of permanence and the lasting power of literature. The sequence revolves around the closely related ideas of the loss of self and the loss of language. It begins when Bernard describes losing his sense of self, which was 'like a death'. He pictures the experience as an eclipse, where self and world disappear: 'The woods had vanished; the earth was a waste of shadow. No sound broke the silence of the wintry landscape. No cock crowed; no smoke rose; no train moved. A man without a self' (*W*, 238). Bernard's loss of self enables him to take a new perspective. In his account of the sunlight returning he recapitulates the opening interlude of the novel, for he sees a 'vapour as if earth were breathing in and out, once, twice, for the first time', echoing the sighing of the waves in the opening scene, and he sees a glimmer of daylight as if 'someone walks with a green light', repeating the earlier image of sunrise as a 'lamp' held over the sea by a woman. The idea of a second creation is stronger in the drafts, where Bernard says, 'Look at the world being reborn without me' (*HD*, I. 390).

Coming at this stage in the novel, the idea of a second creation conjures up images of the Apocalypse, from the Book of Revelation: 'I saw a new heaven and a new earth: for the first heaven and the first earth were passed away; and there was no more sea' (21: 1). This allusion to the last book in the Bible complements the echoes of Genesis in the opening chapter of the novel. The Apocalyptic allusions continue in the picture of Bernard riding against death on horseback, for Revelation depicts a battle in which kings and warriors and the 'Beast' are destroyed by a shadowy, god-like figure on horseback.[23] The image also invokes Plato's image of the soul as a horse in *Phaedrus*, thus evoking alternative (classical) interpretations of the end of life, as the beginning of the novel had suggested alternative views of creation.

Woolf does not accord biblical ideas any authority, for Bernard points at a truth beyond expression in language. Although he feels as though someone is showing him the truth – 'The old nurse who turns the pages of the picture-book had stopped and said, "Look. This is the truth"' (*W*, 240) – nothing is revealed to the reader. Instead, Bernard relays echoes: he quotes the nurse, who is pointing to something which the reader cannot see; he is not narrating the story in her picture-book, but merely adding 'a comment in the margin' (*W*, 200). Woolf implies that while one can hear echoes of voices which hint at the mysterious, no one has the power or authority to describe it directly.

Woolf's denial of the authority of writing is reinforced when Bernard's loss of self is followed by a loss of language. Speaking from a place beyond himself, he says that 'he is dead, the man I called "Bernard", the man who kept a book in his pocket in which he made notes' (*W*, 242–3). The ephemeral nature of language is emphasised when Bernard drops the book containing the phrases he had been collecting all his life, and suggests that there is now no difference between his notebook and other rubbish which the cleaner will sweep away (*W*, 246). Although these reflections on the ephemeral nature of writing echo Wordsworth's concerns in *The Prelude* that though books 'aspire to unconquerable life . . . they must perish' (V. 20, 22), Woolf goes further to suggest that truth evades expression in language. Woolf further questions whether a writer can transcend language and engage with mystery, when she commits Bernard to silence (*W*, 246). Silence means death for a writer, who can have no existence outside words.

Although Woolf ultimately denies that writing can create anything permanent out of the ephemeral, the final paragraphs reinforce the necessity, even the compulsion, to continue the effort of capturing life and truth in art. As Bernard walks out of the restaurant, he sees a new day dawning and becomes aware of the pattern of 'the eternal renewal, the incessant rise and fall and fall and rise again', suggesting that life will continue without him. Bernard's narration closes as he charges to face Death – but the novel still has one narrating voice left, for it ends with an interlude: '*The waves broke on the shore*'. This functions as a reminder of the rhythm of the waves, which are part of this eternal renewal. It suggests that literature is the result of a collective process and not of individual effort alone; that no work of art is a permanent, monumental achievement, for future generations need to sustain the process of renewal and keep attempting to express truths.

III

Woolf's method in Bernard's summing-up demonstrates a form of writing which involves the making and renewing of phrases for, even more than the rest of the novel, it is a palimpsest of quotations from other works, many of which appear in the form of quotations of the quotations which had appeared earlier in *The Waves*, or in other of Woolf's novels. This represents a radical new configuration of her relationship with the literary past.

The summing-up recapitulates the story as it has been told already, but crucially it reiterates the allusions which have become motifs within the novel. Bernard recalls some of his friends through their literary refrains. He recalls Rhoda through her love of Shelley and the only phrase he recalls from a visit to her is a quotation: '"Away!" she said. "The moor is dark beneath the moon"' (*W*, 229). Rhoda's Shelleyan refrain, 'For whom?' is used by Bernard when he recalls his own mourning for Percival, thus making both Rhoda and Shelley part of his own iteration. He remembers going to comfort Susan when she saw Jinny kissing Louis: 'twisting her pocket-handkerchief, Susan cried, "I love, I hate". "A worthless servant," I observed, "laughs upstairs in the attic"' (*W*, 207). Susan's phrase has contestable origins: the more likely source is Catullus's 'Odi et amo' (*W*, 249 n.), but Woolf also made a note of the phrase 'love, hate' in her reading-notes for Dostoevsky's *The Possessed*.[24] In Bernard's recollection of the scene, he adds a reply which did not appear in the first account and recalls the laughter from the attic heard in *Jane Eyre*. Both he and Susan speak in other people's words, thus drawing attention to the inadequacy of language to help us address specific situations. Later in the summing-up, Bernard repeats Susan's phrase in his own voice: 'better to be like Susan and love and hate the heat of the sun' (*W*, 222). Here, Susan's line is allied with Clarissa Dalloway's refrain from *Cymbeline*, thus recalling one of Woolf's earlier novels indirectly by alluding to its most prominent allusion. Further, less obvious examples of this process include the repeated phrase 'mop and mow' (*W*, 213, 214) from *King Lear*, which appeared in *Orlando*; Bernard's description of how 'the earth . . . hangs pendent', which recalls the 'pendent world' from *Measure for Measure* (III. i. 125) quoted in *Night and Day* (*ND*, 158); and 'the savage, the hairy man' Bernard sees in himself, which conjures up Caliban or Comus, both of whom lie behind Dr Lesage in *The Voyage Out*. Through these dense allusions, Woolf develops a voice which is inextricably bound up with the literary past.

The summing-up is unique within the novel for featuring two clusters of assorted quotations. The first occurs when Bernard reflects on the inadequacy of trite phrases used by biographers but concludes that:

> One cannot despise these phrases laid like Roman roads across the tumult of our lives, since they compel us to walk in step like civilized people with the slow and measured tread of policemen though one may be humming any non-sense under one's breath at the same time – 'Hark, hark, the dogs do bark,' 'Come away, come away, death,' 'Let me not to the marriage of true minds'. (*W*, 216–17)

Bernard's mixture of recitations reflects upon the worthlessness of *all* phrases, for a line from a nursery-rhyme and two quotations from Shakespeare – the opening lines of Feste's song from *Twelfth Night* (II. iv. 51) and Sonnet 116, respectively – are alike dismissed as nonsense. The literary past becomes a kind of undertow which continues to sound behind anything we write or say.

The process of 'humming' phrases whilst hearing, reading or writing others suggests a contrapuntal approach, which is highly significant to Woolf's own use of quotation in this part of the novel. In her diary entry for 22 December 1930, she records that she decided on the structure of the summing-up while listening to Beethoven (*D*, III. 339), and in this passage we have a musical effect of phrases being voiced at the same time, like different parts in a classical score, sometimes echoing themes heard earlier in the work, or melodies derived from elsewhere. The second cluster of quotations, much later in the summing-up, also follows this musical model, for two phrases from the first cluster, 'Hark, hark, the dogs do bark' and 'Come away, come away, death', are repeated and interspersed with two new quotations, 'Pillicock sat on Pillicock's hill' – another phrase with a distant origin, for it comes from an old rhyme which Edgar sings in his guise as the madman Poor Tom in *King Lear* (III. iv. 73) – and 'the world's great age begins anew' from Shelley's 'Hellas'. This time, Bernard acknowledges that he is 'mingling nonsense with poetry' (*W*, 236) although tellingly he does not say which is which.

Woolf's method of using quotations in this episode puts into practice the ideas about authorial identity and literary posterity that underlie the novel. The quotations, whether or not they are set in quotation marks, are detached from their original contexts and from their authors. In fact, contexts are called into question for, as we have seen, some quotations have ambiguous origins, or have already been quoted earlier (and so are re-contextualised here). As a result of drawing attention to the ambiguity of origins, Woolf calls into question authorial ownership of any given phrase, most notably in the example where Bernard echoes Edgar's recitation of an old rhyme in *King Lear*. This process suggests that Woolf anticipated Roland Barthes' perception that meaning cannot be overdetermined by the author, but is subject to reinterpretation and reconstitution:

> A text is not a line of words releasing a single 'theological' meaning (the 'message' of the Author-God) but a multi-dimensional space in which a variety of writings, none of them original, blend and clash. The text is a tissue of quotations drawn from the innumerable centres of culture.[25]

In doing so, Woolf challenges the Romantic conception of the author as creative genius; as Banfield notes, she 'reconceived literature to make it, not the Romantic expression of personality, but an impersonal vision'.[26] Woolf proposes a conception of an author who *listens* to the voices of others, retrieves the fragments of what they say and reshapes their words into new forms. This may be seen in Bernard's intention 'to seek among the phrases and fragments something unbroken' (*W*, 222), to use words to suture fragments, 'shattering and piecing together . . . I retrieved them from formlessness with words' (*W*, 225). By extension, Woolf's method implies a fluid form for literary tradition by which each generation and each writer seeks to suture and make whole what has gone before, by allowing the words of past writers to be heard within their own voices.

Notes

1. Indeed, Woolf had described *Jacob's Room* as her first novel using her own method and voice (*D*, II. 186), suggesting that her conception of her 'own' style was in a state of continual change and development.
2. See Introduction, pp. 5–6 above.
3. As Banfield has noted, Woolf's theory of knowledge involved two processes: 'Each aspirant to knowledge must shed the "I" opening to the world, then return to privacy . . . The return to a privacy deep in the perspective's centre . . . paradoxically exits into pure exteriority.' (*The Phantom Table*, pp. 179, 180).
4. Ibid., p. 293.
5. Starr, *Defoe and Spiritual Autobiography*, p. 48.
6. Woolf, 'Woolf and *The Waves*', p. 25.
7. Marcus, 'Britannia Rules *The Waves*', pp. 137, 145.

8. *Don Juan* II, st. 86.
9. *Reading Notebooks*, p. 228.
10. McConnell, '"Death Among the Apple Trees"'. Lee points to Woolf's affinities with Romanticism in 'A Burning Glass'.
11. McNichol, introduction to *Collected Novels of Virginia Woolf*; Flint, introduction to *The Waves* (Penguin); Davida Beth Pines, 'William Wordsworth and Virginia Woolf: Assertion and Dissolution of Self'.
12. Pines, 'William Wordsworth and Virginia Woolf', pp. 33–5. Wordsworth, *Poems, in Two Volumes, and Other Poems, 1800–1807*, p. 428. This note was dictated by Wordsworth to Isabella Fenwick in 1843; Woolf would have known the Fenwick Notes, which appeared in editions of Wordsworth's poems from the 1890s onwards (Logan, *Wordsworthian Criticism*, pp. 75, 78).
13. See Chapter 7, pp. 192–4 below, for an account of how another moment of being described in 'Sketch' is drawn from Coleridge and explored through fiction in *Between the Acts*.
14. Kate Flint, note to the Penguin edition of *The Waves*, p. 229.
15. Richter, *Woolf: The Inward Voyage*, pp. 149, 162.
16. Gill describes Wordsworth as 'a profoundly religious poet' whose poetry 'eschews doctrine and dogma and is not Christ-centred' (*Wordsworth: The Prelude*, pp. 39–40).
17. For Woolf's engagement with Darwinian ideas, see Beer, 'Woolf and Pre-History'.
18. Woolf first mentions reading Dante on 20 August 1930 (*D*, III. 313 and the last reference for several years is on 10 January 1931 (*D*, IV. 5–6). The second typescript is dated 13 June 1930 to 7 February 1931.
19. Dante, *The Inferno*, III. 52–7. Although T. S. Eliot used the last of these lines to describe London in *The Waste Land* ('I had not thought death had undone so many'), it is significant that Woolf circumvents his influence by using her own, more prosaic, translation, 'millions have died'.
20. Here again Woolf sidesteps a quotation used by Eliot, referring to Cleopatra's original 'barge' which Eliot had changed to 'The chair she sat in, like a burnished throne' (*The Waste Land*, l. 77).
21. Wordsworth, *Poetical Works*, p. 494.
22. Jacobus, *Romanticism, Writing and Sexual Difference*, p. 7.
23. Revelation 19: 19–20.
24. Berg, Holograph Reading Notes, vol. 14.
25. Barthes, *Image–Music–Text*, p. 146.
26. Banfield, *Phantom Table*, p. 386.

Bringing the Literary Past to Life in *Between the Acts*

Virginia Woolf's engagement with the literary past was at its most urgent and intense in *Between the Acts*. Written against the backdrop of the escalation of the Fascist threat and the outbreak of the Second World War, a period Woolf feared might signal 'the complete ruin not only of civilization in Europe, but of our last lap' (*D*, V. 162), it betrays a concern to preserve a threatened culture in writing. Set in June 1939, shortly before the outbreak of war, the novel encapsulates a form of English society which was about to disappear. Literature is given a prominent place within this account, both in Miss La Trobe's pageant, which parodies several phases of English literary history and is peppered with allusions, and in the collection of glancing allusions, quotations and misquotations which, as Gillian Beer has noted, are 'combed through' the novel as a whole.[1] However, the novel also reflects an awareness of the difficulties and dangers both in looking back to the literary past and in writing new work at such a crucial point in world history. This awareness was prominent in Woolf's non-fiction at the time and forms a significant part of the dynamic of *Between the Acts*.

Woolf's ambivalence about the value and relevance of literature at a time of danger is central to her argument in *Three Guineas* about whether it is possible to prevent war by protecting culture and intellectual liberty. *Between the Acts*, begun less than a month after *Three Guineas* was completed, continues this debate. Significant tensions emerge clearly at the end of the essay where, having discussed various strategies for preventing war, Woolf remarks to her fictional correspondent that 'even here, even now' she is tempted

> to listen not to the bark of the guns and the bray of the gramophones but to the voices of the poets, answering each other, assuring us of a unity that rubs out divisions as if they were chalk marks only; to discuss with you the capacity of the human spirit to overflow boundaries and make unity out of multiplicity. But that would be to dream . . . the dream of peace, the dream of

freedom. But, with the sound of the guns in your ears you have not asked us to dream. (*3G*, 163)

Woolf now sees reading poetry as a frivolous pleasure, an escapist action which simultaneously tries to ignore the harsh realities of the political situation and seeks false reassurance by celebrating unattainable idealistic values. This is the last in a series of rhetorical turns by which Woolf suggests that literature cannot answer the pressing questions of the time: 'we must cease to hang over old bridges, humming old songs' (*3G*, 28); 'we are not here to sing old songs or to fill in missing rhymes. We are here to consider facts' (*3G*, 77); 'Let us shut the New Testament, Shakespeare, Shelley, Tolstoy and the rest, and face the fact that stares us in the face' (*3G*, 80).

Behind each of these statements, however, lies a strong desire to turn to literature for answers: Woolf has to remind herself to stop singing songs and reading books precisely because she keeps turning to literature for enlightenment on difficult issues. Thus, she discusses instances of male domination in Sophocles' *Antigone* and Thackeray's *Pendennis*; she quotes and discusses Goethe's view of women; and she draws examples from the lives of writers, such as Charlotte Brontë, crushed by patriarchal oppression, and Wilfred Owen, cut down by war. The undertow of the argument in *Three Guineas* is that literature matters and should be a source of help.

That said, the ending of *Three Guineas* also attests to an almost physical discomfort in trying to read literature at a time when more urgent issues command attention. These are represented as auditory disturbances whereby the external noises of the guns and the gramophones interfere with the internalised sound of poetry, the conversation between poets which Woolf habitually staged in her imagination. Woolf's diary entries about her reading whilst writing *Between the Acts* suggest that she wanted to listen to writers' voices but was frustrated by interruptions and disturbances caused by background noises. Two of the authors mentioned most frequently in Woolf's diary from 1938 onwards – Coleridge and Mme de Sévigné – are characterised as great talkers. Woolf's essay on de Sévigné is littered with references to listening: 'we live in her presence, and often fall, as with living people, into unconsciousness. She goes on talking, we half-listen' (*CE*, III. 66). Woolf conveys a similar sense of listening to Coleridge in 'The Man at the Gate': 'We . . . when the voice stops only half an hour before he passed that July day in 1834 into silence, feel bereft' (*CE*, III. 221). Hermione Lee concurs that listening to Coleridge was vital for Woolf at this time: 'Coleridge's voice, from *Three Guineas* onwards through the war, provided her with a life-line, an alternative to the "besieging voices" of radio and loudspeaker and manifestos.'[2]

The interruptions to reading which Woolf felt most keenly were those brought about by the war, although she also bemoaned intrusions by other people and the effects of her own anxieties (such as when she could not concentrate on Coleridge whilst awaiting reviews of her biography of Roger Fry (*D*, V. 307)). In April 1939, she noted that her fears about the coming war prevented her from engaging fully with La Rochefoucauld and Chaucer: 'So if I had any time – but perhaps next week will be more solitudinous – I should, if it weren't for the war – glide my way up and up in to that exciting layer so rarely lived in: where my mind works so quick it seems asleep' (*D*, V. 214). In August 1940, she remarked that noises generated by military exercises prevented her from retreating into the solitude of pure thought, either in reading or writing: 'if I had solitude – no men driving stakes digging fresh gun emplacements & no neighbours, doubtless I cd. expand and soar – into PH. [Pointz Hall] into Coleridge' (*D*, V. 310). The term 'Coleridge' here refers to both Coleridge's writings and two essays Woolf was writing about him: the distractions therefore disrupt the complementary processes of reading and writing by which she 'composed', or formed her own mental image of a work as she read it. In March 1939, whilst lamenting Franco's accession in Spain, she noted 'I have just read [Shelley's] "Mont Blanc" but cant make it "compose"' (*D*, V. 206). In July 1940, she struggled to remember a poem by Shelley, even when trying to draw on him for solace as invasion was threatened: 'Thus our island will be invaded – my season of calm weather. Many ~~an island~~ a green isle – why cant I remember poetry?' (*D*, V. 307).[3]

Woolf dramatises these problems in her description of the library at Pointz Hall in *Between the Acts*. The scene is introduced with the Romantic notion that 'Books are the mirrors of the soul', but this idea is simultaneously undercut by the fact that it is the view of a 'foolish, flattering lady' (*BA*, 15). The lofty ideal is further diminished by the revelation that the library contains a collection of cheap novels left by visitors who had bought them to stave off boredom on their train journeys. This signals that readers' needs and interests extend to areas beyond those addressed in 'high-brow' literature: 'Nobody could pretend, as they looked at the shuffle of shilling shockers that weekenders had dropped, that the looking-glass always reflected the anguish of a Queen or the heroism of King Harry' (*BA*, 15). There is a tension here between deploring contemporary reading habits and suggesting that the literary classics may not be able to help one understand modern life. Furthermore, it is no coincidence that Woolf alludes dismissively to *Henry V*, a play com-

monly hailed as a celebration of military prowess and English nationalism: a hint that literature can sometimes endorse war rather than help
prevent it.

A comparable ambivalence is found in Woolf's description of Isa
Oliver's reading habits. Although the narrator criticises Isa for being
'book-shy', this is not necessarily an authorial judgement, for the
comment comes from the perspective of her father-in-law Bart (the voice
criticises her for being 'gun-shy' too). The comment is also not entirely
true: Isa is not ignorant of literature, for she has just muttered some lines
by Shelley. Rather, Isa finds books unhelpful: 'What remedy was there for
her at her age – the age of the century, thirty-nine – in books?' (*BA*, 18).
Her age makes her representative of a particular generation, so that her
quest for something to read becomes a more general rhetorical question
about how literature might be of help at such a crucial time. We are told
that 'the newspaper was a book' for Isa's generation. Although it does
not reflect well on Isa that she initially turns to the newspaper for entertainment, being attracted by a reference to a fantastic 'horse with a green
tail' (*BA*, 18), the article plunges her into harsh reality, for it leads into
an account of a rape trial. The sequence would have taken Woolf's original readers out of the fictional context and straight into real life, for the
case mentioned was a real one.[4] This shift of focus is analogous to the
moments in *Three Guineas* where the narrator urges the reader to stop
reciting old poems and consider hard facts.

Between the Acts also shows how personal enjoyment of literature can
be disrupted. It is significant that books at Pointz Hall generally remain
closed (Lucy Swithin's reading of *An Outline of History* being one
notable example), for this novel concentrates on the oral delivery of literature, a form which renders it especially prone to the intrusion of
everyday noises. Characters quote literary works frequently but their
quotations are usually inaccurate or unfinished. Sometimes this is due to
memory lapses, such as Bart Oliver's two fragmentary quotations from
Byron (*BA*, 5). At other times, recitations are cut short by everyday concerns, such as when Isa starts to recall Shelley but then breaks off to make
a mundane statement about ordering fish (*BA*, 17).

Woolf's account of Miss La Trobe's play is also a study of an attempt to
recite literature, for it is made up of literary fragments. It also attests to the
difficulties of being creative in the face of the 'torture' of interruptions'
(*BA*, 73). Within the first few moments of the pageant, audience members
whisper to one another, a speaker forgets her lines, the gramophone fails
to work, the words of speakers are blown away by the wind, and a latecomer disturbs both actors and audience. The programme for the pageant
has to allow two intervals to fit in with domestic arrangements, and Miss

La Trobe feels aggrieved at being forced to 'gash' a scene to accommodate a tea-break (*BA*, 85).

Woolf's account of Miss La Trobe's struggle with her production addresses a further, complementary set of questions, concerning the political usefulness of reading literature and the difficulties in writing against the background of dissonant noises. Woolf raised these issues in her essay 'Why Art Follows Politics', published in *The Daily Worker* in 1936. She noted that conditions for creativity had changed in recent years, for the artist's studio was now 'far from being a cloistered spot where he can contemplate his model or his apple in peace', for it was 'beseiged by voices, all disturbing, some for one reason, some for another' (*CE*, II. 232). Here again she characterises political crisis in terms of auditory disturbance or interruption, and she lists as examples the noises of radio news; the voices of dictators addressing the public by megaphone in the streets, and public opinion which, Woolf wrote, called upon artists to prove their social and political usefulness. In totalitarian political systems, artists were forced to compromise and use their work for political purposes – to 'celebrate fascism; celebrate communism' (*CE*, II. 232) in order to be allowed to practise at all.

Although this essay was specifically about a predicament in the plastic arts and acknowledged that writing could and did deal with political issues, Woolf suggested that poetry had been damaged by the intrusion of politics in 'The Leaning Tower' (1940). She expressed anxiety at the pressure placed on the poets of the 1930s to address the public: the poet in the 1930s 'was forced to be a politician. That explains why the artist in the thirties was forced to be a scapegoat' (*CE*, II. 176). She criticised the work of Louis MacNeice, Cecil Day Lewis, Stephen Spender and others whom she saw as adopting intrusive outside voices as their own in 'the pedagogic, the didactic, the loud-speaker strain that dominates their poetry' (*CE*, II. 175).

Woolf's portrait of Miss La Trobe is in many ways a case-study of this predicament. Like the 1930s poets, La Trobe incorporates the noises of modern life into her work: the pageant is driven by the sound of the gramophone, and she addresses the audience through a loudspeaker, an instrument which Woolf associated with Fascist dictators. La Trobe also attempts to be didactic, to make the audience see her point of view, although this didacticism is also shown to be ineffective because she continually despairs of any possibility of 'making them see'. Like the 1930s poets, too, La Trobe has taken the role of the politician, for her aim to teach her audience is dangerously close to a desire to coerce. Nicknamed Bossy, she plans her play like a naval battle: she stands 'in the attitude proper to an Admiral on his quarter-deck' and decides 'to risk the engagement out of doors' (*BA*, 57). The analogy between the staging of a pageant and a military attack plays on an ambiguity implicit in the title of the novel: the acts of the play (between which the narrative of the novel takes place) are analogous to the two 'acts' of the world wars between which the novel is set. La Trobe is, again like the 1930s poets, something of a scapegoat, for she is an outsider to the community: she is not local and is possibly of foreign extraction, she is a lesbian with a mysterious past, and she is not befriended by the locals for she goes to the pub alone after the show.

As the first half of this chapter will demonstrate, Woolf turned to literature to address these dilemmas, for her ongoing reading of Coleridge during the last years of her life helped to inform her thinking on the value and use of reading and writing literature. As we will see, Woolf turned to Coleridge's ideas about unity and integrity as an antidote to the interruptions she faced, adapting and revising Romantic tropes to address a fragmented world in *Between the Acts*. We will also see how Woolf drew on Coleridge's ideas to think through problems concerning the social role of artists in times of war.

I

Although Woolf had read Coleridge regularly throughout her life and had cited him in her earlier works (for example, in drawing on his concept of androgyny in *A Room of One's Own*), she read him intensively whilst writing *Between the Acts*. This heightened engagement began when she studied his essays for *Three Guineas*, as can be seen from the footnotes (*3G*, 205–6). She went on to read a wide selection of his work during her most intensive period of activity on *Between the Acts*, from May to November 1940, including his correspondence with Wordsworth, his poems and *Biographia Literaria* (*D*, V. 289, 289, 300). Although Woolf undertook this reading primarily in preparation for her essays 'Sara Coleridge' and 'The Man at the Gate' (the latter being a review of *Coleridge the Talker*, a collection of memoirs edited by Richard Armor and Raymond Howes), her diaries express pleasure in the project, such as when she anticipates being able to 'settle in very happily I think to Coleridge' (*D*, V. 305).

We have seen that Woolf sought in Coleridge a relief from the interruptions of everyday life, such as when she wanted to 'expand and soar' into his work despite the sounds of military workers outside (*D*, V. 310). Coleridge's work had the potential to satisfy the desire expressed at the end of *Three Guineas* to listen to 'the voices of the poets' and 'make unity out of multiplicity', for he espoused values of unity and harmony, for example in his vision in 'The Eolian Harp' of nature united by 'one intellectual Breeze, | At once the Soul of each, and God of all' (l. 47), and in his quest in *Table Talk* to 'reduce all knowledges into harmony' (*Works*, XIV, i. 248).

Woolf's reading of Coleridge intersected with her own writings of the time in a particularly dynamic way, for it is possible to trace a three-way interaction between *Between the Acts*, Woolf's memoir 'A Sketch of the Past' and her work on Coleridge. Woolf describes her own development as a writer in 'Sketch' in remarkably similar terms to the ones she uses for Coleridge in 'The Man at the Gate'. In a section of the memoir written in April 1939, Woolf describes her own experience of a state of passivity in 'exceptional moments' which 'brought with them a peculiar horror and a physical collapse; they seemed dominant; myself passive' (*MB*, 83); in the essay, Woolf described Coleridge as 'paralysed', 'incapable of action', 'a passive target for innumerable arrows, all of them sharp, many of them poisoned' (*CE*, III. 217). This suggests that her picture of him is drawn through the filter of her own imagination and sensibilities; that she wilfully called him up as an extension or mirror image of herself. Reading between 'The Man at the Gate' and 'A Sketch of the Past', we see that Woolf suggests that both she and Coleridge are writers by virtue of their sensibility and their ability to convert such experiences into words. She imagines Coleridge using words as a comfort: 'he uses words most often to express the crepitations of his apprehensive susceptibility. They serve as a smoke-screen between him and the menace of the real world' (*CE*, III. 219). She describes her own use of words as a form of protection – words provide a way of making a moment 'whole; this wholeness means that it has lost its power to hurt me' (*MB*, 84), although where Woolf sees Coleridge using words to hide, she presents herself as using them to make reality clearer.

An ideal of wholeness, derived from Coleridge himself, lies behind both these accounts. This can be seen in the last of the three 'moments of being' described in 'A Sketch of the Past' where Woolf draws on Coleridge to frame a childhood experience which, she suggests, was one of the things which led to her becoming a writer:

> I was looking at the flower bed by the front door; 'That is the whole', I said. I was looking at a plant with a spread of leaves; and it seemed suddenly plain that the flower itself was a part of the earth; that a ring enclosed what was the flower; and that was the real flower; part earth; part flower. (*MB*, 82)

Although Woolf is describing an incident from early childhood, she reclaims and frames that memory in language and imagery she had acquired later. Here she appropriates a model of poetic creativity from Coleridge to account for her creative response to the plant. As M. H. Abrams has pointed out, Coleridge's 'concept of poetic creativity . . . that self-organizing process, assimilating disparate materials by an inherent lawfulness into an integral whole – borrows many of its characteristic features from the conceptual model of organic growth'.[5] Coleridge used the analogy of the plant growing from a seed to emphasise the importance of fusing elements into unity in poetry:

> In the World we see every where evidences of a Unity, which the component parts are so far from explaining, that they necessarily pre-suppose it as the cause and condition of their existing *as* those parts: or even of their existing at all . . . That the root, stem, leaves, petals, &c., [of this crocus] cohere to one plant, is owing to an antecedent Power or Principle in the Seed, which existed before a single particle of the matters that constitute the *size* and visibility of the Crocus, had been attracted from the surrounding Soil, Air, and Moisture. (*Works*, IX. 75–6)

The growth of the many parts of one plant from one seed here becomes an analogy for a metaphysical unity underlying the world: Coleridge goes on to say that this betokens 'One universal Presence' behind the world, whose existence may be both deduced rationally and experienced spiritually through revelation (*Works*, IX. 77). Woolf attaches importance to revelation when she argues that, following the 'shock' of a 'moment of being' there comes 'a revelation of some order; it is a token of some real thing behind appearances; and I make it real by putting it into words' (*MB*, 84). However, while Coleridge couches his argument in the Unitarian terminology of the 'One universal Presence', Woolf significantly uses a more provisional expression, 'some real thing behind appearances' – a hint that Woolf is not wholly confident in or satisfied by Coleridge's concept of spiritual unity, and as with Lily Briscoe's 'little daily miracles' (*TL*, 218), this vision is fleeting and needs art to give it permanence. Woolf's suspicions about organic wholeness were based partly on an awareness that it could not withstand the outside forces of conflict and fragmentation. This is at the heart of her sense that it was useless to listen to 'poets answering one another' at a time of crisis. Woolf interrogates this concept of wholeness more rigorously in *Between the Acts*. In a section written in April 1938 which effectively becomes a trial run for 'A Sketch of the Past', she describes her vision of the flower from the perspective of George, a small boy looking at a flower as he plays in the grass:

> The flower blazed between the angles of the roots. Membrane after membrane was torn. It blazed a soft yellow, a lambent light under a film of velvet; it filled

the caverns behind the eyes with light. All that inner darkness became a hall,
leaf smelling, earth smelling of yellow light. And the tree was beyond the
flower; the grass, the flower and the tree were entire. Down on his knees grub-
bing he held the flower complete. (*BA*, 10)

George's perception of the integrity of the single flower and its connections with its natural surroundings is drawn from Coleridge's notion of
organic unity in nature. The passage also explores the process by which
the human mind becomes part of nature, as the distinction between inner
and outer space is elided, and George seems to become one with the
flower. This theme found in 'The Eolian Harp' where Coleridge speculates that nature inspires thought and poetry:

> . . . what if all of animated nature
> Be but organic Harps diversly fram'd,
> That tremble into thought, as o'er them sweeps
> Plastic and vast, one intellectual Breeze,
> At once the Soul of each, and God of all? (l. 44)

As in George's vision, inner and outer worlds are elided, for all of nature
– including humankind – is compared to the harp, and all are said to
share one soul, which derives from God. However, Woolf's narration of
the scene from a child's perspective suggests that a belief in unity with
nature might be a naïve one. George's moment of being is shown up as
transitory, for it is interrupted by the intrusion of the adult world, when
Bart frightens him by using a rolled-up newspaper as a mask. We know
that the newspaper carried the story of the rape trial and we can assume
that it also reflected the mounting political crisis, thus drawing attention
to forces which frustrate hopes for unity.

This exemplifies Woolf's sense that Romantic ideas were inadequate
for dealing with the situation in England during the Second World War.
In 'The Leaning Tower' (1940), Woolf drew an explicit contrast between
the Napoleonic Wars of the 1790s when Coleridge and Wordsworth
were writing, when news travelled slowly and the conflict was distant,
and her own time, when she could hear gunfire over the Channel and
Hitler's voice on the radio (*CE*, II. 164). In *Between the Acts*, Woolf
implicitly criticises Coleridge's 'Fears in Solitude', which was concerned
with a threatened invasion by France in April 1798. Coleridge contrasts
the current peace and beauty of the landscape with future destruction, as
he imagines 'What uproar and what strife may now be stirring | This way
or that way o'er these silent hills', and fears 'Carnage and groans beneath
this blessed sun!' (ll. 33, 39), but he concludes that 'solitary musings' and
'nature's quietness' will allay his fears and renew his sense of charity
towards his fellow human beings. Coleridge's fears are echoed in the

thoughts of Giles Oliver as he contemplates a German invasion: 'At any moment guns would rake that land into furrows; planes splinter Bolney Minster into smithereens and blast the Folly.' Yet it is clear that the Romantic love of nature or fellow human beings is unattainable, for Giles 'blamed Aunt Lucy, looking at views, instead of – doing what?' (*BA*, 49).

Woolf rethinks Coleridge's conception of unity in her examination of the relationship between humankind and nature. Coleridge saw nature as having been provided for human contemplation and use. His concept of 'animated nature' in the 'The Eolian Harp' was essentially restricted to humankind: sentient beings capable of thought. Woolf questions this anthropocentric assumption in Giles's prediction that 'guns would rake that land into furrows', which suggests that agricultural cultivation and destruction caused by warfare are much the same and that humankind can be at odds with the natural world.

Woolf further examines the implications of humans using the natural world for their own purposes by considering the relationship between the artist and nature in Miss La Trobe's attempts to stage a village pageant in the grounds of Pointz Hall. La Trobe is caught between imposing meaning on the natural environment and subordinating her own will to nature. For example, as she surveys the performance space she thinks that the trees were

> regular enough to suggest columns in a church; in a church without a roof; in an open-air cathedral, a place where swallows darting seemed . . . to make a pattern, dancing, like the Russians, only not to music, but to the unheard rhythm of their own wild hearts. (*BA*, 59–60)

This passage traces a progression from Miss La Trobe's attempt at artifice – her idea of using the trees to represent a church – to a celebration of the energies of nature itself, where the swallows' movements supplant her intended scenario as the focus of interest. La Trobe's quandary echoes the Romantic preference for art drawn directly from the natural world, rather than based on artistic convention: it can be seen as an extension of Coleridge's suggestion in *Biographia Literaria* that the greatest poetry 'while it blends and harmonises the natural and the artificial, still subordinates art to nature' (*Works*, VII, ii. 17). Woolf takes Coleridge's suggestion to its logical conclusion by suggesting that art breaks down when it encounters the natural world.

The nature which impinges upon La Trobe's play is not simply the spiritual force to which Coleridge responded, but a post-Darwinian nature which acknowledges links between humankind and the animal and vegetable worlds.[6] This can be seen at two points when the narrative of La

Trobe's play breaks down and nature intervenes, and an implicit connection is made between the failure of art, the fall of great civilisations and a resulting resurgence of the natural world. In the first case, the actors have just been singing about the fall of Babylon, Ninevah, Troy and Rome. The words of their song, '*Where the plover nests was the arch . . . through which the Romans trod*' (*BA*, 125; ellipsis and emphasis in original), suggest that nature takes over as birds build their nests in the crumbling architecture of once-great civilisations. Just as La Trobe feels that her illusion has failed, the gap is filled by the noise of a herd of cows like 'the primeval voice sounding loud in the ear of the present moment . . . The cows annihilated the gap; bridged the distance; filled the emptiness and continued the emotion.' (*BA*, 126) The sound of the cows undoes the effects of civilisation, suggesting a return to the primal swamp which Darwin identified as the origin of all life. Even so, there are vestiges here of the Romantic notion of 'sentient' nature, for the mournful sound of the cows articulates the sense of loss which La Trobe is trying to convey.

Nature similarly inscribes a sense of cultural loss the second time it intervenes in the play. Miss La Trobe tries to present a scene entitled, 'The present time. Ourselves', wanting the audience to see present-time reality with no action depicted on stage, but they are awaiting the traditional ensemble ending to an Empire Day pageant, and cannot make sense of the play without it. La Trobe again feels that she has failed; but then the rain falls: 'Down it poured like all the people in the world weeping'. This intervention of nature generates an emotion – not one of triumph, as a jingoistic parade would have done, but one of sorrow – and La Trobe feels that 'Nature once more had taken her part' (*BA*, 162). Untamed nature fills a gap left after art (or 'culture') has broken down, but continues its sentiment.

Although these transitions indicate the breakdown of culture, they also rehearse in an extreme form the Romantic values of expression over form, and rugged nature over structured landscaping. The intervention of nature after the failure of art, and after the song about the fall of great civilisations, is reminiscent of Wordsworth's comment in the *Prelude* that 'power had reverted' to nature at the end of the Reign of Terror in France. Wordsworth had advocated a return to human nature – common sense and intuition – for guidance; Woolf, however, invokes a more fearful image of a surrender to the animal and vegetable elements of nature, rather than celebrating human nature or the 'spiritual' powers of the natural world.

Woolf's reworking of Romantic ideas shapes her ideas of how art might be rebuilt after the breakdown of civilisation. As La Trobe contemplates her disappointment with the pageant, she sees a flock of starlings attacking a tree: 'The whole tree hummed with the whizz they made, as if each bird plucked a wire' (*BA*, 188). She then discovers the germ of her next piece, for 'something rose to the surface' and she imagines a curtain rising to reveal two figures on the stage. Shortly afterwards she hears the first words of the new play: 'Words of one syllable sank down into the mud. She drowsed; she nodded. The mud became fertile' (*BA*, 191). The image of birds plucking wires is suggestive of Coleridge's equation of natural sounds with harp music in 'The Eolian Harp', and in 'The Nightingale' where the birds 'all burst forth in choral minstrelsy, I As if some sudden gale had swept at once I A hundred airy harps!' (l.80), and the analogy of the creative process to the sowing of seeds, echoes Coleridge's organic model for poetic creativity. These ideas are clearly only fragmentary, La Trobe's vision of a new play only hints at a new kind of writing which might emerge through conflict and social upheaval. We do not hear the 'wonderful words' of the new play; the vision prefigures the close of *Between the Acts* ('Then the curtain rose. They spoke'), but there again we are left in ignorance of what happens next. While Woolf cannot look forward, she does look back to adapt the ideas of Coleridge and Wordsworth whose work had also spanned a period of war and cultural revolution.

Woolf's re-reading of Romanticism suggests a conception of nature which was both more inclusive and more heterogeneous than that adopted by Wordsworth or Coleridge. She emphasises heterogeneity – and illustrates the problems inherent in simplistic views of unity – in her depiction of Rev. Streatfield's response to the play:

> 'I thought I perceived that nature takes her part. Dare we, I asked myself, limit life to ourselves? May we not hold that there is a spirit that inspires, pervades . . .' (the swallows were sweeping round him. They seemed cognizant of his meaning . . .) (*BA*, 173)

Streatfield acts as a voice for Romanticism, for his notion of the inspirational power of nature echoes Coleridge's sentiments in 'The Eolian Harp'. While Streatfield's suggestion is partially endorsed, for the appearance of the swallows seems to lend credence to what he says, his analysis is also compromised when his speech is interrupted by intimations of war, as '[t]welve aeroplanes in perfect formation like a flight of wild duck came overhead' (*BA*, 174). The audience goes home disputing Streatfield's words: although they repeat his adage that 'Nature takes part', they also comment that 'if one spirit animates the whole, what about the aeroplanes?' (*BA*, 178). Through the intrusion of the planes, Woolf draws attention to the ways in which war and political conflict interrupt our contemplation of nature and appreciation of literature. It also raises questions about whether one spirit animates the whole: for either the planes are antithetical to the natural world and cannot be subsumed into one spirit; or, resembling *wild* ducks, they represent a possibly malign and certainly uncaring force of nature which cannot be controlled and is indifferent to human suffering. Woolf thus interrogates assumptions about wholeness or unity by suggesting that any attempt to see all things as part of one being must also account for discord and heterogeneity.

The episode also reveals that concepts of unity can be dangerously ideological. Streatfield underlines the importance of the pageant in bringing the villagers together as a community and he interprets the play as an appeal for social unity: 'To me at least it was indicated that we are members one of another. Each is part of the whole' (*BA*, 172). Coming from a clergyman, the speech carries echoes of St Paul's idea that the Christian Church is made up of 'many members, yet but one body' (I Corinthians 12: 12).[7] However, these sentiments are shown to be naïve in view of the social tensions which are clearly present in the community assembled at Pointz Hall – not least their exclusion of the homosexual William Dodge and the lesbian Miss La Trobe. As Judy Little notes, the pageant does not restore a sense of community, even though it resembles a festive comedy or seasonal ritual.[8]

Woolf had exposed a more sinister side of social unity in *Three Guineas*, where she showed how it had become an instrument of Fascism. In the essay, Woolf had used Coleridge and Rousseau to consider ways in which individuals could be part of society but also free. In the last footnote, she quotes Coleridge's argument that the ideal political constitution would be one which all people would obey voluntarily, not by coercion, but by reference to their own reason. Coleridge supported his statement by translating an adage from Rousseau (also quoted by Woolf): 'To find a form of society according to which each one uniting with the whole shall yet obey himself only and remain as free as before' (*Works*, IV, i. 192; *3G*, 206). However, Woolf goes on to note that the rise of Fascism had made the statement problematic, for people were coerced rather than reasoned into obedience. She suggests that such forces should be met with resistance: 'we are not passive spectators doomed to unresisting obedience but by our thoughts and actions can ourselves change that figure. A common interest unites us; it is one world, one life' (*3G*, 163). In the face of Fascism, a sense of common humanity cannot be demonstrated or preserved by giving in to the consensus, but by voicing opposition and entering into conflict if necessary.

Woolf's acknowledgement that discord and dissent were necessary led her to examine and revise Coleridge's view of the social role of writers.

Coleridge argued that poets in a liberal society should draw people in: poetry should be 'the high spiritual instinct of the human being impelling us to seek unity by harmonious adjustment, and thus establishing the principle, that *all* the parts of an organised whole must be assimilated to the more *important* and *essential* parts' (*Works*, VII, ii. 72). Poets and other learned people are attuned to the 'natural' harmony of a society and can help to reconcile individuals to it. Woolf invokes but interrogates these ideas in Miss La Trobe. She acknowledges the formidable obstacles to social unity, which La Trobe notices when she sees the audience gathering and feels aware that their 'minds and bodies were too close, yet not close enough' (*BA*, 60). Woolf also hints at the sinister implications of drawing an audience into an unthinking harmonious group: for example, when the click of a gramophone needle at the start of the play 'seemed to hold them together, tranced' (*BA*, 75), or when La Trobe 'summons' her audience to gather for the second act by playing a gramophone record, which appears to speak to a Romantic 'inner harmony' (*BA*, 107), but is in fact an act of coercion, for La Trobe feels frustrated that '[e]very moment the audience slipped the noose; split up into scraps and fragments' (*BA*, 110). La Trobe's use of the gramophone to unite her audience recalls *Three Guineas*, where gramophones are associated with the establishment and its war machine, suggesting that La Trobe's desire to unite her audience is potentially deeply conformist. Moreover, La Trobe's use of the 'megaphonic, anonymous, loud-speaking' voice (*BA*, 167–8) to make an appeal for social cohesion in the final scene (*'how's this wall, the great wall, which we call, perhaps miscall, civilization, to be built up by . . . orts, scraps and fragments like ourselves?'* (*BA*, 169)) links her to the European dictators whom Woolf associated with the megaphone. All these examples, then, hint that it is dangerous for artists to seek to create social cohesion at a time when social order and conformity were being championed by totalitarian states on both the right and left.

In the closing scene of the pageant, however, Woolf offers a model of how artists might be able to manage the fragmentation of society without resorting to coercive tactics. She does this by revising the romantic tropes of harmony and the mirror to propose a new aesthetic which can deal with contradictions and fragmentation. Jazz music becomes a metaphor for a shift from romantic ideas of harmony to purposeful dissonance. The last scene of the pageant is introduced by a modern tune which some audience members dismiss as cacophony. They see it as typical of the 'young, who can't make, but only break; shiver into splinters the old vision; smash to atoms what was whole' (*BA*, 164). On one level, the comment reflects a sociological shift, for jazz in the 1930s was an emblem of youthful rebellion. As Philip Larkin, recalling his own emerg-ing passion for jazz, notes: 'for the generations that came to adolescence between the wars jazz was that unique private excitement that youth seems to demand. In another age it might have been drink or drugs, relig-ion or poetry'.[9] On another, jazz music symbolises a process of breaking with established structures to form new, complex and (to the untrained ear) distorted ones: new ways of coming together.

The process is given a visual counterpart in the pageant, as the actors appear on stage holding a variety of shiny objects, which they move about so as to reflect the audience in parts rather than as a whole. Although the metaphor of the multiple mirrors had a contemporary counterpart in Cubism,[10] the wall of mirrors also deconstructs the famil-iar notion of art (and drama) as a 'mirror of nature': an idea which Shakespeare had expressed in *Hamlet*, and which became a popular metaphor for poetry among the Romantics, as M. H. Abrams pointed out in *The Mirror and the Lamp*. Coleridge uses the mirror metaphor in *Table Talk* to describe his philosophy:

> My system is the only attempt that I know of ever made to reduce all knowl-edges into harmony . . . I have endeavored to unite the insulated fragments of truth and frame a perfect mirror. I show to each system that I fully understand and rightfully appreciate what that system means; but then I lift up that system to a higher point of view, from which I enable it to see its former position where it was indeed, but under another light and with different relations; so that the fragment of truth is not only acknowledged, but explained. (*Works*, XIV, i. 248–9)

This passage holds fragmentation and unity in tension, for although Coleridge claims that his aim is to 'reduce . . . to harmony' and to 'unite' fragments of truth, he none the less appreciates the discrete nature of each fragment or system, and aims to take it first on its own terms and then to view it from another perspective (as though viewing it in a second mirror) in order to understand it. Thus, his endeavour for unity – or oneness – is undercut by his recognition of the importance of acknowl-edging multiple points of view. Woolf's reading of the mirror imagery in *Between the Acts* picks up on these fault-lines in Coleridge's apparently unified vision. She uses the jumbled mirrors to exploit multiplicity of per-spectives and undermine the possibility of creating unity and coherence out of difference. When the mirrors stop moving, the audience sees itself, but it is 'not whole by any means' (*BA*, 167), thus resisting (and expos-ing as false) the desire to unite the disparate, which Coleridge aimed to do in his philosophy.

Woolf proposes a new aesthetic (founded in a re-reading of Romanticism), which stresses the necessity to accommodate discordant elements without reducing them to harmony, and to take multiple points of view without fusing them into a simple mirror image. Woolf is more concerned with managing and accommodating conflict than with achieving resolution in *Between the Acts*. Even when the audience is united – such as at the end of the mirror scene, when the gramophone plays a conventional piece of music which nobody can name but everybody recognises – there is an undercurrent of dissonance beneath the harmony:

> the distracted united . . . from chaos and cacophony measure; but not the melody of surface sound alone controlled it; but also the warring battle-plumed warriors straining asunder . . . they crashed; solved; united. (*BA*, 169, 170)

The sequence suggests that the resolution achieved at the end of a piece of music is in part the result of discordant notes sounded earlier; that unity can only be achieved (and perhaps only be perceived) through the experience of conflict and fragmentation. The social implications of this are shown at the end of the novel, when the narrator notes that Giles and Isa Oliver must fight before they can embrace and procreate (*BA*, 197). Since war and interpersonal tension cannot simply be eradicated, they must be played through to their conclusion if new creativity is to emerge. Woolf holds unity and dispersity in tension during the novel, for she suggests that unity can only be perceived in contradistinction to fragmentation.

II

Woolf's concerns about managing fragmentation without falling into conventional or simplistic notions of unity may also be seen to inform the structure of *Between the Acts*, particularly in her use of the literary past. An early note, written in April 1938, suggests that she sought to take a compendious approach in order to write a novel which could accommodate disparate texts and ideas:

> Poyntzet Hall: a centre: all lit. discussed in connection with real little incongruous living humour; & anything that comes into my head; but 'I' rejected: 'We' substituted: to whom at the end there shall be an invocation? 'We' . . . composed of many different things . . . we all life, all art, all waifs & strays – a rambling capricious but somehow unified whole – the present state of my mind? (*D*, V. 135, ellipses in original)

Although Woolf starts with the classical unity of place at Pointz Hall, she plans to use it as a space in which to collect disparate elements, including literature and its implied opposite of 'living humour'. As we will see, this plan would provide Woolf with a way of addressing the problem of the multiple interruptions which increasingly beset her as she wrote the novel. It enabled her to accommodate fragments by holding them in tension rather than reducing them to a unified whole: as Jean Wyatt notes, Woolf's use of allusion in *Between the Acts* stresses diversity rather than unity.[11]

Woolf's meditations on identity in this passage are also highly significant for rejecting the monolithic masculine 'I', replacing it with a sense of group identity in 'we'. Melba Cuddy-Keane has shown that these ideas were partly a reaction to Freud's work on group identities which Woolf was reading at this time: in presenting 'the leaderless and fragmented community in *Between the Acts*, Woolf was offering a direct challenge to the powerful, leader-centred group postulated by Freud';[12] additionally, we can see them as rejections of Fascism. They are also bound up with her ongoing quarrel with Romantic ideas about authorial identity, for the shift from 'I' to 'we' dismisses the notion of the author as solitary genius or moral leader, and substitutes a model of creativity as a communal process whereby a writer expresses ideas garnered from a wider community and becomes a medium through which other voices may be heard.

Woolf's comments on Coleridge and Mme de Sévigné suggest that she discerned and admired polyphony in their work. Firstly, Woolf saw the works of both authors as intrinsically bound up with what they had read. In 'How it Strikes a Contemporary', Woolf had argued that Coleridge's critical writings emerged out of a profound engagement with the work of others: she imagined him 'brewing in his head the whole of poetry and letting issue now and then one of those profound general statements which are caught up by the mind when hot with the friction of reading as if they were the soul of the book itself' (*CE*, II. 155). Similarly, she notes that de Sévigné 'has a natural dwelling-place in books, so that Josephus or Pascal or the absurd long romances of the time are not read by her so much as embedded in her mind. Their verses, their stories rise to her lips along with her own thoughts' (*CE*, III. 66–7).

Second, Woolf saw both writers as inextricably linked with the world around them, including the voices of others. Woolf deconstructs Coleridge's ideology of unity by picturing him as multifaceted, fragmented and dispersed:

> For it is vain to put the single word Coleridge at the head of a page – Coleridge the innumerable, the mutable, the atmospheric; Coleridge who is part of Wordsworth, Keats, and Shelley; of his age and of our own; Coleridge whose written words fill hundreds of pages and overflow innumerable margins; whose spoken words still reverberate, so that as we enter his radius he seems not a man, but a swarm, a cloud, a buzz of words, darting this way and that, clustering, quivering, and hanging suspended. (*CE*, III. 217)

The sketch detaches Coleridge from notions of solitary genius to show him caught up in cycles of influence: a view which accords with the more recent critical opinion that, in John Beer's words, 'it is perhaps more accurate . . . to speak of "poetic voices" than of a single "poetic voice" in Coleridge'.[13] Woolf's sense of Coleridge being bound up with others was reinforced by her reading of 'masses' of the letters between him and Wordsworth, 'curiously untwisting and burrowing into that plaited nest' (*D*, V. 289). Furthermore, the sketch gives Coleridge vibrancy and currency, so that he is not a dead writer but one whose words 'still reverberate' and circulate wildly like bees.

Woolf values de Sévigné as a channel for many different voices:

> The month of May, 1678, at Les Rochers in Brittany, thus echoes with different voices. There are the birds singing; Pilois is planting; Madame de Sévigné roams the woods alone; her daughter is entertaining politicians in Provence; not very far away Monsieur de Rochefoucauld is engaged in telling the truth with Madame de La Fayette to prune his words; Racine is finishing the play which soon they will all be hearing together; and discussing afterwards with the King and that lady whom in the private language of their set they called Quanto. The voices mingle; they are all talking together in the garden in 1678. (*CE*, III. 70)

Here, again, is a sense that de Sévigné and her cohorts are not dead, but are still active and, crucially, still talking: as Woolf herself notes, 'it is natural to use the present tense' when discussing her, 'because we live in her presence' (*CE*, III. 68). Woolf valued the way in which de Sévigné could convey lived experience by capturing voices in her letters: she remarked in a note that in de Sévigné, as in the Elizabethans, '[c]olloquial language that comes straight from talk. not only there were people who talked but the writer cd [?use] talk'.[14] Woolf reinforced her sense of de Sévigné's intercourse with others by reading her work alongside that of her associate de Rochefoucauld. As with her comments on Coleridge, Woolf conveys a sense of literature in circulation: for example, Racine's play will be experienced and discussed by the coterie.

If Woolf's comments on Coleridge and de Sévigné – both of whom she had chosen to read extensively at this time – may be taken to reflect her own preoccupations, then they offer insights into her use of allusion and parody in *Between the Acts*. First, Woolf's awareness of the intimate and intricate connections between the words of different writers and the web of conversation is reflected in her own weaving of an almost Barthesian 'tissue of quotations' into her novel, as poetry is bound in with everyday conversation, newspaper reportage, superstition and nursery rhyme. Second, *Between the Acts* may be read as Woolf's own attempt to capture and perpetuate the living word: both in the conversation of the villagers and in the echoes from past literature given currency in passing glances within characters' speeches, narratorial comment and the pageant. The latter additionally offers a forum wherein historical dramatic forms are represented within the present of June 1939.

When read in this light, Woolf's use of the literary fragment can be seen as something far more positive and dynamic than the 'mere cultural detritus, bits of flotsam and jetsam floating about in the characters' minds like fragments of a sunken vessel' described by Alex Zwerdling.[15] Bart's sketchy quotations from Byron, for example, are attached to the fabric of the novel by a series of threads which generate a variety of different meanings from the words. Woolf suggests a 'poetry of place' similar to that evoked in her essay 'Reading',[16] when Bart recalls his mother giving him a copy of the works of Byron 'in that very room' and the memory brings to light two slivers of poetry, as though they linger in the space:

'She walks in beauty like the night,' he quoted.
Then began:
'So we'll go no more a-roving by the light of the moon.' (*BA*, 5)

Whilst these random quotations could be seen to mock Bart, there is sympathy in the portrait for it is clear that he attaches emotions and ideas to the words above and beyond the meanings they hold within the poems, resulting in an explosion of meaning. Bart's recitations from Byron prompt the reader to recall the tenor of the poems, the first of the 'Hebrew Melodies', which speaks of adoration after desire has cooled (the object of the speaker's affections is 'mellow', 'pure' and 'serene') and 'So We'll Go No More A-Roving', a song of a love now becalmed. The mood of the poems offers a suitable complement to Bart's recollection of time gone by and of someone whom he has loved and lost. The meanings of the lines shift as they speak to different contexts within the novel: the references to night and moonlight relate to the setting of the episode on a summer's night, while Isa, hearing the words, associates them with her own preoccupation with the 'gentleman farmer' with whom she dreams of having an affair – 'The words made two rings, perfect rings, that floated them, herself and Haines, like two swans down stream' (*BA*, 5). It is ironically appropriate that Isa's thoughts are stirred by poems of cooling love, for it is clear that her liaison with Haines must remain within the realms of her imagination. Finally, although the quotations are attributed to Byron, both phrases have links to folk culture, one Jewish culture, the other the figure of 'the lady gone a'roving' from English folklore.[17] In doing so, Woolf offers the first of many hints in this novel towards a communal 'we' behind the masculine 'I' of a famous writer.

In these divergent interpretations of the lines we see an example of the kind of reading Woolf described in 'On Being Ill', whereby 'we rifle the poets of their flowers. We break off a line or two and let them open in the depths of the mind.' (*CE*, IV. 199). Such readings have emancipatory potential, for they show that former meanings can be unsettled, that literature is not fixed but in a state of flux; it is not tied to old understandings but can help shape new ways of thinking.

Such shifts in meaning as these often work alongside changes in wording, as quotations are adapted and developed like motifs in music, an analogy which is particularly appropriate to *Between the Acts* where, as Gillian Beer notes, the sonorous quality of words is particularly pronounced.[18] Bart's refrain from Swinburne's 'Itylus' is a case in point, for he initially mutters the opening line accurately – 'Swallow, my sister, O sister swallow' (*BA*, 99), but he misquotes it on picking up the theme again, modulating the next line to ask the question of himself 'How can my heart be full of the spring?' before inventing his own lyrical lines which modulate the theme of the poem: 'What's the use, what's the use . . . O sister swallow, O sister swallow, of singing your song?' (*BA*, 104). By using the first person and changing the phraseology, Bart presents a personal reading of the poem relevant to his own situation: in his anxiety about his son, Giles, he is incredulous of the cheerfulness of others, particularly that of his sister Lucy who is quickly identified as the swallow when she enters and sits 'perched on the edge of a chair like a bird' (*BA*, 105).

As with the quotation from Byron, the significance of these words goes back beyond Swinburne, for Bart's worries about his son pertain to the classical theme of the poem, where the Philomel of Greek myth chides her sister Procne for failing to mourn Procne's son Itylus whom the sisters have slain. In adopting and adapting Swinburne's words, Woolf translates the myth into a different situation: the sisters are replaced by a brother and sister, and the mother and son by a father and son. Although Giles is not dead like Itylus, but is liable to be conscripted during the coming war and, reading between the lines, Bart's military and colonial values would render him culpable of his son's death.

Reading the allusion across the novel, the Procne–Philomel myth offers further intertextual links: between Philomel's rape by Tereus and the newspaper account of the woman raped by guardsmen, and between the image of the swallow and the literal swallows which had played a spontaneous part in the play. Although several critics, such as Jane Marcus, Eileen Barrett and Patricia Cramer, have looked for a schematic use of myth in *Between the Acts*,[19] seeking to view it as a quest to return to the matriarchal origins of culture in pre-classical Greece, the example of 'Itylus' reveals that Woolf's allusions resist the stability of meaning necessary to build them into a plausible scheme. Her allusive strategy also calls the notion of 'origins' and 'originality' into question, for, whereas Swinburne represents one rendering of the myth, the reference to rape calls up an element of the myth not reflected in his poem. Further investigation of the myth itself reveals that the story itself is unstable, for there are several different versions in circulation: in one, Itylus (or Itys) is killed by Procne acting alone, in another by Procne with Philomel, and in another, his mother is called Aëdon, and she kills him accidentally while trying to murder the child of her sister-in-law Niobe. While Procne becomes a swallow and Philomel a nightingale in Greek myth, the metamorphoses happen the other way around in Roman lore: Aëdon becomes a nightingale, but there appear to be no accounts of Niobe being transformed. Woolf emphasises the uncertainty of origins in *Between the Acts* through the repeated unanswered question of 'What's the origin of . . .?' (*BA*, 22, 110). Old phrases and ancient stories reverberate in the present, but they arrive severed from the discursive structures which gave them meaning, allowing new meanings to be made.

The presence of literary quotations within characters' conversations generates further proliferation of meaning. In a household where talk is stilted and often at cross-purposes, quotations provide ready-made phrases for speakers to use, allowing them to exchange utterances without actually conversing with one another. For example, when Mrs Manresa is asked for a recitation and starts but fails to continue Hamlet's soliloquy 'To be or not to be', she asks Giles to take over; Isa, sensing that he does not know the words, begins to recite Keats' 'Ode to a Nightingale': 'Fade far away and quite forget what thou amongst the leaves hast never known . . .' Although Isa's words are simply 'the first . . . that came into her head', they carry on the theme of Hamlet's soliloquy: a desire for oblivion, albeit through inebriation rather than suicide. The lines are also fitting for the situation between Isa and Haines, where it would be better for both if they were to forget their feelings before giving way to them. The exchange continues when William Dodge picks up the next line of Keats' Ode, 'The weariness, the torture and the fret' – lines which may suggest his own anxieties about the awkward gathering (*BA*, 50). On one level, each character speaks of his or her own situation, alienated from the others, but on another level, a choric effect is achieved whereby the words of poets answer one another, producing not unity but creative dissonance.

The allusion to 'Ode to a Nightingale', like the reference to 'Itylus', reverberates beyond this exchange. The poem is echoed a few pages later, when Isa asks for 'a beaker of cold water' (*BA*, 61), inverting Keats' speaker's call for wine ('O for a beaker full of the warm South'). Like

'Itylus', too, it is built around a classical image which has already been made apparent within the novel, for nightingales were heard in the opening pages. The nightingales in *Between the Acts* bring to life Woolf's sense of the continuation of classical Greek culture into the present, which she expressed in 'On Not Knowing Greek', as the song of the nightingale echoing throughout English literature (*CE*, I. 5).The presence of nightingales and swallows in the play serve to enact the Procne–Philomel myth in the present so that the myth survives, not only in quoted words, but in the natural world.

The pageant foregrounds the twin processes of fabricating a living language from fragments of literature and making the literary past live in the present day, for the very nature of performance is to bring scenes to life in real time. The living literary past is seen in the figures identified as Chaucer's pilgrims who pass across the performance space at several points in the play. The device not only enacts the scenario of *The Canterbury Tales* but it suggests that the community spirit described by Chaucer lives on in the present-day village, for the players are described interchangably as 'the villagers' (the actors) and 'the pilgrims' (the characters they are playing) (*BA*, 74). Their appearances subtly recast something which Woolf had stated more explicitly in an extended description of the library in an earlier typescript: 'What Chaucer had begun was continued with certain lapses from his day to this very morning.'[20] Where the typescript had invoked tradition as a link between Chaucer and the latest best-seller (ibid.), the account of the pageant in the final version of the novel suggests something more immediate: a sense of continuing presence.

The three vignettes which make up the main body of the pageant reinforce the relevance of literature to everyday life, for the scenes both parody past theatrical styles and reflect life at Pointz Hall. As Rosemary Sumner notes, the play 'leads out of the world of art into the whole of life'.[21] Jean Wyatt has noted that this reflexivity between life and literature bears out two ideas from Shakespeare: the notion that 'All the world's a stage' from *As You Like It* (II. vii. 138), and Hamlet's advice to the players that the purpose of acting is 'to hold as 'twere the mirror up to nature' (III. ii. 21–2).[22] The sketches also continue the process of weaving literary quotations into the fabric of a living language.

The first vignette is an Elizabethan drama loosely parodying elements of Shakespeare's *Cymbeline*: a Princess disguised as a boy, a missing daughter hidden in a cave, and a missing heir identified by a mole. The text incorporates fragmentary echoes of other works which suit the new context, including the biblical 'sins . . . before cockcrow' of the old woman who has hidden a missing prince, and some elegiac words from

Webster's *The White Devil*. Isa relates the sketch to the real world when she echoes a line 'There is little blood in my arm', to ponder on her own inanition, and recognises three of her own emotions within the scene: 'Love. Hate. Peace' (*BA*, 82, 83).

The second vignette, 'Where there's a Will there's a Way', is a Restoration comedy of love and deception after the manner of Congreve, about whom Woolf had written, with some difficulty, over the summer of 1937. In this scene, too, fragmentary allusions throw out rays of different meanings, such as at the end, where Lady Harridan's maid deserts her, leaving a note which quotes a folk song – '*What care I for your goose-feather bed? I'm off with the raggle-taggle gipsies, O!*' (*BA*, 132). That song tells the tale of a lord's wife who is seduced by a gypsy and renounces her marriage, with its wealth and lands, for a life of pleasure and freedom. Lady Harridan's melodramatic response (*BA*, 132–3) is made suitably pompous by puns on Shakespeare: '*ingratitude, thy name is Deborah*', a play on Hamlet's 'frailty, thy name is woman' (I. ii. 146), and '*Sans niece, sans lover; and sans maid*' a parody of Jaques' 'seven ages of man' speech ('Sans eyes, sans teeth, sans taste, sans everything' (*As You Like It*, II. vii. 165)). Giles, in his reaction to the scene, recognises his own temptation to run away from his family and marriage – 'The words rose and pointed a finger of scorn at him. Off to Gretna Green with his girl; the deed done' (*BA*, 133) – unaware that his own wife is dreaming of going away, if not with the gypsies, then with a gentleman farmer.

The last two scenes reflect village life more directly: the third vignette, a Victorian melodrama of family life, leads two of the locals, Etty Springett and Mrs Lynn Jones, to recall their own childhoods, while the final scene, 'The Present Time', underlines the process of reflexivity by showing the villagers mirror images of themselves.

The link between the play and real life is further cemented by a network of allusions tying the pageant to life at Pointz Hall, and vice versa: characters repeat words from the play and the play echoes characters' words, and literary echoes are present in both. A particularly rich example follows the Elizabethan sketch, where Giles responds with a string of quotations which do not come from the play as we have seen it:

'I fear I am not in my perfect mind,' Giles muttered to the same tune. Words came to the surface – he remembered 'a stricken deer in whose lean flank the world's harsh scorn has struck its thorn . . . Exiled from its festival, the music turned ironical . . . A churchyard haunter at whom the owl hoots and the ivy mocks tap-tap-tapping on the pane . . . For they are dead, and I . . . I . . . I.' (*BA*, 78)

Giles expresses his own state of disquiet by suturing together a set of phrases. The first two phrases, from *King Lear* (IV. vii. 62) and Cowper's *The Task*,[23] are both concerned with insanity. The derivation of the next two phrases is obscure and they may be Woolf's own, but the second of these, concerning the 'churchyard haunter', reflects on mortality to link with the final phrase, which alludes to Wordsworth's 'The Indian Woman': 'For they are dead, and I will die' (l. 14).

Two of these phrases – 'I am not . . . in my perfect mind' and 'The owl hoots and the ivy mocks tap-tap-tapping on the pane' – subsequently become incorporated into the text of the play. This occurs in the mirror scene where the actors, we are told, recite phrases from their parts, although these lines had not formed part of the pageant as we had seen it. The echoes suggest both the reflexivity between theatre and life, and the uncertain or multiple nature of origins: it is unclear whether the lines echo Giles, the literary texts he quoted, or perhaps a part of the play not previously narrated.

This mirror scene represents a gathering of much that has gone before, partly in the pageant but mainly beyond. The ensemble gathers a mosaic of quotations which have not formed a part of the play, none of which is attributed: '*Home is the hunter, home from the hill*' from R. L. Stevenson's 'Requiem'; '*maiden faith is rudely strumpeted*', a misquotation from Shakespeare's Sonnet 66; '*Sweet and low; sweet and low, wind of the western sea*' from Tennyson's 'The Princess'; '*Is that a dagger that I see before me?*' from *Macbeth*; '*Where the worm weaves its winding sheet*' from Blake's 'Sick Rose'; and '*In thy will is our peace*' from Dante's *Paradiso*. These are set alongside a nursery rhyme, '*Hark, hark, the dogs do bark and the beggars*' (*BA*, 166). The mosaic process is epitomised by phrase from the close of the scene, 'scraps and fragments' (*BA*, 169), which also speaks of multiple origins for it is a literary tag with a double derivation: from Shakespeare's *Troilus and Cressida* (V. ii. 157–8) and Wordsworth's 'The Old Cumberland Beggar' (l. 10). This scene, then, sums up much of what the rest of the book has been doing with allusions by practising a polyphony by which the literary past is kept alive by being broken up and woven into living language. The passage calls to question the idea of origins, making it extremely problematic for anyone to claim ownership of literature or to seek to appropriate it for particular ends: the words of famous poets, none of whom is identified, are placed alongside those of anonymous others, and also alongside silences, for the scene is studded with ellipses, resulting in a dense collage which refuses to yield a unified story.

Miss La Trobe's pageant has important implications for Woolf's representation of history in *Between the Acts*. Although the play offers chronological scenes from English history and literature, the narrative presented is fragmentary and episodic. As a result, the play resists national metanarratives of military victory and political leaders – a refusal which is epitomised by the absence of the 'Grand Ensemble' anticipated by Mrs Mayhew (*BA*, 161) – and also literary metanarratives based on great writers – for silences and nursery-rhymes are important elements of the texture of the play. Instead, social and literary history is shown to live on within ordinary people. This in turn leads to a radical reconception of tradition, for the legacy of the past is seen to exist within the villagers, not 'handed down' to them. Woolf's fragmentation of the literary past therefore resists the kind of authoritative structure needed to produce a recognisable tradition. As Christopher Ames notes, Woolf 'uses parody and narrative framing to mitigate the disabling authority of past tradition'.[24] In the face of the rise of Fascism, where history, tradition and culture itself were being dragged into the service of oppression within the state and imperialism beyond it, the undermining of conventional understandings of tradition was both liberating and necessary.

The fragmentary allusions in *Between the Acts* tender the possibility of a literature which could exist among ordinary people and be preserved orally in a form which might survive the upheaval of war. Woolf's interest in oral, communal culture finds a fuller expression in Woolf's late essay 'Anon', where she celebrates the earliest English literature as the product of an unknown balladeer voicing experiences of the common people and reflecting the countryside:

> Every body shared in the emotion of Anons song, and supplied the story. . . . Anon is sometimes man; sometimes woman. He is the common voice singing out of doors. He has no house. He lives a roaming life crossing the fields, mounting the hills, lying under the hawthorn to listen to the nightingale. (*Anon*, 382)

The essay celebrates the lack of fixity of stories before they were printed and the flexibility of early live theatre to respond to its audience. It looks back to an imaginary time when literature was common property, not appropriated by particular authors; indeed, a time when the spirit of literature (represented by the nightingale who sang in ancient Greece and whose song echoes to the present day) was alive in the landscape. Woolf cherishes the possibility that traces of 'Anon' are still to be found 'within ourselves' (*Anon*, 397). *Between the Acts* is a similar attempt to seek the spirit of 'anon' within the present day: a search for a living literature which might survive the coming onslaught.

Notes

1. Beer, *Woolf: The Common Ground*, p. 134.
2. Lee, *Virginia Woolf*, p. 737.
3. 'Many a green isle needs must be | In the deep wide sea of misery', Shelley, 'Lines Written among the Euganean Hills'.
4. Clarke, 'The Horse With a Green Tail'.
5. Abrams, *The Mirror and the Lamp*, p. 124.
6. For Woolf's response to Darwinism in *Between the Acts*, see Beer, 'Woolf and Pre-History'; and Lambert, 'Evolution and Imagination in *Pointz Hall* and *Between the Acts*'.
7. For discussion of Woolf's criticism of St Paul in *Three Guineas*, see Marshik, 'Woolf and Intellectual History'; and Richter, *Virginia Woolf: The Inward Voyage*, pp. 151–2.
8. Little, 'Festive Comedy in Woolf's *Between the Acts*', p. 26.
9. Larkin, *Required Writing*, p. 285.
10. As Roger Fry observed of the work of Henri Matisse: 'By the magic of an intensely coherent style our familiar every day world . . . has been broken to pieces as though reflected in a broken mirror and then put together into a far more coherent unity in which all the visual values are mysteriously changed – in which plastic forms can be read as pattern and apparently flat patterns are read as diversely inclined planes' (*Henri Matisse*, pp. 33–4).
11. Wyatt, 'Art and Allusion in *Between the Acts*', p. 91.
12. Cuddy-Keane, 'The Politics of Comic Modes in Virginia Woolf's *Between the Acts*', p. 274.
13. Beer, Introduction to Coleridge: *Poems*, p. xvi.
14. *Reading Notebooks*, p. 185.
15. Zwerdling, '*Between the Acts* and the Coming of War', p. 231.
16. See Introduction, p. 4 above.
17. For an account of Woolf's use of folk song in *Between the Acts*, see Manhire, ' "The Lady's Gone A-Roving," Woolf and the English Folk Revival'.
18. Beer, *Common Ground*, p. 133.
19. Marcus, 'Some Sources for *Between the Acts*', and 'Liberty, Sorority, Misogyny', in *Virginia Woolf and the Languages of Patriarchy*; Barrett, 'Matriarchal Myth on a Patriarchal Stage'; Cramer, 'Woolf's Matriarchal Family of Origins in *Between the Acts*'.
20. *Virginia Woolf: Pointz Hall: The Earlier and Later Typescripts of* Between the Acts, ed. Leaska, p. 25.
21. Sumner, *Route into Modernism*, p. 156.
22. Wyatt, 'Art and Allusion', pp. 91, 93.
23. 'I was a stricken deer | That left the herd long since; with many an arrow deep infixt | My panting side was charged'.
24. Ames, 'The Modernist Canon Narrative', p. 395.

Conclusion

We can now see that Woolf's novels were informed deeply by her sometimes vexed, sometimes positive conversations with past writers. As the
analyses of her creative processes in the preceding chapters reveal, her
reading and writing practices were closely interfused: quite simply, she
needed to read in order to write, and almost invariably she preferred to
read past writers. Sometimes she needed to read for intellectual stimula-
tion: it is significant that she began to draft *The Voyage Out* after six
years of intensive reading, but even in the 1930s, reading poetry helped
release her from creative deadlock whilst formulating *The Waves*. Woolf
also used past writings to help her make sense of the world and its problems – not least war and patriarchy – and as a consequence these works
informed the thematic content of her novels.

Reading earlier literature also helped Woolf explore her own preoccupations and sensibilities, such as when she read Sterne in 1926 while considering the future of the novel in general and of her own writing in
particular, or when she saw in Coleridge's agonies her own sense of being
overwhelmed by experience. These empathetic readings in turn helped
her articulate traumatic experiences of her own, such as when she used
the classical image of birds singing in Greek in describing her breakdown
of 1904, or when she drew on Romantic models to help develop her
'moments of being'. Reading was so central to Woolf's understanding of
the world that re-reading texts also became a form of self-discovery, a
revisiting of self and past. This is most evident in *The Waves*, where in
an intense reflexive exploration of her own process, she revisited works
which had inspired her: for example, while writing the second typescript
she re-read and quoted from Dante who had stimulated her earliest
sketches for the novel.

It was both a comfort and a challenge for Woolf that past literature
was rich in associations. Past literature was comforting because it helped
her make memorials to people she had known, such as when she remem-

bered Thoby through the Greek classics and Shakespeare in *Jacob's Room* or more powerfully, when she elegised Leslie Stephen through his beloved Milton in *The Voyage Out*. The idea is extended in *Jacob's Room*, *Mrs Dalloway* and *Between the Acts*, to embrace the possibility that culture could be preserved in literary fragments to survive the trauma of war. Woolf found the associative power of literature discomfiting when texts carried shades of patriarchal domination: her novels display strategies for distancing herself from certain elements of the literary past, as she moulds her own writing in contradistinction to what has gone before. Woolf's awkward treatment of the courtship narrative in *The Voyage Out* is an early distancing strategy, before she revisited the pattern ironically in *Night and Day* then in briefer, more critical allusions in *Mrs Dalloway*, *Orlando* and even *To the Lighthouse* with Lily's image of a married couple in an 'old-fashioned scene . . . which required, very nearly, crinolines and peg-top trousers' (*TL*, 267). Other examples of distancing strategies include Woolf's dismissive treatment of eighteenth-century satirists and her mockery of Victorian scholarship in *Orlando*.

This dynamic manifests itself more subtly in Woolf's quest to strip texts of the unhelpful layers of patriarchal interpretation and appropriation, such as when she seeks to 'liberate' classical Greek writings and Shakespeare from establishment ideologies in *Jacob's Room* and *Mrs Dalloway*, or when she digs through mainstream Victorian understandings to discover a Renaissance of her own in *Orlando*. Woolf was forced to address a new manifestation of the problem in *Between the Acts*, as Fascist ideologies threatened to appropriate literature. This archaeological approach is driven partly by an imaginative quest for lost origins, or a dream of a virgin text untouched by patriarchal formulations: a desire for intimacy with the past such as that expressed in 'Byron & Mr Briggs' or 'On Being Ill'. However, in *Between the Acts* and *The Waves* the quest for lost origins is superseded by a recognition that culture has a multiple origins and that literature is a shared legacy, too diffuse for any one person or group to claim exclusively.

Woolf's interaction with the works and legacy of Leslie Stephen was an important, though not the only, focus for this archaeological process. As we have seen, Stephen's view of women writers lay behind Woolf's uncomfortable reception of her female precursors in *The Voyage Out* and *Night and Day*, but *To the Lighthouse* and *Orlando* were important stages for Woolf in acknowledging and dealing with Stephen's legacy directly. In *To the Lighthouse*, she applies Stephen's ideas to develop her own feminist agenda, while in *Orlando*, she satirises his approach to literary history and finally challenges his role as gate-keeper to the past. After writing *Orlando*, Woolf came to see Stephen as a kind of benefactor – the man who gave her books and left her a 'makeshift' inheritance of literature. The process of liberation traced here explains why, by 1940, Woolf could pass on some of Leslie Stephen's advice to working-class women, inviting them to read widely for themselves. Identifying Stephen semi-anonymously as an 'eminent Victorian who was also an eminent pedestrian' – not a literary critic and certainly not a father – and quoting his adage, 'Whenever you see a board up with "Trespassers will be prosecuted", trespass at once'. She urged her audience to 'trespass at once' to recognize that 'literature is common ground' (*CE*, II. 181). Here Stephen is recast as the free-thinker who had his own quarrels with the establishment and opened the gate for others to share literature as common property.

Woolf's varied use of literary quotations reflects these dynamics: she absorbs the words of others into her own voice in acts of intimacy; she uses off-set or ironic quotations as part of a distancing strategy; she moulds quotations to fit new contexts to keep the words of past writers alive in the present; and her frequent use of quotations of quotations in *The Waves* and *Between the Acts* emphasises that literature is common ground, for origins are lost and indeterminate and belong to no one exclusively.

Although much criticism on Woolf and the literary past has sought to place her work within particular traditions, this wider survey reveals a more ambivalent picture. Woolf's work does not fit neatly into any one tradition: her view of different aspects of the literary past changed over her career and she often plays traditions off against one another. Furthermore, Woolf's own idea of 'tradition' changed: for much of her career, she was interested in reinventing traditions by invoking past writers to adopt them as precursors for her own writing and that of other women, in parallel to her project in *A Room of One's Own*. However, *The Waves* and *Between the Acts* give evidence of a profound distrust of the idea of tradition as an interpreting framework, for Woolf began to emphasise tradition as repetition or ritual, as she came to stress the need for repeating and echoing past literature in order to keep its currency in the present.

In so far as it is possible to detect a trend in Woolf's engagement with the past, we can see a critical exploration of Romantic ideas for their potential use to women writers: Woolf used these positively in *Night and Day* to help develop a feminist, modernist aesthetic, but her treatment of Wordsworth in *To the Lighthouse* reveals suspicion about the patriarchal implications of his world-view, and *The Waves* and *Between the Acts* give evidence of wide-ranging scepticism towards Romantic concepts. At the same time, we see Woolf wishing to look beyond Romantic notions of originality and autonomy, and back to the Renaissance, where the emphasis was on rediscovery of the past (particularly the classical past) and the reworking of older material. This dynamic goes hand-in-hand with Woolf's interest in fictional vanishing-points, initially Judith Shakespeare then Anon, which symbolise a lost, communal past which might be refound in the present. That said, however, it is important to recognise that even a book-length study cannot do full justice to the breadth of Woolf's reading, nor can it do more than provide examples of how she brought writings from different eras to bear on her work in creative tensions.

While this study presents Woolf as less 'original' and more 'indebted' than some would choose to see her, it also shows that Woolf herself placed less value on originality than a conventional understanding of her modernism would suggest. Woolf's work appears less new but more rooted; less sweepingly radical but more seriously engaged with currents of thought from classical times onwards.

The literary past sings through Virginia Woolf's novels at every level; its presence should not be ignored.

Select Bibliography

Works by Woolf not listed in the Abbreviations

'A Dialogue upon Mount Pentelicus', *Times Literary Supplement*, 11–17 September 1987, pp. 979.

Orlando: The Original Holograph Draft, transcribed and ed. Stuart N. Clarke (London: Stuart Nelson Clarke, 1993).

Pointz Hall: The Earlier and Later Typescripts of Between the Acts, ed. with introduction, annotations, and afterword by Mitchell Leaska (New York: University Publications, 1983).

Virginia Woolf's Reading Notebooks, ed. Brenda Silver (Princeton, NJ: Princeton University Press, 1983).

Other primary sources not listed in the Abbreviations

Alighieri, Dante, *The Inferno*, tr. Mark Musa (Harmondsworth: Penguin, 1971).

Arber, Edward (ed.) *An English Garner: Ingatherings from our History and Literature*, 8 vols (n.p., 1877–96).

Austen, Jane, *Emma*, ed. Ronald Blythe ([1816]; Harmondsworth: Penguin, 1966).

—, *Northanger Abbey*, ed. Anne Ehrenpreis ([1818]; Harmondsworth: Penguin, 1972).

Burckhardt, Jacob, *The Civilization of the Renaissance in Italy: An Essay* ([1860]: Oxford: Phaidon, 1981).

Byron, George Gordon, *Poetical Works*, ed. Ernest Hartley Coleridge (London: John Murray, 1905).

Coleridge, Samuel Taylor, *Poems*, ed. John Beer ([1963]; London: Everyman, 1983).

Defoe, Daniel, *Roxana: The Fortunate Mistress*, ed. and intro. David Blewett ([1724]; Harmondsworth: Penguin, 1982).

Eliot, George, *Middlemarch*, ed. and intro. W. J. Harvey ([1871–72]; Harmondsworth: Penguin, 1965).

Eliot, T. S., *The Complete Poems and Plays* (London: Faber and Faber, 1969).

—, *Selected Essays* ([1932] London: Faber and Faber, 1986).

Gray, Thomas, *Complete Poems*, ed. H.W. Starr and J. R. Hendrickson (Oxford: Clarendon Press, 1966).

Hume, David, *A Treatise on Human Nature and Dialogues Concerning Natural Religion*, ed. T. H. Green and T. H. Grose, 2 vols ([1736]; London: Longmans and Green, 1874).

Ibsen, Henrik, *A Doll's House*, trans. Kenneth McLeish, ed. Mary Rafferty (Cambridge: Cambridge University Press, 1995).

Keats, John, *The Complete Poems*, ed. Miriam Allott (London: Longman, 1970).

Lee, Vernon, *Euphorion*, 2 vols (London: T. Fisher Unwin, 1884).

—,*Renaissance Fancies and Studies* (London: Smith, Elder, 1895).

Mackail, J. W., intro., trans and notes, *Select Epigrams from the Greek Anthology* (London: Longmans, Green, 1890).

—,*Shakespeare after Three Hundred Years*, The Annual Shakespeare Lecture 1916 (London: British Academy/Oxford University Press, 1916).

Milton, John, *Complete Shorter Poems*, ed. John Carey (Harlow: Longman, 1968).

Pater, Walter, *The Renaissance: Studies in Art and Poetry* ([1873]; London: Macmillan, 1888).

Plato, *The Republic*, trans and intro. Richard W. Sterling and William C. Scott (New York and London: W. W. Norton, 1985).

—, *Phaedrus*, trans with intro., notes and an interpretive essay by James H. Nichols, Jr. (Ithaca, NY and London: Cornell University Press, 1998).

Quiller-Couch, A. T. (ed.), *The Oxford Book of English Verse, 1250–1900* (Oxford: Clarendon Press, 1900).

Raleigh, Walter, *Shakespeare and England*, The Annual Shakespeare Lecture 1918 (London: British Academy, 1918).

Ritchie, Anne Thackeray, *A Book of Sibyls: Miss Barbauld, Miss Edgeworth, Mrs Opie, Miss Austen* (London: Smith & Elder, 1883).

Ruskin, John, *The Stones of Venice*, 3 vols (London: Smith, Elder, 1851).

—,*The Storm Cloud of the Nineteenth Century* (Orpington: George Allen, 1884).

Sackville West, V. (Victoria Mary), *The Heir: A Love Story* (printed for private circulation, 1922).

—,*Knole and the Sackvilles* (London: Heinemann, 1922).

—,*The Land* (London: William Heinemann, 1926).

Shakespeare, William, *The Complete Arden Shakespeare*, general ed. Richard Proudfoot (London and New York: Methuen, 1985).

—,*Sonnets*, ed. W. G. Ingram and Theodore Redpath (London: University of London Press, 1964).

Stephen, Julia, *Stories for Children, Essays for Adults*, ed. Diane F. Gillespie and Elizabeth Steele (New York: Syracuse University Press, 1987).

Stephen, Leslie, *The Playground of Europe* ([1871]; London: Longman, 1901).

—,*Hours in a Library*, 3 vols (London: Smith & Elder, 1874–79).

—, 'Humour', unsigned review in *Cornhill Magazine*, 33 (1876), 318–26.

—,*George Eliot*, English Men of Letters series (London: Macmillan, 1902).

—, *Men, Books and Mountains: Essays* (London: Hogarth Press, 1956).

Symonds, J. A. (ed. A. Pearson), *A Short History of the Renaissance in Italy* (London: Smith, Elder, 1893).

Whitman, Walt, *Leaves of Grass*, ed. J. Loving (Oxford: Oxford University Press, 1990).

Wordsworth, William, *Poetical Works*, with intro. and notes, ed. Thomas Hutchinson; new edn., rev. Ernest de Selincourt (Oxford: Oxford University Press, 1969).

—,*Poems, in Two Volumes, and Other Poems, 1800–1807*, ed. Jared Curtis (Ithaca, NY: Cornell University Press, 1983).

Secondary Reading

Abrams, M. H., *The Mirror and the Lamp: Romantic Theory and the Critical Tradition* ([1953]; New York: Oxford University Press, 1971).

Allen, Graham, *Intertextuality* (London: Routledge, 2000).

Allott, Miriam (ed.), *The Brontës: The Critical Heritage* ([1974]; London and New York: Routledge, 1995).

Ames, Christopher, 'The Modernist Canon Narrative: Woolf's *Between the Acts* and Joyce's "Oxen of the Sun"', *Twentieth-Century Literature*, 37:4 (1991), 390–404.

Annan, Noel, *Leslie Stephen: The Godless Victorian* (New York: Random House, 1984).

Ardis, Ann L., *New Women, New Novels: Feminism and Early Modernism* (New Brunswick and London: Rutgers University Press, 1990).

Bakhtin, Mikhail, *The Dialogic Imagination: Four Essays*, ed. M. Holquist, trans C. Emerson and M. Holquist (Austin: University of Texas Press, 1994).

Banfield, Ann, *The Phantom Table: Woolf, Fry, Russell and the Epistemology of Modernism* (Cambridge: Cambridge University Press, 2000).

Barrett, Eileen, 'Matriarchal Myth on a Patriarchal Stage: Virginia Woolf's *Between the Acts*', *Twentieth-Century Literature*, 33:1 (1987), 18–37.

Barthes, Roland, *Image–Music–Text*, essays selected and trans. Stephen Heath (Glasgow: Fontana, 1977).

Bate, Jonathan, *The Genius of Shakespeare* (London: Picador, 1997).

Beede, Margaret, 'Virginia Woolf – Romantic', *North Dakota Quarterly*, 27: 1 (1959), 21–9.

Beer, Gillian, 'Hume, Stephen, and Elegy in *To the Lighthouse*', *Essays in Criticism*, 34:1 (1984), 33–55.

—,'Virginia Woolf and Pre-History', in *Virginia Woolf: A Centenary Perspective*, ed. Eric Warner (London: Macmillan, 1984), pp. 99–123.

—,*Arguing with the Past: Essays in Narrative from Woolf to Sidney* (London: Routledge, 1989).

—,*Virginia Woolf: The Common Ground* (Edinburgh: Edinburgh University Press, 1996).

Blain, Virginia, 'Narrative Voice and the Female Perspective in Virginia Woolf's Early Novels', in *Virginia Woolf: New Critical Essays*, ed. Patricia Clements and Isobel Grundy (London: Vision, 1983), pp. 115–36.

Bloom, Harold, *The Anxiety of Influence: A Theory of Poetry* (New York and Oxford: Oxford University Press, 1973; second edition 1997).

Booth, Alison, *Greatness Engendered: George Eliot and Virginia Woolf* (Ithaca, NY and London: Cornell University Press, 1992).

Briggs, Julia, 'In Search of New Virginias', in *Virginia Woolf: Turning the Centuries: Selected Papers from the Ninth Annual Conference on Virginia Woolf*, ed. Ann Ardis and Bonnie Kime Scott (New York: Pace University Press, 2000), pp. 166–76.

Brownstein, Rachel, *Becoming a Heroine: Reading about Women in Novels* (Harmondsworth: Penguin, 1984).

Butler, Judith, *Bodies that Matter: On the Discursive Limits of 'Sex'* (New York and London: Routledge, 1993).

Cafarelli, Annette Wheeler, 'How Theories of Romanticism Exclude Women: Radcliffe, Milton, and the Legitimation of the Gothic Novel', in *Milton, the Metaphysicals, and Romanticism*, ed. Lisa Low and Anthony John Harding (Cambridge: Cambridge University Press, 1994), pp. 84–113.

Clarke, Stuart N., 'The Horse With a Green Tail', *Virginia Woolf Miscellany*, 34 (1990), pp. 3–4.

Clayton, Jay and Eric Rothstein (eds), *Influence and Intertextuality in Literary History* (Madison: University of Wisconsin Press, 1991).

Clements, Patricia and Isobel Grundy (eds), *Virginia Woolf: New Critical Essays* (London: Vision, 1983).

Cohen, Steven, 'Why Mr Ramsay Reads *The Antiquary*', *Women and Literature*, 7:2 (1979), 14–24.

Comstock, Margaret, '"The Current Answers Don't Do": The Comic Form of *Night and Day*', *Women's Studies*, Virginia Woolf Special Issue, ed. Madeline Moore, 4 (1977), 153–71.

Costello, Bonnie, 'Response to "Tradition and the Female Talent"', in *Literary History: Theory and Practice: Proceedings of the Northeastern University Center for Literary Studies*, 2, ed. H. L. Sussman (Boston, MA: Northeastern University Press, 1984).

Cramer, Patricia, 'Virginia Woolf's Matriarchal Family of Origins in *Between the Acts*', *Twentieth-Century Literature*, 39:2 (1993), 166–84.

Cuddy-Keane, Melba, 'The Politics of Comic Modes in Virginia Woolf's *Between the Acts*', *PMLA*, 105:2 (1990), 273–85.

—, 'Virginia Woolf and the Varieties of Historicist Experience', in Beth Carole Rosenberg and Jeanne Dubino (eds), *Virginia Woolf and the Essay* (Basingstoke: Macmillan, 1997), pp. 59–77.

Davies, Stevie, *Virginia Woolf, To the Lighthouse* (Harmondsworth: Penguin, 1989).

Dawson, Anthony B., *Hamlet*, Shakespeare in Performance (Manchester: Manchester University Press, 1995).

de Gay, Jane, 'Behind the Purple Triangle: Art and Iconography in *To the Lighthouse*', in *Woolf Studies Annual* (New York: Pace University Press, 1999).

Delgarno, Emily, *Virginia Woolf and the Visible World* (Cambridge: Cambridge University Press, 2001).

De Salvo, Louise A., *Virginia Woolf's First Voyage: A Novel in the Making* (London and Basingstoke: Macmillan, 1980).

Dettmar, Kevin J. H. (ed.), *Rereading the New: A Backward Glance at Modernism* (Ann Arbor, MI: University of Michigan Press, 1992).

di Battista, Maria, 'Joyce, Woolf and the Modern Mind', in *Virginia Woolf: New Critical Essays* ed. Patricia Clements and Isobel Grundy (London: Vision Press, 1983), pp. 96–114.

Dick, Susan, 'The Tunnelling Process: Some Aspects of Virginia Woolf's Use of Memory and the Past', in *Virginia Woolf: New Critical Essays*, ed. Patricia Clements and Isobel Grundy (London: Vision Press, 1983), pp. 176–99.

Dictionary of National Biography, ed. Leslie Stephen and Sidney Lee, 22 vols (Oxford: Oxford University Press, 1917–).

Dole, Carol M., 'Oppression, Obsession: Virginia Woolf and Henry James', *Southern Review*, 24:2 (1988), 253–71.

Du Plessis, Rachel Blau, *Writing Beyond the Ending: Narrative Strategies of Twentieth-Century Women Writers* (Bloomington, IN: Indiana University Press, 1985).

Dusinberre, Juliet, *Virginia Woolf's Renaissance: Woman Reader or Common Reader?* (Basingstoke: Macmillan, 1997).

Fetterley, Judith, *The Resisting Reader: A Feminist Approach to American Fiction* (Bloomington: Indiana University Press, 1978).

Fisher, Jane Elizabeth, 'The Seduction of the Father: Virginia Woolf and Leslie Stephen', *Women's Studies*, 18:1 (1990), 31–48.

Flint, Kate, *The Woman Reader: 1837–1914* (Oxford: Clarendon Press, 1993).

—,Introduction and editorial matter in Virginia Woolf, *The Waves* (Harmondsworth: Penguin, 1992).

Fogel, Daniel Mark, *Covert Relations: James Joyce, Virginia Woolf, and Henry James* (Charlottesville and London: University Press of Virginia, 1990).

Fowler, R., '"On Not Knowing Greek": The Classics and the Women of Letters', *Classical Journal*, 78 (1983), 337–49.

—,'Moments and Metamorphoses: Virginia Woolf's Greece', *Comparative Literature*, 51 (1999), 217–42.

Fox, Alice, 'Literary Allusion as Feminist Criticism in *A Room of One's Own*', *Philological Quarterly*, 63 (1984), 145–61.

—, *Virginia Woolf and the Literature of the English Renaissance* (Oxford: Clarendon Press, 1990).

Fraser, Hilary, *The Victorians and Renaissance Italy* (Oxford: Blackwell, 1992).

Froula, Christine, 'Virginia Woolf as Shakespeare's Sister: Chapters in a Woman Writer's Autobiography', in *Women's Re-Visions of Shakespeare: On the Responses of Dickinson, Woolf, Rich, H.D., George Eliot, and Others*, ed. Marianne Novy (Urbana, IL and Chicago: University of Illinois Press, 1990), pp. 123–42.

Fry, Roger, *Henri Matisse* (London: Zwemmer, 1930).

Fussell, Paul, *The Great War and Modern Memory* (Oxford: Oxford University Press, 1975).

Gay, Penny, *As She Likes It: Shakespeare's Unruly Women* (London: Routledge, 1994).

Gérin, Winifred, *Anne Thackeray Ritchie: A Biography* (Oxford: Oxford University Press, 1983).

Gilbert, Sandra M. and Susan Gubar, *The Madwoman in the Attic: The Woman Writer and the Nineteenth-Century Literary Imagination* (New Haven, CT and London: Yale University Press, 1979).

—, *No Man's Land: The Place of the Woman Writer in the Twentieth Century*, 3 vols (New Haven, CT and London: Yale University Press, 1988–94).

Gill, Stephen, *Wordsworth: The Prelude*, Landmarks of World Literature (Cambridge: Cambridge University Press, 1991).

Gordon, Lyndall, *Virginia Woolf: A Writer's Life* (Oxford: Oxford University Press, 1984).

Graham, J.W., 'The "Caricature Value" of Parody and Fantasy in *Orlando*', *University of Toronto Quarterly*, 30:4 (1961), 345–66.

Greenblatt, Stephen, *Renaissance Self-Fashioning: From More to Shakespeare* (Chicago and London: Chicago University Press, 1980).

Greene, Sally (ed.), *Virginia Woolf: Reading the Renaissance* (Athens, OH: Ohio University Press, 1999).

Gualtieri, Elena, *Virginia Woolf's Essays: Sketching the Past* (Basingstoke: Macmillan, 2000).

Hafley, James, *The Glass Roof: Virginia Woolf as Novelist* (Berkeley and Los Angeles: University of California Press, 1954).

Hanson, Clare, '"As a woman I have no country": Woolf and the Construction of National Identity', in *Contemporary Writing and National Identity*, ed. Tracy Hill and William Hughes (Bath: Sulis Press, 1995), pp. 54–64.

Hill, Katherine C., 'Virginia Woolf and Leslie Stephen: History and Literary Revolution', *PMLA*, 96 (1981), 351–62.

Hobsbawm, Eric and Terence Ranger (eds), *The Invention of Tradition* (Cambridge: Cambridge University Press, 1983).

Hussey, Mark (ed.), *Virginia Woolf and War: Fiction, Reality, and Myth* (New York: Syracuse University Press, 1991).

Hutcheon, Linda, *A Theory of Parody: The Teachings of Twentieth-Century Art Forms* (New York and London: Methuen, 1985).

Hyman, Virginia R., 'The Metamorphosis of Leslie Stephen', *Virginia Woolf Quarterly*, 2:1–2, (1975–6), 48–65.

—, 'Reflections in the Looking-Glass: Leslie Stephen and Virginia Woolf', *Journal of Modern Literature*, 10 (1983), 197–215.

Ingelbien, Raphaël, 'Intertextuality, Critical Politics and the Modernist Canon: The Case of Virginia Woolf', *Paragraph*, 22 (1999): 278–92.

Jacobus, Mary, *Romanticism, Writing and Sexual Difference: Essays on* The Prelude (Oxford: Clarendon Press, 1989).

Johnston, Judith L., 'The Remediable Flaw: Revisioning Cultural History in *Between the Acts*', in *Virginia Woolf and Bloomsbury: A Centenary Celebration*, ed. Jane Marcus (Basingstoke: Macmillan, 1987), pp. 253–77.

Jones, Danell, 'The Chase of the Wild Goose: The Ladies of Llangollen and *Orlando*', in *Virginia Woolf: Themes and Variations: Selected Papers from the Second Annual Conference on Virginia Woolf*, ed. Vara Neverow-Turk and Mark Hussey (New York: Pace University Press, 1993), pp. 181–9.

Joseph, Gerhard, 'The Antigone as Cultural Touchstone: Matthew Arnold, Hegel, George Eliot, Virginia Woolf, and Margaret Drabble', *PMLA*, 96:1 (1981), 22–35.

Kellerman, Frederick, 'A New Key to Virginia Woolf's *Orlando*', *English Studies: A Journal of English Language and Literature*, 59 (1978), 138–50.

Kristeva, Julia, *The Kristeva Reader*, ed. Toril Moi (Oxford: Blackwell, 1986).

Laity, Cassandra, *H.D. and the Victorian Fin de Siècle: Gender, Modernism, Decadence* (Cambridge: Cambridge University Press, 1996).

Lambert, Elizabeth, 'Evolution and Imagination in *Pointz Hall* and *Between the Acts*', in *Virginia Woolf: Themes and Variations: Selected Papers from the Second Annual Conference on Virginia Woolf*, ed. Vara Neverow-Turk and Mark Hussey (New York: Pace University Press, 1993), pp. 83–9.

Larkin, Philip, *Required Writing: Miscellaneous Pieces 1955–1982* (London: Faber, 1983).

Laurence, Patricia Ondek, *The Reading of Silence: Virginia Woolf in the English Tradition* (Stanford, CA: Stanford University Press, 1991).

Lee, Hermione, 'A Burning Glass: Reflection in Virginia Woolf', in *Virginia Woolf: A Centenary Perspective*, ed. Eric Warner (London: Macmillan, 1984), pp. 12–27.

—, *Virginia Woolf* (London: Chatto & Windus, 1996).

Lee, Judith, '"Without Hate, Without Bitterness, Without Fear, Without Protest, Without Preaching": Virginia Woolf Reads Jane Austen', *Persuasions*, Journal of the Jane Austen Society of North America, 12 (1990), 111–16.

Lilienfeld, Jane, '"The Deceptiveness of Beauty": Mother Love and Mother Hate in *To the Lighthouse*', *Twentieth-Century Literature*, 23:3 (1977), 345–76.

—, Jeffrey Oxford and Lisa Low (eds), *Woolf Studies Annual 9* and *10*: Special Issues on Virginia Woolf and Literary History (New York: Pace University Press, 2003–4).

Little, Judy, 'Festive Comedy in Woolf's *Between the Acts*', *Women and Literature* 5:1 (1977), 26–37.

—, '(En)gendering Laughter: Woolf's *Orlando* as Contraband in the Age of Joyce', *Women's Studies*, 15:2 (1988), 179–91.

Litvak, Joseph, *Caught in the Act: Theatricality in the Nineteenth-Century English Novel* (Berkeley: University of California Press, 1992).

Logan, James V., *Wordsworthian Criticism: A Guide and Bibliography* (Columbus, OH: Ohio State University Press, 1961).

Low, Lisa, 'Two Figures Standing in Dense Violet Light: John Milton, Virginia Woolf, and the Epic Vision of Marriage', in *Virginia Woolf Miscellanies: Proceedings of the First Annual Conference on Virginia Woolf*, ed. Mark Hussey and Vara Neverow-Turk (New York: Pace University Press, 1992), pp. 144–5.

—, '"Thou Canst Not Touch the Freedom of My Mind": Fascism and Disruptive Female Consciousness in *Mrs Dalloway*', in Merry M. Pawlowski (ed.) *Virginia Woolf and Fascism: Resisting the Dictators' Seduction* (Basingstoke: Palgrave, 2001), pp. 92–104.

—, 'Feminist Elegy/Feminist Prophecy: Lycidas, *The Waves*, Kristeva, Cixous', in Jane Lilienfeld, Jeffrey Oxford and Lisa Low (eds) *Woolf Studies Annual 9*: Special Issue on Virginia Woolf and Literary History (New York: Pace University Press, 2003), pp. 221–42.

MacKay, Carol Hanbery, 'The Thackeray Connection: Virginia Woolf's Aunt Anny', in *Virginia Woolf and Bloomsbury: A Centenary Celebration*, ed. Jane Marcus (Basingstoke: Macmillan, 1987), pp. 68–95.

—, 'Hate and Humor as Empathetic Whimsy in Anne Thackeray Ritchie', *Women's Studies*, Special Issue on women and comedy, ed. Regina Barreca, 15:1–3 (1988), 117–33.

Maitland, Frederic W., *The Life and Letters of Leslie Stephen* (London: Duckworth, 1906).

Majumdar, Robin and Allen McLaurin (eds), *Virginia Woolf: The Critical Heritage* ([1975]; London and New York: Routledge & Kegan Paul, 1997).

Manhire, Vanessa, '"The Lady's Gone A-Roving," Woolf and the English Folk Revival', in *Virginia Woolf: Out of Bounds*, ed. Jessica Berman and Jane Goldman (New York: Pace University Press, 2001), pp. 236–42.

Marcus, Jane, 'Some Sources for *Between the Acts*', *Virginia Woolf Miscellany*, 6 (1977), 1–3.

—, *Virginia Woolf and the Languages of Patriarchy* (Bloomington and Indianapolis: Indiana University Press, 1987).

—, 'Britannia Rules *The Waves*', in *Decolonizing Tradition: New Views of Twentieth-Century 'British' Literary Canons*, ed. Karen R. Lawrence (Urbana, IL: University of Illinois Press, 1992), pp. 136–62.

Marshik, Celia J., 'Virginia Woolf and Intellectual History: The Case of Josephine Butler and *Three Guineas*', in *Virginia Woolf and Her Influences: Selected Papers from the Seventh Annual Conference on Virginia Woolf*, ed. Laura Davis and Jeanette McVicker (New York: Pace University Press, 1998), pp. 91–6.

McConnell, Frank D., '"Death Among the Apple Trees": *The Waves* and the World of Things', in *Virginia Woolf: A Collection of Critical Essays*, ed. Claire Sprague (Englewood Cliffs, NJ: Prentice-Hall, 1971), pp. 117–29.

McGavran, J. Holt, Jr, 'Shelley, Woolf, and *The Waves*: A Balcony of One's Own', *South Atlantic Review*, 48:4 (1983), 58–73.

McNichol, Stella, Introduction to *Collected Novels of Virginia Woolf: Mrs Dalloway, To the Lighthouse, The Waves* (Basingstoke: Macmillan, 1992).

McWhirter, David, 'The Novel, the Play, and the Book: *Between the Acts* and the Tragicomedy of History', *English Literary History*, 60:3 (1993), 787–812.

Meisel, Perry, *The Absent Father: Virginia Woolf and Walter Pater* (New Haven, CT and London: Yale University Press, 1980).

Miller, Jane E., *Rebel Women: Feminism, Modernism and the Edwardian Novel* (London: Virago, 1994).

Miller, Nancy K., *Subject to Change: Reading Feminist Writing* (New York: Columbia University Press, 1988).

Minow-Pinkney, Makiko, *Virginia Woolf and the Problem of the Subject* (Brighton: Harvester, 1987).

Naremore, James, *The World Without a Self: Virginia Woolf and the Novel* (New Haven, CT: Yale University Press, 1973).

—, 'The "Orts and Fragments" in *Between the Acts*', *Ball State University Forum*, 14:1 (1973), 59–69.

Nicolson, Nigel, *Portrait of a Marriage* (London: Weidenfeld and Nicolson, 1973).

Paul, Janis M., *The Victorian Heritage of Virginia Woolf: The External World in her Novels* (Norman, OK: Pilgrim Books, 1987).

Pierce, David and Peter de Voogd (eds), *Laurence Sterne in Modernism and Postmodernism* (Amsterdam: Rodopi, 1996).

Pykett, Lyn, *Engendering Fictions: The English Novel in the Early Twentieth Century*, Writing in History (London: Edward Arnold, 1995).

Rackin, Phyllis, 'Androgyny, Mimesis, and the Marriage of the Boy Heroine on the English Renaissance Stage', *PMLA*, 102:1 (1987), 29–41.

Raitt, Suzanne, *Virginia Woolf's To the Lighthouse* (Hemel Hempstead: Harvester Wheatsheaf, 1990).

—, *Vita and Virginia: The Work and Friendship of V. Sackville-West and Virginia Woolf* (Oxford: Oxford University Press, 1993).

Ramsay, Stephen J., '"On Not Knowing Greek": Virginia Woolf and the New Ancient Greece', in *Virginia Woolf: Turning the Centuries: Selected Papers from the Ninth Annual Conference on Virginia Woolf*, ed. Ann Ardis and Bonnie Kime Scott (New York: Pace University Press, 2000), pp. 6–11.

Richter, Harvena, *Virginia Woolf: The Inward Voyage* (Princeton, NJ: Princeton University Press, 1970).

—, 'The Ulysses Connection: Clarissa Dalloway's Bloomsday', *Studies in the Novel*, 21 (1989), 305–19.

Roe, Sue, Introduction and editorial matter in Virginia Woolf, *Jacob's Room* (Harmondsworth: Penguin, 1992).

Rose, Phyllis, *Woman of Letters: A Life of Virginia Woolf* ([1978]; London: Pandora, 1986).

Rosenbaum, S. P., 'The Philosophical Realism of Virginia Woolf', in *English Literature and British Philosophy: A Collection of Essays*, ed. and intro. by S. P. Rosenbaum (Chicago and London: University of Chicago Press, 1971), pp. 316–56.

—, 'An Educated Man's Daughter: Leslie Stephen, Virginia Woolf, and the Bloomsbury Group', in *Virginia Woolf: New Critical Essays*, ed. Patricia Clements and Isobel Grundy (London: Vision, 1983), pp. 32–56.

Rosenberg, Beth Carole, *Virginia Woolf and Samuel Johnson: Common Readers* (New York: St Martin's Press, 1995).

Rosenman, Ellen Bayuk, *The Invisible Presence: Virginia Woolf and the Mother–Daughter Relationship* (Baton Rouge, LA and London: Louisiana State University Press, 1986).

Ruddick, Sara, 'Private Brother, Public World', in *New Feminist Essays on Virginia Woolf*, ed. Jane Marcus (London and Basingstoke: Macmillan, 1981), pp. 185–215.

Schlack, Beverly Ann, *Continuing Presences: Virginia Woolf's Use of Literary Allusion* (University Park, PA and London: Pennsylvania State University Press, 1979).

—, 'Fathers in General: The Patriarchy in Virginia Woolf's Fiction', in *Virginia Woolf: A Feminist Slant*, ed. Jane Marcus (Lincoln, NB: University of Nebraska Press, 1983), pp. 52–77.

Schneidau, Herbert N., *Waking Giants: The Presence of the Past in Modernism* (New York: Oxford University Press, 1991).

Schwartz, Beth C., 'Thinking Back Through our Mothers: Virginia Woolf Reads Shakespeare', *English Literary History*, 58:3 (1991), 721–46.

Schweickart, Patrocinio P., 'Reading Ourselves: Toward a Feminist Theory of Reading' (1986), in *Feminisms: An Anthology of Literary Theory and Criticism*, revised edition, ed. Robyn R. Warhol and Diane Price Herndl (Basingstoke: Macmillan, 1997), pp. 609–34.

Scott, Bonnie Kime, *Refiguring Modernism*, 2 vols (Bloomington and Indianapolis: Indiana University Press, 1995).

—, *The Gender of Modernism: A Critical Anthology* (Bloomington and Indianapolis: Indiana University Press, 1990).

Showalter, Elaine, *A Literature of Their Own: From Charlotte Brontë to Doris Lessing* (London: Virago, 1978).

Silver, Brenda R., 'Virginia Woolf and the Concept of Community: The Elizabethan Playhouse', *Women's Studies*, 4:2–3 (1977), 291–8.

Snaith, Anna, *Virginia Woolf: Public and Private Negotiations* (Basingstoke: Macmillan, 2000).

Southam, B. C. (ed.), *Jane Austen: The Critical Heritage*, 2 vols ([1968–87]; London and New York: Routledge, 1995).

Squier, Susan M., 'Tradition and Revision in Woolf's *Orlando:* Defoe and "The Jessamy Brides"', *Women's Studies*, 12:12 (1986), 167–77.

Starr, G. A., *Defoe and Spiritual Autobiography* (Princeton, NJ: Princeton University Press, 1965).

Steele, Elizabeth, *Virginia Woolf's Literary Sources and Allusions: A Guide to the Essays* (New York and London: Garland Publishing, 1983).

—, *Virginia Woolf's Rediscovered Essays: Sources and Allusions* (New York and London: Garland Publishing, 1987).

Strauss, Nina Pelikan, 'The Exclusion of the Intended from Secret Sharing in Conrad's *Heart of Darkness*', in Andrew Michael Roberts (ed.), *Conrad*, Longman Critical Readers (Harlow: Longman, 1998), pp. 171–88.

Sumner, Rosemary, *A Route to Modernism: Hardy, Lawrence, Woolf* (Basingstoke: Macmillan, 2000).

Tate, Trudi, 'HD's War Neurotics', in *Women's Fiction and the Great War*, ed. Suzanne Raitt and Trudi Tate (Oxford: Clarendon Press, 1997), pp. 241–62.

Taylor, Gary, *Reinventing Shakespeare* (London: Hogarth, 1989).

Todd, Janet, 'Who's Afraid of Jane Austen?', in *Jane Austen: New Perspectives*, ed. Janet Todd, Women & Literature, New Series 3 (New York and London: Holmes and Meier, 1983), pp. 107–27.

Tremper, Ellen, *'Who Lived at Alfoxton?': Virginia Woolf and English Romanticism* (London: Associated University Presses, 1998).

Wallace, Miriam, 'Thinking Back Through our Others: Rereading Sterne and Rethinking Joyce in *The Waves*', in Jane Lilienfeld, Jeffrey Oxford and Lisa Low (eds), *Woolf Studies Annual*, 9: Special Issue on Virginia Woolf and Literary History (New York: Pace University Press, 2003), pp. 193–220.

Watkins, Renée, 'Survival in Discontinuity: Virginia Woolf's *Between the Acts*', *Massachusetts Review*, 10:2 (1969), 356–76.

Webb, Caroline, '"All was dark; all was doubt; all was confusion": Nature, Culture, and Orlando's Ruskinian Storm-Cloud', in *Virginia Woolf: Out of Bounds*, ed. Jessica Berman and Jane Goldman (New York: Pace University Press, 2001), pp. 243–9.

Wilson, J. J., 'Why is *Orlando* Difficult?', in *New Feminist Essays on Virginia Woolf*, ed. Jane Marcus (London and Basingstoke: Macmillan, 1981), pp. 170–84.

Woolf, Leonard, 'Virginia Woolf and *The Waves*', *Radio Times* (23 June 1957), 25.

Worton, Michael and Judith Still (eds), *Intertextuality: Theories and Practices* (Manchester and New York: Manchester University Press, 1990).

Wright, G. Patton, 'Virginia Woolf's Uncommon Reader: Allusions in *Between the Acts*', in *Virginia Woolf Miscellanies: Proceedings of the First Annual Conference on Virginia Woolf*, ed. Mark Hussey and Vara Neverow-Turk (New York: Pace University Press, 1992), 230–3.

Wright, T. R., 'George Eliot and Positivism: A Reassessment', *Modern Language Review*, 76 (1981), 257–72.

Wyatt, Jean, 'Art and Allusion in *Between the Acts*', *Mosaic*, 9:4 (1978), 91–100.

Zuckerman, Joanne P., 'Anne Thackeray Ritchie as the Model for Mrs Hilbery in Virginia Woolf's *Night and Day*', *Virginia Woolf Quarterly*, 1:3 (1973), 32–46.

Zwerdling, Alex, '*Between the Acts* and the Coming of War', *Novel: A Forum on Fiction*, 10:3 (1977), 220–36.

Unpublished sources

Booth, Alison, 'Virginia Woolf and Collective Biographies of Women', paper given at the Seventh Annual Virginia Woolf Conference, 12 June 1997. Abstract in *Virginia Woolf and Her Influences: Selected Papers from the Seventh Annual Conference on Virginia Woolf*, ed. Laura Davis and Jeanette McVicker (New York: Pace University Press, 1998), pp. 58–9.

Cuddy-Keane, Melba, 'Thinking Historically about Historical Thinking', paper given at the Seventh Annual Virginia Woolf Conference (Plymouth State College, NH, June 1997). Abstract in *Virginia Woolf and Her Influences: Selected Papers from the Seventh Annual Conference on Virginia Woolf*, ed. Laura Davis and Jeanette McVicker (New York: Pace University Press, 1998), pp. 59–60.

Lyons, Brenda, 'Textual Voyages: Platonic Allusions in Virginia Woolf's Fiction' (D.Phil thesis, University of Oxford, 1995).

Pines, Davida Beth, 'William Wordsworth and Virginia Woolf: Assertion and Dissolution of Self' (M.Phil thesis, University of Oxford, 1993).

Saunders, Max, 'War, History, and Madness in Ford Madox Ford's *Parade's End*', paper given at 'The Cultural and Intellectual Contexts of Modernism' conference, Centre for English Studies, University of London, 31 May–1 June 1996.

Smart, Nick, '"Never See Rachel Again": Virginia Woolf and Domestic Fiction', paper given at 'Voyages Out, Voyages Home': The Eleventh Annual Conference on Virginia Woolf, University of Wales, Bangor, 13–16 June 2001.

Warner, Eric, 'Some Aspects of Romanticism in the Work of Virginia Woolf' (D.Phil thesis, University of Oxford, 1980).

Index